S0-BZK-259

AMERICAN HEART ASSOCIATION

BRAND NAME

FAT
AND
CHOLESTEROL

COUNTER

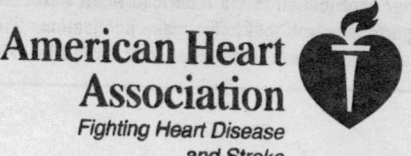

American Heart Association
Fighting Heart Disease and Stroke

BRAND NAME

FAT
AND
CHOLESTEROL

COUNTER

TIMES 𝕿 BOOKS

RANDOM HOUSE

Your contribution to the American Heart Association supports research that helps make publications like this possible. For more information, call 1-800-AHA-USA 1.

Copyright © 1994 by American Heart Association

All rights reserved under International and Pan-American Copyright Conventions. Published in the United States by Times Books, a division of Random House, Inc., New York, and simultaneously in Canada by Random House of Canada Limited, Toronto.

Library of Congress Cataloging-in-Publication Data

American Heart Association brand name fat and cholesterol counter/by the American Heart Association—1st ed.

p.   cm.

ISBN 0-8129-2366-9 (pbk.)

1. Food—Cholesterol content—Tables. 2. Food—Fat content —Tables. 3. Food—Sodium content—Tables. I. American Heart Association.   II. Title: Brand name fat and cholesterol counter.

TX553.C43A42   1994

641.1′4—dc20   94-14293

Designed by M. Kristen Bearse

Manufactured in the United States of America

9 8 7 6 5 4 3 2

First Edition

ACKNOWLEDGMENTS

The dedication, talent and untiring efforts of many people made this book a reality. Special thanks, however, go to the staff of the Diet Modification Center of Baylor College of Medicine, Houston, Texas, for compiling the database used for this publication. Lynne W. Scott, M.A., R.D./L.D., and her staff, especially Mary Carole McMann, M.P.H., R.D./L.D., were always available for consultation. Their expertise, cheerfully shared, is very much appreciated.

Janice R. Moss edited and oversaw the production of this book, and Cheryl Bates kept the many lines of communication open. Word processors Gerre Gilford and Debra Bond never complained when asked to make one more change to the manuscript.

All of us hope that this book will serve three primary purposes: first and most important, to help you develop a more healthful eating plan; second, to show you the tremendous variety of foods you can choose from to make this plan as enjoyable as possible; and finally, to shorten and simplify your food shopping trips.

Mary Winston, Ed.D., R.D.,
Senior Science Consultant,
Office of Scientific Affairs,
American Heart Association
National Center

CONTENTS

EATING YOUR HEART OUT

The evidence is in. We can't ignore it.

Hundreds of scientific studies show a strong link between a diet high in saturated fat and cholesterol and the development of atherosclerosis. We know that atherosclerosis is one of the major causes of heart attack and stroke.

Atherosclerosis is a progressive disease of the blood vessels. Fatty substances, mostly cholesterol, build up in the inner lining of the arteries. This can eventually block an artery and stop the flow of blood. When this happens in an artery that supplies blood to your heart, you have a heart attack. When it happens in an artery feeding your brain, you have a stroke.

Cholesterol is a major part of the fatty buildup known as atherosclerotic plaque. Cholesterol comes mostly from your bloodstream. The cholesterol in your blood comes from two places: Your body produces a great deal of it, and you get some of it from the foods you eat. People with a high level of cholesterol in their blood are at much higher risk of having a heart attack than those who keep their cholesterol levels low.

Although it's important to keep your blood cholesterol level below 200 mg/dl (milligrams per deciliter), your body does need some cholesterol. It helps produce sex hormones and helps form cell membranes and protective sheaths around your nerves. Fortunately, your body manufactures the amount of cholesterol you need for

these functions. You don't really need any of the cholesterol that comes from food.

DOWN WITH HIGH CHOLESTEROL

Most heart attacks that happen in middle age and later
life are caused by long-standing high blood cholesterol,
often a result of eating a diet high in total fat, saturated
fat and cholesterol.

Studies show that the higher your blood cholesterol
rises above 200 mg/dl, the more likely you are to have a
heart attack.

The National Cholesterol Education Program is a program of the National Heart, Lung, and Blood Institute
(NHLBI) of the National Institutes of Health. It has established the following guidelines for determining how
blood cholesterol levels relate to the risk of heart disease.

Classification Based on Total Cholesterol and HDL Cholesterol

Cholesterol Level

Less than 200 mg/dl	Desirable
200–239 mg/dl	Borderline high
240 mg/dl or greater	High
	Low HDL cholesterol
	Less than 35 mg/dl

CHOLESTEROL ISN'T YOUR ONLY WORRY

Besides high blood cholesterol, several other major factors can increase your risk for heart disease. These include
cigarette smoking, physical inactivity, high blood pressure, obesity, diabetes and low HDL cholesterol.

To help control high blood cholesterol, one of the risk
factors for heart attack, it's important to cut down on the
saturated fat and cholesterol in your diet. It's also impor-

tant to limit your sodium intake, quit smoking, control your blood pressure, be physically active and keep your weight at its optimum level.

A DIET YOU CAN PUT YOUR HEART INTO

The American Heart Association Diet, outlined below, is a simple eating plan for all healthy Americans over the age of two.

It offers a few easy-to-follow guidelines that can help you control your blood cholesterol level by controlling the amount and kind of fat you eat and by limiting your dietary cholesterol. It recommends moderate sodium intake (no more than 3,000 mg per day) as a means of controlling your blood pressure and, in some instances, of preventing it from becoming too high.

When you compare the diet recommendations from the American Heart Association, the American Cancer Society, the American Diabetes Association and the United States Department of Agriculture/Health and Human Services (USDA/HHS) Dietary Guidelines, you'll find that they share the same basic concept. Therefore, when you follow the American Heart Association guidelines, you're not only taking steps to prevent heart disease but also may be helping prevent some forms of cancer and control diabetes.

Our basic eating plan provides about 1,600 calories daily and gives you all the nutrients your body needs. If your caloric requirements are higher than this, select additional foods from all the food groups except Meat, Poultry, Seafood and Eggs (you may have extra dried beans and peas from that group, however).

When eaten in moderation, all the foods listed in this guide can be part of a heart-healthful eating plan for most healthy adults. You should not assume that each of these foods can be eaten in unlimited quantities. They are meant to be evaluated as part of an overall eating plan. Some of them may not be appropriate for every person.

If you are on a more restricted diet for cardiovascular disease, you may need to further limit your food choices. If you are on a low-sodium diet, you will need to restrict those foods high in sodium. If you are on a weight-reduction diet, you may need to restrict the high-calorie foods listed here and limit the quantities of food you eat.

When a low-fat, low-cholesterol, moderate-sodium eating plan becomes your usual way of eating, you can splurge once in a while with no ill effects! For the rest of that day or the next day, make choices so you balance your intake. As an alternate plan, when the desire for a high-fat, high-cholesterol or high-sodium food overtakes you, here's something that works for lots of people: Eat a small serving or share the food with your dining partner or partners.

AMERICAN HEART ASSOCIATION DIET GUIDELINES

- Limit your intake of meat, fish and poultry to no more than 6 ounces per day.
- Eat fish and poultry more frequently than lean meat.
- When selecting meat, be sure to look for lean cuts.
- Frequently use meatless main dishes as entrées, or cook "low-meat" entrées by combining small amounts of meat with rice, pasta, beans or vegetables.
- Use approximately 5 to 8 teaspoons of fat and oils per day for cooking, baking, salad dressings and spreads. The amount may vary according to your caloric needs.
- Use cooking methods that require little or no fat: boiling, broiling, baking, roasting, poaching, microwaving and steaming.
- Eat no more than 3 to 4 egg yolks per week, including those used in cooking, baking and store-bought baked goods. (You may eat all the egg whites you want.)
- Limit your intake of organ meats, such as livers, brains, chitterlings, kidneys, hearts, gizzards, sweetbreads and pork maws.
- Eat at least 5 servings of fruits and vegetables per day.
- Eat 6 or more servings of cereals and grains daily.
- Choose skim or 1% milk and use the nonfat or low-fat varieties of other dairy products.
- Limit your sodium intake to no more than 3,000 mg daily.

MEAT, POULTRY, SEAFOOD, DRIED BEANS AND PEAS, AND EGGS

Choose: the leanest cuts of meat; eat poultry and fish more frequently than meat. Trim all visible fat before cooking. Unless roasting poultry, remove the skin before cooking.

Daily Servings: no more than 6 ounces of cooked poultry, seafood or lean meat per day, or 2 or more servings of dried beans and peas. No more than 3 or 4 egg yolks a week (you may eat all the egg whites you like).

Serving Size: 3 ounces cooked (or 4 ounces raw) meat, poultry or fish; 1 cup cooked beans, peas or legumes. (Three ounces of meat is about the size of a deck of cards; three ounces is also about half a chicken breast, a chicken leg with a thigh, or about ½ cup of flaked fish.)

VEGETABLES AND FRUITS

Choose: all vegetables and fruits except coconut. Olives and avocados should be counted as fats because of their high fat content (see the "Fats, Oils, Seeds and Nuts" category below). Oranges, grapefruit, melons and strawberries are excellent sources of vitamin C. Deep yellow fruits, such as apricots and cantaloupe, are high in vitamin A. Dark green vegetables, such as spinach and broccoli, provide vitamin C and along with deep yellow vegetables, such as carrots, are excellent sources of vitamin A.

Daily Servings: 5 or more.

Serving Size: 1 medium-size piece of fruit or ½ cup of fruit juice; ½ to 1 cup of cooked or raw vegetables.

BREADS, CEREALS, PASTA AND STARCHY VEGETABLES

Choose: low-fat breads, rolls, crackers and snacks; hot or cold cereals (except granola, which may be high in saturated fatty acids); homemade quick breads made with low-fat or skim milk and fats or oils low in saturated fatty acids; rice; pasta made without egg yolk; starchy vegetables; low-fat soups.

Daily Servings: 6 or more.

Serving Size: 1 slice of bread; ¼–1 cup cereal (hot or cold); 1 cup cooked rice or pasta; ¼–½ cup starchy vegetables; 1 cup low-fat soup.

MILK PRODUCTS

Choose: skim or 1% milk; low-fat or nonfat dairy products, such as cheese, yogurt and frozen desserts, where available.

Daily Servings: 2 or more for adults over 24 and children 2–10; 3–4 for ages 11–24 and women who are pregnant or lactating.

Serving Size: 8 ounces skim or 1% milk; 8 ounces low-fat yogurt; 1 ounce low-fat cheese; ½ cup low-fat cottage cheese (nonfat varieties of some dairy products are available in various parts of the country).

FATS, OILS, SEEDS AND NUTS

Choose: vegetable oils (canola, corn, olive, safflower, sesame, soybean, sunflower) and margarines made with these oils, with no more than 2 grams of saturated fatty acids per tablespoon; salad dressings and mayonnaise with no more than 1 gram of saturated fatty acids per tablespoon.

Daily Servings: 5–8 teaspoons, depending on your caloric needs.

Serving Size: 1 teaspoon vegetable oil or regular margarine; 2 teaspoons diet margarine; 1 tablespoon salad dressing; 2 teaspoons mayonnaise or peanut butter; 3 teaspoons seeds or nuts; ⅛ medium avocado; 10 small or 5 large olives.

DESSERTS

Choose: desserts made with acceptable ingredients or low in fat, cholesterol and calories. You can also make your own desserts by using ingredients from the above lists.

SNACKS

Choose: snacks such as fruits, raw vegetables and dips, nutritious cookies (for example, oatmeal cookies, newton-type cookies and gingersnaps), low-fat crackers and pretzels, seeds and nuts. Nonfat varieties of some snack foods are available. However, note that they are usually no lower in calories than the low-fat varieties.

BEVERAGES

Choose: fruit or vegetable juices, coffee, tea, mineral water. If you drink, have no more than 1 ounce of pure alcohol per day, which is about 8 fluid ounces of wine, 24 fluid ounces of beer, or 2 fluid ounces of 100-proof distilled spirits. If you don't drink, don't start.

FIGURING YOUR FAT ALLOWANCE AND SODIUM INTAKE

The first step is to determine the maximum amount of total fat and saturated fat you can eat every day—and still keep your blood cholesterol at a safe level. To discover this, you must first know how many calories you need to maintain your ideal weight. Here's an easy way to find the approximate number of calories you'll need. It is simply a guide. People who are very active will need more calories. Children and pregnant and lactating women also have special caloric needs. Ask your physician to guide you. Start by finding your ideal weight in the table that follows.

Desirable Body Weight Ranges

Height Without Shoes (ft./in.)	Weight Without Shoes	
	Men (pounds)	Women (pounds)
4'10"	—	92–121
4'11"	—	95–124
5'0"	—	98–127
5'1"	105–134	101–130
5'2"	108–137	104–134
5'3"	111–141	107–138
5'4"	114–145	110–142
5'5"	117–149	114–146
5'6"	121–154	118–150
5'7"	125–159	122–154
5'8"	129–163	126–159
5'9"	133–167	130–164
5'10"	137–172	134–169
5'11"	141–177	—
6'0"	145–182	—
6'1"	149–187	—
6'2"	153–192	—
6'3"	157–197	—

This table is adapted from the Desirable Weight Tables prepared in 1959 by the Metropolitan Life Insurance Company. It is based on weights associated with the lowest mortality. For women 18 to 25 years old, subtract one pound for each year under 25.

The 1983 revision of the Metropolitan Life Insurance Company's Height and Weight Tables allow increased weight for certain heights. However, because obesity is a contributing factor for heart disease, the American Heart Association did not adapt the 1983 version.

Next, to find your caloric needs, multiply your ideal weight by 15 if you're moderately active or 20 if you are very active. From that total, subtract the following numbers according to your age:

Age 25 to 34, subtract 0
Age 35 to 44, subtract 100
Age 45 to 54, subtract 200

Age 55 to 64, subtract 300
Age 65+, subtract 400

For example, if you're a forty-five-year-old man whose desirable weight is 145 pounds and who is moderately active, take 145 pounds and multiply by 15, to get 2,175 calories; then subtract 200, totaling 1,975 calories. For a moderately active 120-pound woman of thirty-five, you'd figure it like this: $120 \times 15 = 1,800 - 100 = 1,700$.

After you figure how many calories you need daily, you can determine the maximum amount of fat that should be in your diet. At the American Heart Association, we recommend that your total fat intake be less than 30 percent of your total calories. We suggest keeping saturated fatty acids to less than 10 percent of total calories.

To find out how many grams of fat you can allow yourself, take your daily calories and multiply by .30. That will give you the maximum daily calories you can have from fat. Then divide that number by 9 (1 gram of fat has 9 calories), which will give you the number of total grams of fat you can have each day. For example, $2,000 \times .30 = 600 \div 9 = 67$ grams of total fat (rounded from 66.6).

Then you do the same thing with saturated fatty acids. Multiply your total calories by .10, then divide that number by 9. Example: $2,000 \times .10 = 200 \div 9 = 22$ grams of saturated fatty acids (rounded from 22.2). The table on page xxii shows the maximum grams of total fat and saturated fatty acids for a variety of calorie levels. Remember that your total fat intake includes saturated, mono-unsaturated and polyunsaturated fat.

Suggested Daily Fat Intake

Daily Calories	Maximum Grams of Total Fat	Maximum Grams of Saturated Fat
1,200	40	13
1,400	47	16
1,600	53	18
1,800	60	20
2,000	67	22
2,200	73	24
2,400	80	27
2,600	87	29
2,800	93	31
3,000	100	33

Check the food listings in this guide, as well as the labels on prepared foods, to see how many grams of fat are in one serving of the product you want to eat. For example, the label opposite shows 3 grams of fat and no saturated fat in each ½-cup portion of the product. (See page xxvii for a discussion about the government's new nutrition labeling regulations.)

Just keep track of the number of grams of total fat and saturated fatty acids you eat every day. See whether your intake of fat and saturated fatty acids is within the guidelines listed on the chart above. If not, use this *Brand Name Fat and Cholesterol Counter* to help you adjust your eating habits.

The AHA also recommends that you limit your daily sodium intake to 3,000 mg or less. One way to begin is to use the lists in this guide to note the sodium level of foods. When buying products that are canned, frozen or prepared, select those without added salt when possible. Be adventurous—prepare foods with a variety of herbs and spices rather than salt. And avoid salting your food before eating—break the habit of reaching for the salt shaker as soon as you sit at the table.

Nutrition Facts

Serving Size ½ cup (114g)
Servings Per Container 4

Amount Per Serving

Calories 90   Calories from Fat 30

                                    % Daily Value*

Total Fat 3g	**5%**
Saturated Fat 0g	**0%**
Cholesterol 0mg	**0%**
Sodium 300mg	**13%**
Total Carbohydrate 13g	**4%**
Dietary Fiber 3g	**12%**
Sugars 3g	
Protein 3g	

Vitamin A	80%	• Vitamin C	60%
Calcium	4%	• Iron	4%

* Percent Daily Values are based on a 2,000
calorie diet. Your daily values may be higher or
lower depending on your calorie needs:

	Calories	2,000	2,500
Total Fat	Less than	65g	80g
Sat Fat	Less than	20g	25g
Cholesterol	Less than	300mg	300mg
Sodium	Less than	2,400mg	2,400mg
Total Carbohydrate		300g	375g
Fiber		25g	30g

Calories per gram:
Fat 9   •   Carbohydrate 4   •   Protein 4

The AHA has prepared this *Brand Name Fat and Cholesterol Counter* for people interested in making some healthful life-style changes. It may also be helpful to those of you following a modified diet for the treatment of cardiovascular disease, as prescribed by your doctor.

Compare your present diet with the AHA eating plan that begins on page xvi. Perhaps you are not eating the variety of foods you need and thus are not getting the recommended amounts of minerals and vitamins, or perhaps you are consuming many high-fat, high-sodium foods.

Once you've mastered the principles of the AHA eating plan and determined the number of calories and the amount of fat and saturated fat you should eat, you can make a few heart-healthy substitutions for specific foods you're eating now. For example, you can replace whole milk with skim milk or 1% milk. Or you might start by eating a lower-fat version of one of your favorite foods. This book is intended to make it easier for you to work your way through the hundreds of food products in the grocery store and to make educated choices.

By choosing a variety of foods from each group, you can build an eating plan that's low in fat and sodium and high in nutrition. Such an eating plan can also help keep your cholesterol level—and thereby one of your risks for heart attack—on the low side.

HOW TO READ THE FOOD TABLE

You'll find more than 4,000 foods listed in this guide. All these products were included on the basis of their nutritional content. They do not contain more than a specific amount of fat, saturated fat and cholesterol per serving; we refer to these maximum amounts as the AHA criteria. Since the composition of a product may change because of reformulation after the AHA's review, you should always read the nutrition label on any product you buy.

The information on the branded products—product name, serving size and nutritional values—was obtained directly from the food manufacturers and is current as of the time of their review by the AHA. This guide will be revised annually so that you will have the most up-to-date information possible. Also, by using the tables at the beginning of each chapter, you will be able to find additional foods that meet the AHA criteria and fit into your eating plan. You will even be able to evaluate foods for which we don't have nutritional information and foods introduced after this book was published.

Because of the enormous negative impact on public health caused by tobacco products and because of the activities of tobacco companies and their affiliates concerning public health issues regarding regulation of tobacco products, food products made by tobacco companies or their corporate subsidiaries or parents are identified by a † symbol. The source used to identify tobacco-owned companies was derived from a list compiled by the American Lung Association, American Cancer Society and American Heart Association in 1992. Health-conscious consumers may wish to consider this background, as well as the nutritional content of a product, when making a food selection.

By policy, the AHA does not endorse any commercial product, and the AHA is not suggesting the nutritional superiority of any product listed in this guide over any other product not listed in this guide.

The listings are divided into 20 chapters by type of food product. Portion size, grams of total fat and saturated fatty acids, milligrams of cholesterol and sodium, and number of calories are given for each food. Parentheses around an amount in the listings indicate that specific information was not available for that item. A value was therefore estimated, either by analyzing the ingredients listed on the label or by gathering information from the USDA Handbook Series 8. When foods contain only a small amount of a given nutrient, the table reads "tr," for "trace." Other abbreviations used are as follows:

approx	approximately
cal.	calorie(s)
chol.	cholesterol
env	envelope
fl oz	fluid ounce(s)
g	gram(s)
<	less than
mg	milligram(s)
n/a	not available
oz	ounce(s)
pkg	package
pkt	packet
sat.	saturated
sod.	sodium
tbsp	tablespoon(s)
tsp	teaspoon(s)
tot.	total

If it has been determined that most brands of a specific food contain approximately the same amounts of various nutrients, you will find a generic entry among the brand name entries. For example, listed with brand name entries for canned fish, you will see a generic entry for tuna packed in water because many brands of water-packed tuna will provide about the same amounts of total fat, saturated fat, cholesterol, sodium and calories.

If a product, either generic or brand name, does not fit into a subcategory, it will be listed at the end of the category as "other." For example, in the chapter "Breads and Bread Products," there is a miscellaneous subcategory called "Other Breads."

As of May 8, 1994, food manufacturers must comply with the National Label Education Act regulations. All nutrition labels will be standard and meet standard serving sizes for various food categories established by the Food and Drug Administration.

In 1994, a transition year, you will probably continue to see some products with the old labels and serving sizes. However, when the AHA selected products for this guide, we adjusted the serving sizes to meet FDA requirements for serving sizes and determined by mathematical calculation that such foods would meet our criteria. For more information on the new nutritional labeling regulations, contact the American Heart Association at 1-800-AHA-USA 1. Our brochures "Facts About the New Food Label" and "How To Read The New Food Label" may be of particular interest.

In addition to the lists of foods, you will also find two tables at the beginning of each chapter. The first, the AHA criteria table, shows the maximum allowable amounts of total fat, saturated fat and cholesterol in general categories, such as main dishes, processed luncheon meats and snack crackers.*

A second table lists a few generic foods that are not

* In most instances, the AHA criteria are consistent with the FDA nutrient content claims for fat, saturated fat and cholesterol. The exception is the category of fats and oils. Although high in fat, the food products included there are important components of the AHA diet. They can contribute to lowering blood cholesterol levels. Although the total fat content of these oils and fats is approximately the

recommended for frequent eating because they are so high in total fat, saturated fat and/or cholesterol. These foods and their values are provided for comparison with more wholesome, lower-fat items found in the listings.

With these tables and the food product listings, you can select healthful, nutritious foods that can help keep your weight down, your cholesterol level low and your heart healthy.

FOODS WE DIDN'T INCLUDE

Some of your favorite foods may not be listed in the following pages. Often that is because they exceed at least one of the AHA criteria for fat, saturated fat and cholesterol, discussed earlier. Another reason is that some products became available after this book went to press. Yet another possibility is that the manufacturer did not supply the needed information about its products. Finally, some foods are available that we are not aware of. If you know of foods that should be listed but aren't, you can help us include them in future editions of the *Brand Name Fat and Cholesterol Counter*. Just send us the following information:

- Exact name of the product;
- Name of the manufacturer (and address if possible); and
- Fat, saturated fat, cholesterol, sodium and calorie values.

Address your correspondence to:

Diet Modification Center
6565 Fannin, F770
Houston, TX 77030

same, the amount of saturated fat varies from type to type. Therefore, we determined the maximum amount of this nutrient that each type of fat may contain.

On the other hand, you may wonder why some foods that contain ingredients such as cream, egg yolks, butter, palm kernel oil and coconut oil are listed. They are included because the high-fat or high-cholesterol ingredients are present in such very small amounts that the foods are able to meet the AHA criteria.

The truth is, choice is everything.

Armed with this table, you will find that trying to eat healthfully can be an enjoyable experience.

Here's to good eating—and good health!

Atherosclerosis A blood vessel disease in which the inner linings of arteries become thick and irregular because of deposits of fat, cholesterol and other substances. These arteries then become narrowed, and the flow of blood is reduced.

Calorie The unit of measurement of the heat or energy supplied by food when it is broken down in the body. Carbohydrates, protein, fat and alcohol supply calories.

Cholesterol A fatlike substance produced by your body and contained in foods of animal origin only. Your body produces all the cholesterol it needs. The cholesterol from foods can raise your blood cholesterol level and thus increase your risk of heart disease. Cholesterol is found in egg yolks, organ meats, meats, fish, other seafood, poultry and dairy products.

Hydrogenated Fat The type of fat resulting from a chemical process that changes a liquid oil that is naturally high in unsaturated fats to a more solid and more saturated form. This process helps the fat in food products stay fresh longer. The greater the degree of hydrogenation, the more saturated the fat becomes. Hydrogenated margarines and spreads are acceptable if they contain no more than 2 grams of saturated fatty acids per tablespoon.

Monounsaturated Fatty Acids Fats that are found in canola, olive and peanut oils. They are also found in foods such as meats, nuts and seeds. Like polyunsaturated fatty acids, monounsaturated fatty acids tend to lower blood cholesterol, especially when they're used to replace saturated fatty acids in the diet.

Polyunsaturated Fatty Acids Fats such as safflower, sunflower, corn and soybean oils. They are also found in foods such as nuts and seeds. They tend to lower blood cholesterol when they are used as part of a low-saturated-fat, low-cholesterol eating plan.

Saturated Fatty Acids The main culprit in raising blood cholesterol. Saturated fatty acids are found in both animal and plant foods. Animal foods containing large amounts of saturated fatty acids include beef, veal, lamb, pork, butter, cream, whole milk, and cheese and other dairy products made from whole milk. The plant sources of saturated fatty acids include coconut oil, cocoa butter, palm and palm kernel oil, and some shortenings and margarines. Many commercial baked goods are made with these oils.

Sodium An element that is essential for good health. The body needs only a tiny amount each day. Most foods in their natural state contain small amounts of sodium. Table salt (sodium chloride) is 40 percent sodium by weight. Most Americans consume far more sodium than their bodies need. In some people, this can contribute to high blood pressure.

AMERICAN HEART

FOOD
TABLES

ASSOCIATION

BEVERAGES AND BEVERAGE MIXES

Most beverages and beverage mixes contain very little or no fat. However, many of the flavored coffees that contain chocolate and/or creamer are too high in fat and saturated fat to be included in this book. The beverages and beverage mixes in this chapter were evaluated the way they will be consumed—as purchased, prepared according to package directions or prepared with skim milk (as indicated on the following pages).

Products listed in this book vary in sodium content. Use the values appearing on the following pages to help plan a daily intake providing no more than 3,000 milligrams of sodium.

Most of the foods in this book are brand name products; however, when a brand name is not specified, it means that most brands of that product provide about the same amount of fat, saturated fat and cholesterol and that these amounts do not exceed AHA criteria.

You can use those generic entries and the tables below to evaluate products introduced since this book went to press.

AHA Criteria for Beverages and Beverage Mixes*

	Tot. Fat (g)	Sat. Fat (g)	Chol. (mg)
Alcoholic, carbonated and noncarbonated beverages, coffee and tea	<0.5	<0.5	<2
Cocoa, flavored milk beverage and instant breakfast mixes (prepared)	3	2	20

* Per serving.

Beverages Not Recommended
for Frequent Consumption

A type of beverage that is usually too high in fat, saturated fat and/or cholesterol to be recommended for frequent consumption is shown in the table below. Values that exceed AHA criteria are followed by asterisks. The AHA does not have criteria for sodium.

You can use the values in the table to compare this beverage with more-healthful alternatives listed on the following pages.

Beverages High in Fat,
Saturated Fat and/or Cholesterol

	Tot. Fat (g)	Sat. Fat (g)	Chol. (mg)	Sod. (mg)	Cal.
Cappuccino-flavored instant coffee, sugar sweetened, made with 2 rounded teaspoons powder and 6 fluid ounces water	2.1*	1.8*	(0)	104	62

Adapted from USDA Handbook No. 8 series.
* These values exceed AHA criteria for beverages.

	Tot. Fat (g)	Sat. Fat (g)	Chol. (mg)	Sod. (mg)	Cal.
ALCOHOLIC BEVERAGES					
Beer					
Light (12 fl oz)	0.0	0.0	0	10	100
Regular (12 fl oz)	0.0	0.0	0	19	146
Gin (1½ fl oz)	0.0	0.0	0	1	110
Liqueur					
Coffee (1½ fl oz)	0.1	0.1	0	4	174
Creme de menthe (1½ fl oz)	0.1	0.0	0	3	186
Rum (1½ fl oz)	0.0	0.0	0	0	97
Vodka (1½ fl oz)	0.0	0.0	0	0	97
Whiskey (1½ fl oz)	0.0	0.0	0	0	105
Wine					
Dessert (2 fl oz)	0.0	0.0	0	5	90
Table (3½ fl oz)	0.0	0.0	0	8	72

Mixers for Alcoholic Beverages

	Tot. Fat (g)	Sat. Fat (g)	Chol. (mg)	Sod. (mg)	Cal.
Bacardi Frozen Concentrated Tropical Fruit Mixers, made with water only					
Banana Daiquiri (8 fl oz)	0.8	(0.2)	{0}	17	104
Margarita Mix (8 fl oz)	0.0	0.0	{0}	20	99
Peach Daiquiri (8 fl oz)	0.0	0.0	{0}	21	131
Raspberry Daiquiri (8 fl oz)	0.0	0.0	{0}	20	187
Strawberry Daiquiri (8 fl oz)	0.0	0.0	{0}	20	139
Libby's Bloody Mary Mix (6 fl oz)	0.0	0.0	{0}	1120	40
Romanoff Grenadine (1.17 oz)	0.0	0.0	{0}	5	92
Schweppes					
Bitter Lemon (6 fl oz)	<1.0	0.0	0	30	80
Collins Mixer (6 fl oz)	<1.0	(0.0)	0	40	70

CARBONATED BEVERAGES

	Tot. Fat (g)	Sat. Fat (g)	Chol. (mg)	Sod. (mg)	Cal.
Barq's Root Beer, Diet (6 fl oz)	0.2	(0.0)	{0}	35	2
Clearly Canadian Sparkling Water					
Blackberry (6 fl oz)	0.0	0.0	{0}	8	68
Cherry (6 fl oz)	0.0	0.0	{0}	8	64
Cranberry (6 fl oz)	0.0	0.0	{0}	8	63

	Tot. Fat (g)	Sat. Fat (g)	Chol. (mg)	Sod. (mg)	Cal.
Loganberry (6 fl oz)	0.0	0.0	(0)	8	55
Peach (6 fl oz)	0.0	0.0	(0)	8	63
Raspberry (6 fl oz)	0.0	0.0	(0)	8	55
Club soda (12 fl oz)	0.0	0.0	0	75	0
Cola (12 fl oz)	0.0	0.0	0	14	151
Diet (sweetened with aspartame) (12 fl oz)	0.0	0.0	0	21	2
Cream soda (12 fl oz)	0.0	0.0	0	43	191
Evian Natural Spring Water (8 fl oz)	(0.0)	(0.0)	(0)	1	(0)
Fresca (6 fl oz)	(0.0)	(0.0)	0	tr	2
Ginger ale (12 fl oz)	0.0	0.0	0	25	124
Grape soda (12 fl oz)	0.0	0.0	0	57	161
Hansen's Natural Soda					
Cherry (12 fl oz)	0.6	(0.0)	(0)	<10	149
Grapefruit (12 fl oz)	0.4	(0.0)	(0)	<10	152
Mandarin Lime (12 fl oz)	0.4	(0.0)	(0)	<10	152
Raspberry (12 fl oz)	0.6	(0.0)	(0)	<10	149
I.B.C. Root Beer Soft Drink					
Diet (12 fl oz)	0.0	0.0	(0)	6	2
Regular (12 fl oz)	0.0	0.0	(0)	16	168
IGA Soft Drink					
Black Cherry (6 fl oz)	0.0	0.0	0	(35)	78
Cherry Cola (6 fl oz)	0.0	0.0	0	(35)	82
Ginger Ale, Diet (6 fl oz)	0.0	0.0	0	(33)	2
Grape, Diet (6 fl oz)	0.0	0.0	0	(80)	0
Punch (6 fl oz)	1.5	(0.0)	0	(35)	88
Red Pop (6 fl oz)	0.0	0.0	0	(22)	84
Koala Springs Water					
Apple and Black Currant (6 fl oz)	0.0	0.0	0	41	67
Cranberry, Melon and Apple (6 fl oz)	0.0	0.0	0	41	71
Kiwi, Lime and Grapefruit (6 fl oz)	0.0	0.0	0	41	59
Lemon, Lime and Orange (6 fl oz)	0.0	0.0	0	40	60
Mandarin and Orange (6 fl oz)	0.0	0.0	0	39	58
Natural Mineral Water (6 fl oz)	0.0	0.0	0	0	0
Orange and Mango (6 fl oz)	0.0	0.0	0	41	67
Orange and Passionfruit (6 fl oz)	0.0	0.0	0	41	61
Raspberry, Guava and Apple (6 fl oz)	0.0	0.0	0	42	48
Sparkling Lemonade (6 fl oz)	0.0	0.0	0	41	72
Wild Cherry and Apple (6 fl oz)	0.0	0.0	0	41	149
Lemon-lime soda (12 fl oz)	0.0	0.0	0	41	149

	Tot. Fat (g)	Sat. Fat (g)	Chol. (mg)	Sod. (mg)	Cal.
Mello Yello (6 fl oz)	(0.0)	(0.0)	0	14	87
Diet (6 fl oz)	(0.0)	(0.0)	0	tr	3
Orange soda (12 fl oz)	0.0	0.0	0	46	177
Perrier Mineral Water (8 fl oz)	(0.0)	(0.0)	(0)	4	(0)
Root beer (12 fl oz)	0.0	0.0	0	49	152
Schweppes Club Soda, Sodium Free (6 fl oz)	<1.0	(0.0)	0	0	0
Schweppes Flavored Seltzer					
Black Cherry (6 fl oz)	<1.0	0.0	0	varies	0
Lemon (6 fl oz)	<1.0	0.0	0	varies	0
Lime (6 fl oz)	<1.0	0.0	0	varies	0
Orange (6 fl oz)	<1.0	0.0	0	varies	0
Peaches 'N Cream (6 fl oz)	<1.0	0.0	0	varies	0
Wild Raspberry (6 fl oz)	<1.0	0.0	0	varies	0
Schweppes Ginger Ale					
Diet (6 fl oz)	<1.0	0.0	0	55	2
Raspberry (6 fl oz)	<1.0	0.0	0	35	65
Raspberry, Diet (6 fl oz)	<1.0	0.0	0	55	2
Schweppes Seltzer Water					
Lemon-Lime (6 fl oz)	<1.0	(0.0)	0	varies	0
Plain (6 fl oz)	<1.0	(0.0)	0	varies	0
Sodium Free (6 fl oz)	0.0	0.0	0	<5	0
Very Low Sodium (6 fl oz)	0.0	0.0	0	7	0
Schweppes Soft Drink					
Ginger Beer (6 fl oz)	<1.0	0.0	0	55	70
Grapefruit (6 fl oz)	<1.0	(0.0)	0	55	80
Lemon Sour (6 fl oz)	0.0	0.0	0	40	79
Schweppes Sparkling Water					
Black Cherry (6 fl oz)	<1.0	(0.0)	0	varies	0
Lemon (6 fl oz)	<1.0	(0.0)	0	varies	0
Lemon-Lime (6 fl oz)	<1.0	(0.0)	0	varies	0
Lime (6 fl oz)	<1.0	(0.0)	0	varies	0
Orange (6 fl oz)	<1.0	(0.0)	0	varies	0
Plain (6 fl oz)	<1.0	(0.0)	0	varies	0
Wild Raspberry (6 fl oz)	<1.0	(0.0)	0	varies	0
Schweppes Tonic Water, Diet (6 fl oz)	<1.0	(0.0)	0	60	0
Schweppes Vichy Water (6 fl oz)	<1.0	(0.0)	0	105	0
Tonic water (12 fl oz)	0.0	0.0	0	15	125

	Tot. Fat (g)	Sat. Fat (g)	Chol. (mg)	Sod. (mg)	Cal.
COCOA MIXES					
Carnation Hot Cocoa Mix					
70-Calorie (1 env)	<1.0	0.2	1	135	70
Milk Chocolate (1 env)	1.0	0.9	1	130	110
Rich Chocolate (1 env)	1.0	1.0	1	130	110
with Chocolate Marshmallows (1 env)	1.0	1.0	2	120	110
with Marshmallows (1 env)	1.0	0.9	1	120	110
Carnation Sugar Free Hot Cocoa Mix					
Diet (1 env)	<1.0	0.2	0	150	25
Mocha (1 env)	<1.0	0.2	2	140	50
Rich Chocolate (1 env)	<1.0	0.2	3	160	50
Featherweight Sugar Free Hot Cocoa Mix (1 env)	1.0	(0.6)	0	110	50
Nestle Hot Cocoa Mix					
Rich Chocolate Flavor, made with water (6 fl oz)	1.0	(0.6)	0	200	120
Rich Chocolate Flavor with Marshmallows, made with water (6 fl oz)	1.0	(0.6)	0	200	110
Swiss Miss Cocoa Mix					
Diet, made with water (6 oz)	<1.0	(0.0)	2	180	20
Lite, made with water (6 oz)	<1.0	(0.0)	1	180	70
Sugar Free, made with water (6 oz)	<1.0	(0.0)	2	190	50
with Sugar Free Marshmallows, made with water (6 oz)	<1.0	(0.0)	2	180	50
Weight Watchers Hot Cocoa Mix (1 env)	<1.0	<1.0	5	160	60
COFFEE/TEA					
Cafix Instant Beverage, made with water (1 cup)	0.0	0.0	(0)	3	6
Coffee					
Brewed, regular or decaffeinated, unsweetened (1 cup)	0.0	0.0	0	5	5
Instant, regular or decaffeinated, made with water (1 cup)	0.0	0.0	0	8	5

	Tot. Fat (g)	Sat. Fat (g)	Chol. (mg)	Sod. (mg)	Cal.
Lipton Flavored Teas, brewed, all flavors (1 cup)	0.0	0.0	0	0	0-4
Lipton Iced Tea Mix with Sugar, Lemon Lime (8 fl oz)	(0.0)	0.0	(0)	0	60
Lipton Instant Tea, Raspberry Flavored (8 fl oz)	0.0	0.0	0	0	2
Lipton Sugar Free Iced Tea Mix, Mandarin Orange (8 fl oz)	(0.0)	0.0	(0)	0	4
Natural Touch Kaffree Roma, dry (1 tsp)	0.0	0.0	0	1	6
Natural Touch Kaffree Tea, brewed (8 fl oz)	0.0	0.0	0	<1	(6)
Nestea Ice Teasers, Citrus, Lemon, Orange, Tropical or Wild Cherry (8 fl oz)	0.0	0.0	0	0	6
Postum Instant Hot Beverage Coffee Flavor (6 oz)	0.0	0.0	0	0	12
Regular (6 fl oz)	0.0	0.0	0	0	12
Tea					
Brewed or instant, regular or herbal, unsweetened (8 fl oz)	0.0	0.0	0	2-8	3
Instant, regular or decaffeinated Presweetened with artificial sweetener, dry (2 tsp)	0.0	0.0	0	17	5
Presweetened with sugar, made with water (8 fl oz)	0.0	0.0	0	0	87

FLAVORED MILK BEVERAGES

	Tot. Fat (g)	Sat. Fat (g)	Chol. (mg)	Sod. (mg)	Cal.
Carnation Malted Milk Chocolate, made with 8 fl oz skim milk (3 heaping tsp)	1.4	0.8	5	181	166
Original, made with 8 fl oz skim milk (3 heaping tsp)	2.4	(1.2)	8	231	176
Kraft† Instant Malted Milk, Chocolate, made with 8 fl oz skim milk (3 tsp)	1.4	0.9	(4)	171	176
Nestle Quik Chocolate, dry, made with 8 fl oz skim milk (2½ heaping tsp)	1.4	(0.9)	(4)	151	176

	Tot. Fat (g)	Sat. Fat (g)	Chol. (mg)	Sod. (mg)	Cal.
Strawberry, dry, made with 8 fl oz skim milk (2½ tsp)	0.4	0.3	(4)	126	166
Sugar Free, Chocolate, dry, made with 8 fl oz skim milk	1.0	(<1.0)	(4)	(160)	104
Nestle Quik Syrup, Strawberry Flavor, made with 8 fl oz skim milk (1²/₃ tbsp)	0.4	0.3	(4)	126	186
Weight Watchers Shake Mix Chocolate Fudge, made with water (1 env)	<1.0	(<1.0)	5	150	70
Orange Sherbet, made with water (1 env)	<1.0	0.0	0	210	70

FRUIT-FLAVORED BEVERAGES

Powdered Drink Mixes

	Tot. Fat (g)	Sat. Fat (g)	Chol. (mg)	Sod. (mg)	Cal.
Country Time Sugar Free Drink Mix, Lemonade or Pink Lemonade (8 fl oz)	0.0	0.0	0	0	4
Country Time Sugar Sweetened Drink Mix					
Iced Tea (8 fl oz)	0.0	0.0	0	0	70
Lemonade or Pink Lemonade (8 fl oz)	0.0	0.0	0	15	70
Lemonade Punch (8 fl oz)	0.0	0.0	0	10	70
Crystal Light Sugar Free Diet Soft Drink Mix, all flavors, made with water (8 fl oz)	0.0	0.0	0	0	4
Hi-C Powder Drink Mixes Cherry, made with water (6 fl oz)	0.0	0.0	(0)	25	75
Fruit Punch, made with water (6 fl oz)	0.0	0.0	(0)	0	76
Grape, made with water (6 fl oz)	0.0	0.0	(0)	0	76
Lemonade (pink or white), made with water (6 fl oz)	0.0	0.0	(0)	5	74
Light Fruit Punch, made with water (6 fl oz)	0.0	0.0	(0)	7	3
Light Lemon, made with water (6 fl oz)	0.0	0.0	(0)	3	7
Orange, made with water (6 fl oz)	0.0	0.0	(0)	0	75

	Tot. Fat (g)	Sat. Fat (g)	Chol. (mg)	Sod. (mg)	Cal.
Peach, made with water (6 fl oz)	0.0	0.0	(0)	20	76
Whipped Orange, made with water (6 fl oz)	0.0	0.0	(0)	30	92
Whipped Strawberry, made with water (6 fl oz)	0.0	0.0	(0)	30	91
Knox Drinking Gelatin with Nutrasweet, Orange Flavored (1 env)	0.0	0.0	0	15	40
Kool-Aid Sugar Free Soft Drink Mix					
Cherry, Grape, Great Bluedini, Lemonade, Rock-A-Dile Red or Sharkleberry Fin, made with water (8 fl oz)	0.0	0.0	0	0	4
Mountain Berry Punch, made with water (8 fl oz)	0.0	0.0	0	35	4
Purplesaurus Rex, made with water (8 fl oz)	0.0	0.0	0	5	4
Tropical Punch, made with water (8 fl oz)	0.0	0.0	0	10	4
Kool-Aid Sugar Sweetened Soft Drink Mix					
Cherry, Grape, Great Bluedini, Mountain Berry Punch, Purplesaurus Rex, Raspberry, Rock-A-Dile Red, Sharkleberry Fin, Strawberry, Tropical Punch, made with water (8 fl oz)	0.0	0.0	0	0	70
Lemonade, made with water (8 fl oz)	0.0	0.0	0	0	70
Orange, made with water (8 fl oz)	0.0	0.0	0	5	70
Kool-Aid Unsweetened Soft Drink Mix					
Black Cherry, Cherry, Grape, Great Bluedini, Lemon-Lime, Orange, Rock-A-Dile Red, Sharkleberry Fin, or Tropical Punch, made with sugar and water (8 fl oz)	0.0	0.0	0	0	100
Lemonade or Pink Lemonade, made with sugar and water (8 fl oz)	0.0	0.0	0	10	100
Mountain Berry Punch, made with sugar and water (8 fl oz)	0.0	0.0	0	15	100

BEVERAGES AND BEVERAGE MIXES

11

	Tot. Fat (g)	Sat. Fat (g)	Chol. (mg)	Sod. (mg)	Cal.
Purplesaurus Rex, made with sugar and water (8 fl oz)	0.0	0.0	0	5	100
Raspberry or Strawberry, made with sugar and water (8 fl oz)	0.0	0.0	0	25	100
Tang Beverage Crystals					
Mango Flavored, made with water (6 fl oz)	0.0	0.0	0	0	80
Orange Flavored, made with water (6 fl oz)	0.0	0.0	0	0	70
Sugar Free Orange Flavored, made with water (6 fl oz)	0.0	0.0	0	0	6
Wyler's Flavor Crystals					
Lemonade, made with water (8 fl oz)	(0.0)	(0.0)	0	50	80
Tropical Punch (8 fl oz)	0.0	0.0	(0)	0	80
Wild Strawberry (8 fl oz)	0.0	0.0	(0)	35	80
Wyler's Sweetened Drink Mix					
Bunch 'O Berries, made with water (8 fl oz)	(0.0)	(0.0)	0	15	80
Pink Lemonade, made with water (8 fl oz)	(0.0)	(0.0)	0	50	80
Strawberry Split, made with water (8 fl oz)	(0.0)	(0.0)	0	15	80
Wild Cherry, made with water (8 fl oz)	(0.0)	(0.0)	0	0	80
Wild Grape, made with water (8 fl oz)	(0.0)	(0.0)	0	0	80
Ready-to-Drink					
Bama Fruit Juice Drink					
Fruit Punch (with 10% fruit juice) (8.45 fl oz)	0.0	0.0	(0)	15	130
Grape (with 10% fruit juice) (8.45 fl oz)	0.0	0.0	(0)	25	120
Orange (with 10% fruit juice) (8.45 fl oz)	0.0	0.0	(0)	60	120
Betty Crocker Squeezit					
Cherry or Green Punch (6.75 fl oz)	0.0	0.0	0	0	100
Grape or Red Punch (6.75 fl oz)	0.0	0.0	0	0	90
Orange (6.75 oz)	0.0	0.0	0	50	90

	Tot. Fat (g)	Sat. Fat (g)	Chol. (mg)	Sod. (mg)	Cal.
Strawberry or Wild Berry (6.75 fl oz)	0.0	0.0	0	0	100
Bright & Early Breakfast Beverage (6 fl oz)	0.2	(0.0)	(0)	18	90
Citrus fruit juice drink (6 fl oz)	0.0	0.0	0	6	84
Cranberry juice cocktail (6 fl oz)	0.0	0.0	0	6	102
Five Alive					
Berry Citrus (6 fl oz)	0.1	(0.0)	(0)	21	88
Tropical Citrus (6 fl oz)	0.1	(0.0)	(0)	19	85
Five Alive To-Go Box, Citrus (8.45 fl oz)	0.0	0.0	(0)	32	123
Hawaiian Punch Fruit Juicy, all flavors (8 fl oz)	0.0	0.0	0	30	110
Hi-C Fruit Drink					
Boppin' Berry (6 fl oz)	0.0	0.0	(0)	20	90
Double Fruit Cooler (6 fl oz)	0.0	0.0	(0)	18	93
Fruit Punch (6 fl oz)	0.0	0.0	(0)	17	96
Grape (6 fl oz)	0.1	(0.0)	(0)	17	96
Hula Cooler (6 fl oz)	0.0	0.0	(0)	17	97
Hula Punch (6 fl oz)	0.0	0.0	(0)	17	87
Jammin' Apple (6 fl oz)	0.0	0.0	(0)	16	86
Orange (6 fl oz)	0.0	0.0	(0)	17	95
Peach (6 fl oz)	0.0	0.0	(0)	18	101
Wild Berry (6 fl oz)	0.1	(0.0)	(0)	17	92
Hi-C To-Go Box					
Candy Apple Cooler (8.45 fl oz)	0.0	0.0	(0)	25	132
Cherry (8.45 fl oz)	0.1	(0.0)	(0)	24	141
Double Fruit Cooler (8.45 fl oz)	0.0	0.0	(0)	25	131
Fruit Punch (8.45 fl oz)	0.0	0.0	(0)	24	135
Grape (8.45 fl oz)	0.1	(0.0)	(0)	24	136
Lemonade (8.45 fl oz)	0.1	(0.0)	(0)	73	109
Orange (8.45 fl oz)	0.0	0.0	(0)	24	134
Wild Berry (8.45 fl oz)	0.1	(0.0)	(0)	24	129
IGA Drinks					
Apple Cherry Berry (6 fl oz)	0.0	0.0	0	(20)	100
Cranberry Apple (6 fl oz)	0.0	0.0	0	(10)	120
Cranberry Cocktail (6 fl oz)	0.0	0.0	0	(10)	100
Fruit Punch (6 fl oz)	0.0	0.0	0	(35)	90
Grape (6 fl oz)	0.0	0.0	0	(20)	100
Orange Banana (6 fl oz)	0.0	0.0	0	(5)	100
Papaya Punch (6 fl oz)	0.0	0.0	0	(20)	90

	Tot. Fat (g)	Sat. Fat (g)	Chol. (mg)	Sod. (mg)	Cal.
Pineapple Orange (6 fl oz)	0.0	0.0	0	(20)	90
Pink Grapefruit Cocktail (6 fl oz)	0.0	0.0	0	(10)	90
Tropical Punch (6 fl oz)	0.0	0.0	0	(20)	90
Kern's Islander Punch (8 fl oz)	0.0	0.0	(0)	40	120
Kool-Aid Kool Bursts Soft Drink					
Cherry, Great Bluedini or Tropical					
Punch (6.75 fl oz)	0.0	0.0	0	10	110
Grape or Rock-A-Dile Red (6.75 fl oz)	0.0	0.0	0	10	110
Orange (6.75 fl oz)	0.0	0.0	0	10	130
Kool-Aid Koolers Juice Drink					
Cherry (8.45 fl oz)	0.0	0.0	0	10	140
Grape (8.45 fl oz)	0.0	0.0	0	10	140
Great Bluedini (8.45 fl oz)	0.0	0.0	0	10	110
Lemonade (8.45 fl oz)	0.0	0.0	0	10	120
Orange (8.45 fl oz)	0.0	0.0	0	10	110
Purplesaurus Rex (8.45 fl oz)	0.0	0.0	0	10	130
Rainbow Punch (8.45 fl oz)	0.0	0.0	0	10	130
Rock-A-Dile Red (8.45 fl oz)	0.0	0.0	0	10	130
Sharkleberry Fin (8.45 fl oz)	0.0	0.0	0	10	140
Tropical Punch (8.45 fl oz)	0.0	0.0	0	10	130
Libby's Juice Drink					
Fruit Medley (6 fl oz)	0.0	0.0	(0)	0	80
Grape Medley (6 fl oz)	0.0	0.0	(0)	0	90
Lemonade (6 fl oz)	0.0	0.0	(0)	10	80
McCain Beverages					
Apple Peach (¾ cup)	0.1	0.0	0	11	78
Pineapple Grapefruit (8 fl oz = 1 box)	0.2	0.1	0	8	115
Minute Maid Juices and Punches					
Concord Punch (11.5 fl oz = 1 can)	0.1	(0.0)	(0)	74	178
Fruit Punch (11.5 fl oz = 1 can)	0.1	(0.0)	(0)	33	174
Pink Grapefruit Juice Cocktail					
(11.5 fl oz = 1 can)	0.2	(0.0)	(0)	34	163
Tropical Punch (11.5 fl oz = 1 can)	0.0	0.0	(0)	33	176
Minute Maid On-The-Go Bottle					
Concord Punch (10 fl oz)	0.1	(0.0)	(0)	29	155
Fruit Punch (10 fl oz)	0.1	(0.0)	(0)	29	152
Orange (10 fl oz)	0.6	(0.0)	(0)	32	155
Minute Maid To-Go Box					
Concord Punch (8.45 fl oz)	0.1	(0.0)	(0)	25	131

	Tot. Fat (g)	Sat. Fat (g)	Chol. (mg)	Sod. (mg)	Cal.
Fruit Punch (8.45 fl oz)	0.1	(0.0)	(0)	24	128
Tropical Punch (8.45 fl oz)	0.0	0.0	(0)	24	130
Newman's Own Roadside Virgin Lemonade (8 fl oz)	<1.0	(0.0)	0	0	100
Ocean Spray Drinks					
Cran•Blueberry Blueberry Cranberry (6 fl oz)	0.0	0.0	(0)	10	120
Cran•Grape Grape Cranberry (6 fl oz)	0.0	0.0	(0)	5	130
Cran•Raspberry Raspberry Cranberry (6 fl oz)	0.0	0.0	(0)	5	110
Cran•Raspberry Raspberry Cranberry, Low Calorie (6 fl oz)	0.0	0.0	(0)	10	40
Cran•Strawberry (6 fl oz)	0.0	0.0	(0)	10	110
Cran•Tastic (6 fl oz)	0.0	0.0	(0)	15	110
Cranapple Cranberry Apple (6 fl oz)	0.0	0.0	(0)	10	130
Low Calorie (6 fl oz)	0.0	0.0	(0)	5	40
Cranberry Juice Cocktail, Low Calorie (6 fl oz)	0.0	0.0	(0)	10	40
Cranicot Cranberry Apricot Juice (6 fl oz)	0.0	0.0	(0)	5	110
Mauna La'i Hawaiian Guava (6 fl oz)	0.0	0.0	(0)	10	100
Mauna La'i Hawaiian Guava•Passion Fruit (6 fl oz)	0.0	0.0	(0)	5	100
Pineapple Grapefruit Juice Cocktail (6 fl oz)	0.0	0.0	(0)	5	110
Pink Grapefruit Juice Cocktail (6 fl oz)	0.0	0.0	(0)	15	80
PowerAde, all flavors (6 fl oz)	(0.0)	(0.0)	0	21	54
R.W. Frookie Cool Fruits, Cherry, Grape or Orange (1 fruit squeezer)	0.0	0.0	0	5	35
Sundance Natural Juice Sparklers					
Apple (10 oz)	0.0	0.0	0	23	119
Black Currant (10 oz)	0.0	0.0	0	12	119
Cranberry (10 oz)	0.0	0.0	0	48	133
Kiwi Lime (10 oz)	0.0	0.0	0	34	119
Raspberry (10 oz)	0.0	0.0	0	35	128
Sour Cherry (10 oz)	0.0	0.0	0	20	133
Tropical Lemon (10 oz)	0.0	0.0	0	23	126
Sunny Delight Plus Calcium (8 fl oz)	<1.0	0.0	0	135	135

	Tot. Fat (g)	Sat. Fat (g)	Chol. (mg)	Sod. (mg)	Cal.
Tang Fruit Box Juice Drink					
Berry Blend or Mixed Fruit (8.45 fl oz)	0.0	0.0	0	10	140
Cherry (8.45 fl oz)	0.0	0.0	0	10	130
Grape (8.45 fl oz)	0.0	0.0	0	10	130
Orange (8.45 fl oz)	0.0	0.0	0	10	130
Tropical Orange (8.45 fl oz)	0.0	0.0	0	10	150
Treehouse Beverages					
Apple Cherry (6 fl oz)	0.0	0.0	0	8	66
Apple Cranberry (8.3 fl oz = 1 drinking box)	0.1	0.0	0	7	131
Grape Raspberry (6 fl oz)	0.0	0.0	0	6	72
Orange Banana (6 fl oz)	0.0	0.0	0	5	73
Orange Peach (6 fl oz)	0.0	0.0	0	5	70
Pineapple Tangerine (8.3 fl oz = 1 drinking box)	0.1	0.0	0	6	113
TreeSweet Beverage, Awake					
Orange (6 fl oz)	0.0	0.0	0	10	80
Orange Plus Citrus (6 fl oz)	0.0	0.0	0	20	100
Welch's Juice Cocktail					
Apple Cranberry (6 fl oz)	0.0	0.0	0	20	110
Apple Grape Cherry (6 fl oz)	0.0	0.0	0	20	110
Apple Grape Raspberry (6 fl oz)	0.0	0.0	0	20	110
Fruit Punch (6 fl oz)	0.0	0.0	0	20	100
Grape (6 fl oz)	0.0	0.0	0	20	100
Orange-Pineapple-Apple (6 fl oz)	0.0	0.0	0	20	110
Tropical (6 fl oz)	0.0	0.0	0	20	110
Welch's Orchard Juice Cocktail					
Apple-Orange-Pineapple (6 fl oz)	0.0	0.0	0	20	110
Grape (6 fl oz)	0.0	0.0	0	20	110
Grape-Apple (bottle) (6 fl oz)	0.0	0.0	0	20	110
Harvest Blend (6 fl oz)	0.0	0.0	0	20	110
Welch's Orchard Tropical Drink					
Passion Fruit (6 fl oz)	0.0	0.0	0	20	100
Pineapple Banana (6 fl oz)	0.0	0.0	0	20	100
Wyler's Flavored Drink					
Fruit Punch (8 fl oz)	0.0	0.0	(0)	5	130
Lemonade (8 fl oz)	(0.0)	(0.0)	(0)	30	110

Reconstituted from Frozen

	Tot. Fat (g)	Sat. Fat (g)	Chol. (mg)	Sod. (mg)	Cal.
Five Alive, Citrus, made with water (6 fl oz)	0.0	0.0	(0)	6	87
Hi-C Fruit Punch, made with water (6 fl oz)	0.4	(0.0)	(0)	10	95
Minute Maid Punch					
Apple, made with water (6 fl oz)	0.0	0.0	(0)	0	90
Citrus, made with water (6 fl oz)	0.0	0.0	(0)	18	93
Fruit, made with water (6 fl oz)	0.1	(0.0)	(0)	17	91
Grape, made with water (6 fl oz)	0.0	0.0	(0)	3	89
Welch's Juice Cocktail					
Cranberry, no sugar added, made with water (6 fl oz)	0.0	0.0	0	5	40
Cranberry Apple, made with water (6 fl oz)	0.0	0.0	0	0	120
Cranberry Cherry, made with water (6 fl oz)	0.0	0.0	0	0	110
Cranberry Orange, made with water (6 fl oz)	0.0	0.0	0	0	110
Cranberry Raspberry, made with water (6 fl oz)	0.0	0.0	0	0	110
Cran-Raspberry, no sugar added, made with water (6 fl oz)	0.0	0.0	0	0	40
Grape, no sugar added, made with water (6 fl oz)	0.0	0.0	0	0	40
Orange-Pineapple-Apple, made with water (6 fl oz)	0.0	0.0	0	0	110
Welch's Orchard Juice Cocktail					
Apple-Grape-Cherry, made with water (6 fl oz)	0.0	0.0	0	0	110
Apple-Grape-Raspberry, made with water (6 fl oz)	0.0	0.0	0	0	110
Fruit Harvest Punch, made with water (6 fl oz)	0.0	0.0	0	0	100
Grape-Apple, made with water (6 fl oz)	0.0	0.0	0	0	110
Harvest Blend, made with water (6 fl oz)	0.0	0.0	0	0	110

	Tot. Fat (g)	Sat. Fat (g)	Chol. (mg)	Sod. (mg)	Cal.

INSTANT BREAKFAST MIXES

Carnation Diet Instant Breakfast

	Tot. Fat (g)	Sat. Fat (g)	Chol. (mg)	Sod. (mg)	Cal.
Chocolate, made with 8 fl oz skim milk (1 env)	1.2	0.8	6	241	156
Chocolate Malt, made with 8 fl oz skim milk (1 env)	2.0	1.0	6	261	156
Strawberry, made with 8 fl oz skim milk (1 env)	0.7	0.4	7	246	156
Vanilla, made with 8 fl oz skim milk (1 env)	0.6	0.4	7	246	156

Carnation Instant Breakfast

	Tot. Fat (g)	Sat. Fat (g)	Chol. (mg)	Sod. (mg)	Cal.
Chocolate, made with 8 fl oz skim milk (1 env)	1.3	0.8	6	261	216
Chocolate Malt, made with 8 fl oz skim milk (1 env)	1.7	1.0	7	286	216
Coffee, made with 8 fl oz skim milk (1 env)	0.7	0.4	7	276	216
Strawberry, made with 8 fl oz skim milk (1 env)	0.6	0.4	7	336	216
Vanilla, made with 8 fl oz skim milk (1 env)	0.6	0.4	7	261	216

Pillsbury Instant Breakfast

	Tot. Fat (g)	Sat. Fat (g)	Chol. (mg)	Sod. (mg)	Cal.
Chocolate, made with skim milk (8 fl oz)	<1.0	(<1.0)	(8)	326	216
Chocolate Malt, made with skim milk (8 fl oz)	<1.0	(<1.0)	(8)	346	216
Strawberry, made with skim milk (8 fl oz)	<1.0	(<1.0)	(8)	306	216
Vanilla, made with skim milk (8 fl oz)	<1.0	(<1.0)	(8)	336	226

TEA—see **COFFEE/TEA**

† = tobacco company, corporate subsidiary or parent

BEVERAGES AND BEVERAGE MIXES

BREADS AND BREAD PRODUCTS

The breads and bread products in this section are low in fat, saturated fat and cholesterol as purchased or when prepared according to package directions.

"Complete" mixes for biscuits, pancakes and waffles already contain fat and usually call only for the addition of water. If you follow the manufacturer's directions for most "incomplete" mixes, the products will not meet AHA criteria. If you use egg substitute or egg white, skim milk and less oil or margarine, however, the result can be a prepared product that is lower in fat, saturated fat and cholesterol than one made with a complete mix.

Products listed in this book vary in sodium content. Use the values appearing on the following pages to help plan a daily intake providing no more than 3,000 milligrams of sodium.

Most of the foods in this book are brand name products; however, when a brand name is not specified, it means that most brands of that product provide about the same amount of fat, saturated fat and cholesterol and that these amounts do not exceed AHA criteria.

You can use those generic entries and the tables below to evaluate products introduced since this book went to press.

	Tot. Fat (g)	Sat. Fat (g)	Chol. (mg)
Bagels, biscuits, breads, cornbread, English muffins, French toast, hamburger and hot dog buns, pancakes, pita bread, rolls, soft breadsticks, stuffing mixes (prepared), tortillas and waffles	3	1	<2
Batter mixes, bread crumbs, croutons and hard breadsticks	3	<0.5	<2

* Per serving.

Breads and Bread Products Not Recommended for Frequent Consumption

Some types of bread and bread products that are usually too high in fat, saturated fat and/or cholesterol to be recommended for frequent consumption are shown in the table below. Values that exceed AHA criteria are followed by asterisks. The AHA does not have criteria for sodium.

You can use the values in the table to compare these breads and bread products with more-healthful alternatives listed on the following pages.

Breads and Bread Products High in Fat, Saturated Fat and/or Cholesterol

	Tot. Fat (g)	Sat. Fat (g)	Chol. (mg)	Sod. (mg)	Cal.
Biscuit, made from mix with 2% milk (1 3-inch-diameter biscuit)	6.9*	1.6*	(2)	544	191
Buttermilk pancakes, made from mix with egg, oil and 2% milk (3 4-inch-diameter pancakes)	8.7*	2.3*	81*	576	249
Cheese croissant (1 medium)	11.9*	5.5*	(27)*	316	236
Cornbread, made from mix with egg and 2% milk (3³/₄ inches by 2¹/₂ inches by ³/₄ inch)	6.0*	1.6*	37*	467	189
Cornbread stuffing, made from mix with stick margarine (¹/₂ cup)	8.8*	1.8*	0	455	179
Crescent roll, made from refrigerated dough (2¹/₂ inches in diameter or about 2 ounces)	8.0*	2.0*	0	648	186

Adapted from USDA Handbook No. 8 series.

* These values exceed AHA criteria for breads and bread products.

	Tot. Fat (g)	Sat. Fat (g)	Chol. (mg)	Sod. (mg)	Cal.
BAGELS					
Cinnamon Raisin Bagels					
David's Deli Bagels, Cinnamon Raisin (2.85 oz = 1 bagel)	0.0	0.0	0	375	200
Lender's					
Bagelettes, Cinnamon'n Raisin (.9 oz)	1.0	(0.2)	0	115	70
Bagels, Cinnamon'n Raisin (2.5 oz)	2.0	(0.3)	0	310	190
Big'n Crusty Bagels, Cinnamon'n Raisin (3 oz)	2.0	(0.3)	0	330	230
Sara Lee					
Bagels, Cinnamon Raisin (2.5 oz = 1 bagel)	2.0	(0.3)	0	230	200
Deli Style Bagels, Cinnamon Raisin (2.8 oz = 1 bagel)	2.0	(0.2)	0	280	240
Egg Bagels					
David's Deli Bagels (2.85 oz = 1 bagel)	<1.0	0.0	0	390	208
Lender's					
Bagels (2 oz)	1.0	(0.1)	0	310	150
Big'n Crusty Bagels (3 oz)	1.0	(0.1)	0	400	210
Garlic Bagels					
Lender's					
Bagels (2 oz)	1.0	(0.2)	0	280	140
Big'n Crusty Bagels (3 oz)	1.0	(0.2)	0	420	210
Onion Bagels					
David's Deli Bagels (2.85 oz = 1 bagel)	<1.0	0.0	0	390	208
Lender's					
Bagelettes (.9 oz)	<1.0	(0.0)	0	110	70
Bagels (2 oz)	1.0	(0.2)	0	300	150
Big'n Crusty Bagels (3 oz)	1.0	(0.2)	0	410	210

	Tot. Fat (g)	Sat. Fat (g)	Chol. (mg)	Sod. (mg)	Cal.
Sara Lee					
Bagels (2.5 oz = 1 bagel)	1.0	(0.2)	0	450	190
Deli Style Bagels (2.8 oz = 1 bagel)	1.0	(0.2)	0	630	230

Plain Bagels

	Tot. Fat (g)	Sat. Fat (g)	Chol. (mg)	Sod. (mg)	Cal.
Plain bagels (2.5 oz = 1 med)	1.1	0.2	0	379	195
David's Deli Bagels (2.85 oz = 1 bagel)	0.0	0.0	0	375	208
Lender's					
Bagelettes (.9 oz)	<1.0	(0.0)	0	130	70
Bagels (2 oz)	1.0	(0.2)	0	320	150
Big'n Crusty Bagels (3 oz)	2.0	(0.3)	0	430	210
Sara Lee					
Bagels (2.5 oz = 1 bagel)	1.0	(0.2)	0	460	190
Deli Style Bagels (2.8 oz = 1 bagel)	1.0	(0.2)	0	540	230

Poppy Seed Bagels

	Tot. Fat (g)	Sat. Fat (g)	Chol. (mg)	Sod. (mg)	Cal.
Sara Lee					
Bagels (2.5 oz = 1 bagel)	1.0	(0.2)	0	450	190
Deli Style Bagels (2.8 oz = 1 bagel)	1.0	(0.2)	0	580	230

Sesame Bagels

	Tot. Fat (g)	Sat. Fat (g)	Chol. (mg)	Sod. (mg)	Cal.
David's Deli Bagels (2.85 oz = 1 bagel)	<1.0	0.0	0	375	208
Lender's Bagels (2 oz)	1.0	(0.2)	0	280	150
Sara Lee					
Bagels (2.5 oz = 1 bagel)	1.0	(0.2)	0	440	190
Deli Style Bagels (2.8 oz = 1 bagel)	3.0	(0.5)	0	570	260

Other Bagels

	Tot. Fat (g)	Sat. Fat (g)	Chol. (mg)	Sod. (mg)	Cal.
Lender's Bagels					
Blueberry (2.5 oz)	2.0	(0.3)	0	320	190
Oat Bran (2.5 oz)	2.0	(0.4)	0	300	170
Poppy Seed (2 oz)	1.0	(0.2)	0	290	140
Pumpernickel (2 oz)	1.0	(0.1)	0	330	140
Rye (2 oz)	1.0	(0.1)	0	320	140
Sara Lee Bagels, Oat Bran (2.5 oz = 1 bagel)	1.0	(0.2)	0	360	180

BREADS AND BREAD PRODUCTS

	Tot. Fat (g)	Sat. Fat (g)	Chol. (mg)	Sod. (mg)	Cal.
BATTER MIXES/BREAD CRUMBS					
Devonsheer Bread Crumbs, Plain					
(1 oz)	1.4	(0.4)	0	272	108
Dixie Fry (1 oz)	1.2	(0.4)	(0)	710	96
Kellogg's Corn Flakes Crumbs (1 oz)	0.0	0.0	0	290	100
Croutettes (1 oz)	0.0	0.0	0	370	100
Mrs. Dash Crispy Coating Mix (17 g)	0.1	(0.0)	0	3	(60)
Old London Bread Crumbs					
Italian Style (1/2 oz)	0.6	0.0	0	200	50
Plain (1/2 oz)	0.5	0.0	0	80	50
Progresso Bread Crumbs					
Italian Style (2 tbsp)	<1.0	(0.0)	0	240	60
Plain (2 tbsp)	<1.0	(0.0)	0	110	60
Shake 'N Bake Seasoning and Coating Mixture					
Original Barbecue Recipe for Pork (1/8 pkt)	0.0	0.0	0	260	35
Original Recipe for Fish (1/4 pkt)	1.0	(0.3)	0	410	70
Tone's Bread Crumbs					
Italian (1 tsp)	0.1	0.0	0	15	8
Plain (1 tsp)	0.1	0.0	0	15	8
Tone's Cajun Batter					
Chicken (1 tsp)	0.1	0.0	0	75	12
Fish (1 tsp)	0.1	0.0	0	49	12
BISCUITS					
Ballard					
Extra Lights Ovenready Biscuits (1 biscuit)	<1.0	0.0	0	180	50
Extra Ready Ovenready Buttermilk Biscuits (1 biscuit)	<1.0	0.0	0	180	50
La Loma Ruskets Biscuits (1 oz = 2 biscuits)	0.0	0.0	0	95	110
Pillsbury					
Butter Biscuits (1 biscuit)	<1.0	0.0	0	180	50
Buttermilk Biscuits (1 biscuit)	1.0	0.0	0	180	50
Country Biscuits (1 biscuit)	1.0	0.0	0	180	50

	Tot. Fat (g)	Sat. Fat (g)	Chol. (mg)	Sod. (mg)	Cal.
Hungry Jack Extra Rich Buttermilk Biscuits (1 biscuit)	1.0	0.0	0	180	50
Tender Layer Buttermilk Biscuits (1 biscuit)	1.0	0.0	0	170	50
Roman Meal Biscuits, Mixed Grain, refrigerated (2 biscuits)	3.8	0.9	0	456	180

BREADS

Bran Breads

	Tot. Fat (g)	Sat. Fat (g)	Chol. (mg)	Sod. (mg)	Cal.
Brownberry Bread, Bran'nola Nutty Grains (1 slice)	2.4	0.5	0	120	90
Country Harvest Bread, Prairie Bran (1 slice)	1.4	0.2	0	(180)	83
Grant's Farm Bread, Honey Wheat Bran (1 oz = 1 slice)	1.0	(0.2)	0	120	70
Pepperidge Farm Bread, Honey Bran (1 slice)	1.0	(0.2)	0	160	90
Stonehouse Farm Bread, Honey Bran (1 slice)	1.4	(0.3)	(0)	(185)	91
Wheat bran bread (1 oz = 1 slice)	1.0	0.2	0	138	70

Diet/Light Breads—see also specific types of bread

	Tot. Fat (g)	Sat. Fat (g)	Chol. (mg)	Sod. (mg)	Cal.
Brownberry Bakery Bread, Light Italian (.8 oz = 1 slice)	0.5	0.1	0	70	40
Colonial Bread, Light Oat Bran (3/4 oz = 1 slice)	<1.0	(0.0)	0	100	40
Diet, light, lite, thin or very thin bread (1.2 oz = 2 slices)	1.2	0.3	0	208	96
Earth Grains Bread					
Light Rye (1 oz)	1.0	(0.2)	0	240	70
Light Sour Dough (3/4 oz)	1.0	0.2	0	115	40
Grant's Farm Bread, Light 7-Grain (3/4 oz = 1 slice)	<1.0	(0.0)	0	115	40
Kilpatrick's Bread, Light Oat Bran (3/4 oz = 1 slice)	<1.0	(0.0)	0	100	40
Oatmeal Goodness Light Bran (9/10 oz = 1 slice)	<1.0	<1.0	0	95	40

	Tot. Fat (g)	Sat. Fat (g)	Chol. (mg)	Sod. (mg)	Cal.
Wheat (8/10 oz = 1 slice)	<1.0	<1.0	0	90	40
Pepperidge Farm Light Style					
Oatmeal (.7 oz = 1 slice)	0.0	0.0	0	95	45
Seven Grain (.7 oz)	0.0	0.0	0	135	40
Vienna (.7 oz = 1 slice)	0.0	0.0	0	100	45
Rainbo Bread, Light Oat Bran (3/4 oz = 1 slice)	<1.0	(0.0)	0	100	40
Roman Meal Light Bread					
Oat Bran (.8 oz = 1 slice)	0.4	0.0	0	100	42
Seven Grain (.8 oz = 1 slice)	0.5	0.0	0	101	42
Sourdough (.8 oz = 1 slice)	0.4	0.0	0	115	41
Twelve Grain (.8 oz = 1 slice)	0.5	0.0	0	104	42
Wheatberry (.8 oz = 1 slice)	0.4	0.0	0	102	42
Whole Grain Sourdough (.8 oz = 1 slice)	0.3	0.0	0	104	40
Wonder Light Bread					
Italian (8/10 oz = 1 slice)	0.0	0.0	0	115	40
Sourdough (8/10 oz = 1 slice)	0.0	0.0	0	115	40

French Breads

	Tot. Fat (g)	Sat. Fat (g)	Chol. (mg)	Sod. (mg)	Cal.
Dicarlo's Parisian French (1 oz = 1 slice)	1.0	<1.0	0	170	70
French bread (1 oz = 1 slice)	0.8	0.2	0	172	78
Pepperidge Farm Hearth Bread, French Style Enriched					
Fully Baked (1 oz)	1.0	0.0	0	140	80
Sliced French (1 oz)	1.0	(0.2)	(0)	160	80
Twin French (1 oz)	1.0	(0.0)	0	160	80

Italian Breads

	Tot. Fat (g)	Sat. Fat (g)	Chol. (mg)	Sod. (mg)	Cal.
Italian bread (1 oz = 1 slice)	0.2	0.0	0	166	77
Pepperidge Farm Hearth Bread, Italian, sliced (.9 oz = 1 slice)	1.0	0.0	0	125	70
Weight Watcher's Bread, Italian (.8 oz = 1 slice)	0.4	0.0	0	99	38

Light Breads—see
Diet/Light Breads

	Tot. Fat (g)	Sat. Fat (g)	Chol. (mg)	Sod. (mg)	Cal.

Multigrain Breads

Brownberry Natural Bread, 12 Grain
(.8 oz = 1 slice)...................................1.2 | 0.2 | 0 | 90 | 50

Colonial Family Recipe Bread, Honey
Grain (1 oz = 1 slice)........................1.0 | (0.2) | 0 | 180 | 70

Country Hearth Bread, Grainola
(1 oz = 1 slice)...................................1.0 | (0.2) | (0) | 240 | 70

Grant's Farm Bread, Honey Grain
(1 oz = 1 slice)...................................1.0 | (0.2) | 0 | 170 | 70

Kilpatrick's
Family Recipe Bread, Honey Grain
(1 oz = 1 slice)...................................1.0 | (0.2) | 0 | 180 | 70

Honey Grain (1 oz = 1 slice)...................1.0 | (0.2) | 0 | 170 | 70

Multigrain (1 oz = 1 slice)......................1.1 | 0.2 | 0 | 138 | 71

Rainbo Family Recipe Bread, Honey
Grain (1 oz = 1 slice)........................1.0 | (0.2) | 0 | 180 | 70

Roman Meal Bread
Sun Grain (1 oz = 1 slice)......................1.6 | 0.2 | 0 | 135 | 70

Twelve Grain (1 oz = 1 slice)..................1.7 | 0.2 | 0 | 140 | 70

Rubschlager Cocktail Bread, Honey
Whole Grain (¾ oz = 2 slices)........<1.0 | (0.0) | 0 | 100 | 50

Seven-grain breads (1 oz = 1 slice)..........1.1 | 0.2 | 0 | 138 | 71

Weight Watcher's Bread, Multi-Grain
(.8 oz = 1 slice).................................0.5 | 0.1 | 0 | 98 | 41

Oat Breads

Arnold Bakery Bread
Oatmeal (.9 oz = 1 slice)......................1.2 | (0.2) | <1 | 93 | 60

Oatmeal Raisin (1 slice)........................0.7 | (0.2) | 0 | 91 | 58

Brownberry Natural Bread, Oatmeal
(1 slice)..1.1 | 0.4 | 0 | 140 | 65

Colonial Family Recipe Bread, Split
Top Oat (1 oz = 1 slice)......................1.0 | (0.2) | 0 | 140 | 70

Country Harvest Bread
Oat Bran (2 slices)...............................3.2 | 0.8 | 0 | (335) | 186

Oat 'N' Honey (1 slice)..........................1.4 | 0.2 | 0 | (195) | 106

Country Hearth Bread, Honey & Oat
(1 oz = 1 slice)...................................1.0 | (0.3) | (1) | 180 | 70

	Tot. Fat (g)	Sat. Fat (g)	Chol. (mg)	Sod. (mg)	Cal.
Earth Grains Bread					
Honey Oat Bran (1 oz = 1 slice)	1.0	(0.3)	0	105	80
Honey Oatberry (1 oz = 1 slice)	1.0	(0.2)	0	135	70
Grant's Farm Bread, Oatmeal &					
Toasted Almond (1 oz = 1 slice)	1.0	(0.2)	0	135	80
Kilpatrick's Family Recipe Bread, Split					
Top Oat (1 oz = 1 slice)	1.0	(0.2)	0	140	70
Oatmeal Goodness					
Oatmeal/Bran (1²/₁₀ oz = 1 slice)	1.0	<1.0	0	150	80
Oatmeal/Sunflower Seeds (1²/₁₀ oz =					
1 slice)	1.0	<1.0	0	150	80
Oatmeal/Wheat (1²/₁₀ oz = 1 slice)	1.0	<1.0	0	150	80
Pepperidge Farm Bread, Hearty					
Crunchy Oat (2.7 oz = 2 slices)	4.0	1.0	0	290	190
Rainbo Family Recipe Bread, Split Top					
Oat (1 oz = 1 slice)	1.0	(0.2)	0	140	70
Roman Meal Bread					
Honey Nut Oat Bran (1 oz = 1 slice)	1.7	0.2	0	129	72
Honey Oat Bran (1 oz = 1 slice)	1.2	0.2	0	132	70
Stonehouse Farm Bread, Oat 'N' Fibre					
(1 slice)	1.3	0.4	0	(170)	97
Weight Watcher's Bread, Oat (.8 oz =					
1 slice)	0.5	0.1	0	102	41

Pumpernickel Breads

	Tot. Fat (g)	Sat. Fat (g)	Chol. (mg)	Sod. (mg)	Cal.
Earth Grains Bread, Pumpernickel Rye					
(1 oz)	<1.0	(0.2)	0	220	70
Pepperidge Farm Party Bread,					
Pumpernickel (.85 oz = 4 slices)	1.0	0.0	0	160	60
Pumpernickel bread (1 oz = 1 slice)	0.9	0.1	0	190	71
Rubschlager Bread					
Cocktail Bread, Pumpernickel (³/₄ oz =					
2 slices)	1.0	(0.2)	0	125	60
Danish Pumpernickel (1 oz = 1 slice)	<1.0	(0.0)	0	140	70
Westphalian Pumpernickel (1 oz =					
1 slice)	<1.0	(0.0)	0	130	70

	Tot. Fat (g)	Sat. Fat (g)	Chol. (mg)	Sod. (mg)	Cal.
Raisin Breads					
B & M Brown Bread, Raisin (1.6 oz)	0.0	0.0	0	320	94
Brownberry Bread					
Orange Raisin (1 slice)	1.2	(0.3)	0	83	67
Raisin Bran (1 slice)	1.3	(0.3)	0	108	61
Raisin Cinnamon (1 slice)	1.3	(0.3)	0	107	66
Raisin bread (1 oz = 1 slice)	1.3	0.3	0	111	78
Rubschlager Bread, Raisin Pumpernickel (¾ oz = 1 slice)	<1.0	(0.0)	0	105	60
Sun•Maid Raisin Bread (1 oz = 1 slice)	1.0	(0.2)	(0)	105	80
Weight Watcher's Bread, Raisin (.8 oz = 1 slice)	0.4	0.1	0	95	55
Rye Breads					
Beefsteak Rye Bread					
Hearty (9/10 oz = 1 slice)	1.0	<1.0	0	170	60
Onion (9/10 oz = 1 slice)	1.0	<1.0	0	170	60
Earth Grains Bread					
Dill Rye (1 oz = 1 slice)	1.0	0.4	0	190	80
Extra Sour Rye (1 oz = 1 slice)	1.0	0.3	0	200	70
Very Thin Light Rye (1 oz)	1.0	(0.2)	0	230	70
Grant's Farm Bread, Honey Cracked Rye (1 oz = 1 slice)	1.0	(0.4)	0	190	70
Pepperidge Farm Bread					
Dijon Rye (.8 oz = 1 slice)	1.0	0.0	0	180	50
Family Bread, Seedless Rye (1.15 oz = 1 slice)	1.0	0.0	0	210	80
Party Bread, Rye (.85 oz = 4 slices)	1.0	0.0	0	250	60
Rubschlager Bread					
Cocktail Bread, Rye (¾ oz = 2 slices)	1.0	(0.2)	0	135	50
Jewish Deli Rye (1 oz = 1 slice)	1.0	(0.2)	0	150	70
Swedish Limpa Rye (¾ oz = 1 slice)	1.0	(0.1)	0	95	60
Rye bread (1 oz = 1 slice)	0.9	0.2	0	187	73
Weight Watcher's Bread, Rye (.8 oz = 1 slice)	0.3	0.0	0	100	38

	Tot. Fat (g)	Sat. Fat (g)	Chol. (mg)	Sod. (mg)	Cal.
Sourdough Breads					
Roman Meal Bread, Whole Grain Sourdough (1 oz = 1 slice)	0.9	0.1	0	141	65
Sourdough bread (1 oz = 1 slice)	0.8	0.2	0	172	78
Wheat Breads					
B & M Brown Bread, Plain (1.6 oz)	0.0	0.0	0	345	92
Bread du Jour, Austrian Wheat (1 oz = 1 slice)	1.0	<1.0	0	140	70
Bridgeford Bread Dough, Honey Wheat (1 oz)	1.0	(0.2)	0	150	80
Colonial Family Recipe Bread, Honey Buttered Split Top Wheat (1 oz = 1 slice)	1.0	(0.2)	0	140	70
Earth Grains Bread, Honey Wheat Berry (1 oz = 1 slice)	1.0	(0.2)	0	160	70
Grant's Farm Bread, Wheatberry (1 oz = 1 slice)	1.0	(0.2)	0	150	70
Kilpatrick's Family Recipe Bread, Honey Buttered Split Top Wheat (1 oz = 1 slice)	1.0	(0.2)	0	140	70
Pepperidge Farm Bread, Hearty Sesame Wheat (2 slices)	3.0	1.0	0	340	190
Rainbo Family Recipe Bread, Honey Buttered Split Top Wheat (1 oz = 1 slice)	1.0	(0.2)	0	140	70
Roman Meal Bread, Honey Wheat-Berry (1 oz = 1 slice)	0.9	0.1	0	139	67
Rubschlager Bread, 100% Stone Ground Whole Wheat (1 oz = 1 slice)	1.0	(0.2)	0	130	70
Whole wheat bread (1 oz = 1 slice)	1.2	0.3	(1)	149	70
White Breads					
Bridgeford Bread Dough, White (1 oz)	1.0	(0.3)	0	160	80
Colonial Family Recipe Bread, Honey Buttered Split Top White (1 oz = 1 slice)	1.0	(0.3)	0	140	80

	Tot. Fat (g)	Sat. Fat (g)	Chol. (mg)	Sod. (mg)	Cal.
Earth Grains Bread, Salt Free Sandwich (1 oz = 1 slice)	1.0	(0.3)	0	20	80
Grant's Farm Bread, Buttermilk (1 oz = 1 slice)	1.0	(0.3)	0	190	70
Kilpatrick's Family Recipe Bread, Honey Buttered Split Top White (1 oz = 1 slice)	1.0	(0.3)	0	140	80
Rainbo Bread					
Family Recipe Bread, Honey Buttered Split Top White (1 oz = 1 slice)	1.0	(0.3)	0	140	80
IronKids (1 oz = 1 slice)	1.0	(0.2)	0	140	60
White bread (1 oz = 1 slice)	1.2	0.3	(0)	149	70

Other Breads

	Tot. Fat (g)	Sat. Fat (g)	Chol. (mg)	Sod. (mg)	Cal.
Earth Grains Bread, Onion & Garlic (1 oz)	1.0	0.2	0	140	70
Nature's Grain Bread, Cinnamon Hot Bread (2 oz = 1 section)	2.0	(0.3)	(0)	260	140
Pepperidge Farm Swirl Bread, Apple Walnut (1 oz = 1 slice)	1.0	0.0	0	130	80
Rubschlager Bread					
Bagel (1⅓ oz = 1 slice)	2.0	(0.4)	0	175	90
German-Style Kommissbrot (1 oz = 1 slice)	1.0	(0.1)	0	150	70
Marble (.8 oz = 1 slice)	1.0	(0.2)	0	125	50
Stonehouse Farm Bread, Potato Scone (1 slice)	0.8	(0.2)	(0)	(195)	90
Tortilla, corn (.9 oz = 1 tortilla)	0.6	0.1	0	40	56

BREADSTICKS

	Tot. Fat (g)	Sat. Fat (g)	Chol. (mg)	Sod. (mg)	Cal.
Angonoa Breadsticks					
Cheese (1 oz)	2.0	(0.3)	0	210	110
Garlic (1 oz)	2.0	(0.3)	0	160	120
Italian (1 oz)	2.0	(0.3)	0	240	120
Mini Cheese (1 oz)	2.0	(0.3)	0	160	110
Mini Pizza (1 oz)	2.0	(0.3)	0	220	120
Barbara's Bakery Breadsticks (1 oz = 8 sticks)	3.0	(0.4)	0	170	120

	Tot. Fat (g)	Sat. Fat (g)	Chol. (mg)	Sod. (mg)	Cal.
Italian Style (1 oz = 8 sticks)	3.0	(0.4)	0	170	120
Breadsticks, 9¼″ × ⅜″ diam					
(5 breadsticks)	3.0	0.4	0	195	125
Delicious Breadsticks					
Cheese (1 oz)	1.3	0.3	<1	259	111
Garlic (1 oz)	1.5	0.4	0	171	113
Italian (1 oz)	1.4	0.4	0	330	108
Sesame (1 oz)	2.5	0.6	0	208	117
Whole Wheat Sesame (1 oz)	3.1	0.8	0	124	117
Fattorie & Pandea Grissini Breadsticks					
Pizza (½ oz = 3 sticks)	1.0	(0.1)	(0)	100	59
Sesame (½ oz = 3 sticks)	2.0	(0.3)	(0)	100	65
Traditional (½ oz = 3 sticks)	1.0	(0.1)	(0)	100	60
Whole Wheat (½ oz = 3 sticks)	1.0	(0.1)	(0)	100	57
Lance Breadsticks					
Cheese (2 breadsticks)	<1.0	0.0	0	40	20
Garlic (2 breadsticks)	<1.0	0.0	0	40	30
Plain (2 breadsticks)	<1.0	0.0	0	50	30
Pepperidge Farm Crunchy Baked Snacks, Thin Breadsticks					
Onion (½ oz)	1.0	0.0	0	75	60
Sesame (.5 oz)	2.0	0.0	0	90	60
Pillsbury Breadsticks (1 breadstick)	2.0	<1.0	0	230	100
Roman Meal Breadsticks, Brown & Serve, Soft (2.7 oz = 1 breadstick)	2.9	0.1	0	366	181

COATINGS—see
BATTER MIXES/BREAD CRUMBS

CROUTONS

	Tot. Fat (g)	Sat. Fat (g)	Chol. (mg)	Sod. (mg)	Cal.
Arnold Crispy Croutons, Fine Herbs (½ oz)	0.8	(0.7)	0	151	53
Brownberry Croutons					
Caesar Salad (½ oz)	2.7	0.6	0	150	60
Cheese & Garlic (½ oz)	2.1	(0.4)	0	120	60
Ranch (½ oz)	2.4	0.5	0	170	60
Pepperidge Farm Croutons					
Cheddar and Romano Cheese (½ oz)	2.0	0.0	0	200	60

	Tot. Fat (g)	Sat. Fat (g)	Chol. (mg)	Sod. (mg)	Cal.
Olive Oil and Garlic (.5 oz)	2.0	0.0	0	160	60
Onion and Garlic (1/2 oz)	3.0	0.0	0	160	70
Prepco Francisco Croutons (1/2 oz)	2.0	(0.5)	0	195	65

CRUMPETS—see
ENGLISH MUFFINS, Crumpets

ENGLISH MUFFINS

Cinnamon Raisin/Raisin English Muffins

	Tot. Fat (g)	Sat. Fat (g)	Chol. (mg)	Sod. (mg)	Cal.
Arnold English Muffins, Raisin (1 muffin)	1.4	(0.2)	0	220	150
Crystal Farms English Muffins, Raisin (2 oz)	1.0	<1.0	0	190	140
Earth Grains English Muffins, Raisin (2.3 oz = 1 muffin)	2.0	0.3	0	300	160
Oatmeal Goodness English Muffins, Cinnamon Raisin (1 muffin)	2.0	<1.0	0	190	140
Pepperidge Farm English Muffins Cinnamon Raisin Bran (1 muffin)	2.0	0.0	0	200	150
Wholesome Choice English Muffins, Cinnamon Raisin (2.05 oz = 1 muffin)	1.0	0.0	0	120	120
Sun•Maid English Muffins, Raisin (2.5 oz = 1 muffin)	1.0	0.4	0	180	160
Thomas' English Muffins, Raisin with Cinnamon (1 muffin)	1.2	(0.2)	0	180	140
Wolferman's Deluxe English Muffins, Cinnamon Raisin (1/2 muffin)	<1.0	(0.0)	0	229	110

Crumpets

	Tot. Fat (g)	Sat. Fat (g)	Chol. (mg)	Sod. (mg)	Cal.
Wolferman's Crumpets Brown Sugar Cinnamon (1 crumpet)	2.0	(0.3)	0	220	110
Buttermilk (1 crumpet)	<1.0	(0.0)	0	230	100

	Tot. Fat (g)	Sat. Fat (g)	Chol. (mg)	Sod. (mg)	Cal.
Fruit English Muffins					
Amana English Muffins					
Apple Cinnamon (1/2 muffin)	0.0	0.0	(0)	105	41
Blueberry (1/2 muffin)	0.0	0.0	(0)	105	56
Pepperidge Farm English Muffins,					
Cinnamon Apple (1 muffin)	1.0	0.0	0	210	140
Wolferman's Deluxe English Muffins,					
Apple Strudel (1/2 muffin)	2.0	(0.3)	0	220	110
Oat English Muffins					
Earth Grains English Muffins, Oat					
Bran (2 oz = 1 muffin)	1.0	0.4	0	410	120
Oatmeal Goodness English Muffins,					
Honey and Oatmeal (1 muffin)	2.0	<1.0	0	210	140
Roman Meal English Muffins, Honey					
Nut & Oat Bran, Refrigerated (1/2					
muffin)	1.3	0.2	0	114	81
Thomas' English Muffins, Oat Bran (1					
muffin)	1.1	0.5	0	210	120
Plain/Regular English Muffins					
Arnold English Muffins, Extra Crisp (1					
muffin)	1.4	(0.2)	0	230	125
Crystal Farms English Muffins, Plain					
(2 oz = 1 muffin)	1.0	<1.0	<2	300	140
Earth Grains English Muffins, Plain					
(2 oz = 1 muffin)	1.0	0.2	0	390	120
English muffins, plain (1 muffin)	1.0	0.1	0	265	134
Pepperidge Farm English Muffins					
Plain (1 muffin)	1.0	0.0	0	220	140
Wholesome Choice English Muffins,					
Country White (2.05 oz = 1 muffin)	1.0	0.0	0	150	130
Thomas' English Muffins, Regular (1					
muffin)	1.1	0.3	0	210	120
Wolferman's Deluxe English Muffins,					
Plain (1/2 muffin)	1.0	(0.1)	0	219	120

	Tot. Fat (g)	Sat. Fat (g)	Chol. (mg)	Sod. (mg)	Cal.
Raisin English Muffins—see **Cinnamon Raisin/Raisin English Muffins**					

Sourdough English Muffins

	Tot. Fat (g)	Sat. Fat (g)	Chol. (mg)	Sod. (mg)	Cal.
Arnold English Muffins, Sourdough (1 muffin)	1.3	(0.2)	0	250	120
Crystal Farms English Muffins, Sour Dough (2 oz = 1 muffin)	1.0	<1.0	<2	220	140
Earth Grains English Muffins, Sourdough (2 oz = 1 muffin)	1.0	0.2	0	390	120
Pepperidge Farm English Muffins, Sourdough (1 muffin)	1.0	0.0	0	260	135
Thomas' English Muffins, Sour Dough (1 muffin)	0.8	0.1	0	210	125
Wolferman's Deluxe English Muffins, Sourdough (1/2 muffin)	<1.0	(0.0)	0	281	110
Wonder English Muffins, Sourdough (1 muffin)	1.0	<1.0	0	240	120

Wheat English Muffins

	Tot. Fat (g)	Sat. Fat (g)	Chol. (mg)	Sod. (mg)	Cal.
Amana English Muffins, Honey Wheat (1/2 muffin)	0.0	0.0	(0)	105	47
Crystal Farms English Muffins, Wheat (2 oz = 1 muffin)	1.0	<1.0	0	190	110
Earth Grains English Muffins Wheatberry (2.3 oz = 1 muffin)	1.0	0.4	0	470	140
Whole Wheat (2.3 oz = 1 muffin)	1.0	0.4	0	420	130
Roman Meal English Muffins Original (1 muffin)	1.2	0.1	0	332	135
Refrigerated (1/2 muffin)	0.5	0.1	0	95	66
Thomas' English Muffins, Honey Wheat (1 muffin)	1.2	0.1	0	200	115

Other English Muffins

	Tot. Fat (g)	Sat. Fat (g)	Chol. (mg)	Sod. (mg)	Cal.
Pepperidge Farm English Muffins, Cinnamon Chip (1 muffin)	3.0	0.0	0	180	160

BREADS AND BREAD PRODUCTS

	Tot. Fat (g)	Sat. Fat (g)	Chol. (mg)	Sod. (mg)	Cal.
HAMBURGER/HOT DOG BUNS					
Arnold Bran'nola Natural Buns (1 bun)	0.8	(0.2)	0	164	99
Hamburger bun, small (1.5 oz = 1 bun)	2.2	0.5	(1)	241	123
Hot dog bun, small (1.5 oz = 1 bun)	2.2	0.5	(1)	241	123
Pepperidge Farm Sandwich Rolls, Onion with Poppy Seeds (1.85 oz = 1 roll)	3.0	1.0	0	260	150
Rainbo Hamburger Buns, IronKids (1.75 oz = 1 bun)	2.0	(0.5)	0	250	120
Wonder Buns					
Honey Wheat (1 bun)	2.0	<1.0	0	230	130
Light Hamburger (1 bun)	1.0	<1.0	0	210	80
Light Hot Dog (1 bun)	1.0	<1.0	0	210	80

HOT DOG BUNS—see
HAMBURGER/HOT DOG BUNS

MUFFINS—see **"DESSERTS,"**
MUFFINS, page 117

	Tot. Fat (g)	Sat. Fat (g)	Chol. (mg)	Sod. (mg)	Cal.
PANCAKES/WAFFLES					
Aunt Jemima Lite Healthy Waffles, frozen (1 waffle)	1.0	(0.1)	0	240	60
Kellogg's Special K Waffles, Fat Free, Cholesterol Free (1 waffle)	0.0	0.0	0	130	80
Krusteaz Pancake Mix, Oat Bran Lite Complete, made with water (3 4" pancakes)	1.0	(0.2)	0	370	130
Pillsbury Extra Lights Complete Pancake Mix, made with water (3 4" pancakes)	3.0	0.0	0	730	180
Pre-Measured Packets Pancake Mix, made with water (3 4" pancakes)	3.0	<1.0	0	650	180
PITA BREAD					
Athens Mini Pita Hi Fiber (1 pita)	0.4	0.0	0	105	70

BREADS AND BREAD PRODUCTS

36

	Tot. Fat (g)	Sat. Fat (g)	Chol. (mg)	Sod. (mg)	Cal.
Onion (1 pita)	0.4	0.0	0	90	80
Sourdough (1 pita)	0.4	0.0	0	105	80
Pepperidge Farm Wholesome Choice Sandwich Pockets, White (2 oz = 1 pocket)	1.0	0.0	0	410	140
White pita					
Mini, 4″ diam (1 oz = 1 pita)	0.4	0.0	0	152	78
Regular, 6½″ diam (2 oz = 1 pita)	0.7	0.1	0	322	165
Whole wheat or seasoned pita					
Mini, 4″ diam (1 oz = 1 pita)	0.7	0.1	0	151	76
Regular, 6½″ diam (2¼ oz = 1 pita)	1.7	0.3	0	340	170

ROLLS

French Rolls

	Tot. Fat (g)	Sat. Fat (g)	Chol. (mg)	Sod. (mg)	Cal.
Dicarlo's Rolls, French (1 roll)	2.0	<1.0	0	390	180
Earth Grains Rolls					
French (1 roll)	1.0	(0.2)	0	270	100
Sourdough French (1 roll)	1.0	(0.2)	0	160	100
Francisco International French Rolls					
Large (2.3 oz = 1 roll)	2.6	(0.4)	0	484	183
Small (1.4 oz = 1 roll)	1.5	(0.2)	0	285	108

Hard Rolls

	Tot. Fat (g)	Sat. Fat (g)	Chol. (mg)	Sod. (mg)	Cal.
Pepperidge Farm Hard Rolls					
French Style Enriched (9 per pkg) (1.35 oz = 1 roll)	1.0	0.0	0	230	100
Seven Grain French (9 per pkg) (1.35 oz = 1 roll)	2.0	1.0	0	270	100
Sourdough Style French Enriched (1.35 oz = 1 roll)	1.0	0.0	0	240	100
Rolls, hard, 3½″ diam (1 roll)	2.4	0.3	0	310	167

Kaiser/Submarine Rolls

	Tot. Fat (g)	Sat. Fat (g)	Chol. (mg)	Sod. (mg)	Cal.
Earth Grains Rolls					
Kaiser (1 roll)	2.0	(0.5)	0	520	190
Submarine (½ roll)	1.0	(0.3)	0	500	180

	Tot. Fat (g)	Sat. Fat (g)	Chol. (mg)	Sod. (mg)	Cal.
Levy's Old Country Deli Rolls, Sub (1 roll)	2.3	(0.6)	0	388	163

Wheat Rolls

	Tot. Fat (g)	Sat. Fat (g)	Chol. (mg)	Sod. (mg)	Cal.
Bread du Jour Rolls, Bavarian Wheat (1 roll)	1.0	<1.0	0	180	80
Earth Grains Rolls, Wheat (1 roll)	1.0	(0.2)	0	260	110
Rubschlager Dinner Rolls					
Honey Whole Grain (1 roll)	1.0	(0.2)	0	160	80
Wheat (1 roll)	1.0	(0.2)	0	180	90
Wonder Bakery Style Rolls, Wheat (1 roll)	2.0	<1.0	0	300	150

White Rolls

	Tot. Fat (g)	Sat. Fat (g)	Chol. (mg)	Sod. (mg)	Cal.
Pepperidge Farm Deli Classic Rolls, Brown 'N Serve					
Club Enriched (1.35 oz = 1 roll)	1.0	0.0	0	190	100
Hearth Enriched (.7 oz = 1 roll)	1.0	0.0	0	100	50
Pepperidge Farm Dinner Rolls, Country Style Classic (.7 oz = 1 roll)	1.0	0.0	0	90	50
Roman Meal Dinner Rolls, Original (2 rolls)	2.2	0.1	0	282	136
Rubschlager Dinner Rolls, Original Recipe (1 roll)	1.0	(0.3)	0	170	70
Wonder Bakery Style Rolls, Original (1 roll)	2.0	<1.0	0	280	140
Wonder Pan Rolls					
Brown 'N Serve (1 roll)	1.0	<1.0	0	135	70
Brown 'N Serve with Buttermilk (1 roll)	1.0	<1.0	0	135	70
Dinner (1 roll)	1.0	<1.0	0	140	80

Other Rolls

	Tot. Fat (g)	Sat. Fat (g)	Chol. (mg)	Sod. (mg)	Cal.
Arnold Rolls, Soft Sandwich (1 roll)	2.3	(0.6)	1	194	110
Bread du Jour Rolls, Crusty Italian (1 roll)	1.0	<1.0	0	190	80
Dicarlo's Rolls, Sourdough (1 roll)	3.0	<1.0	0	310	200
Earth Grains Rolls, Onion (1 roll)	2.0	(0.3)	0	53	490

BREADS AND BREAD PRODUCTS

	Tot. Fat (g)	Sat. Fat (g)	Chol. (mg)	Sod. (mg)	Cal.
Rubschlager Dinner Rolls					
Pumpernickel (1 roll)	2.0	(0.2)	0	210	90
Rye (1 roll)	2.0	(0.2)	0	220	80
Wonder Bakery Style Rolls, Sourdough					
(1 roll)	2.0	<1.0	0	300	150
Wonder Pan Rolls, Biscuit (1 roll)	1.0	<1.0	0	140	80

SUBMARINE ROLLS—*see*
ROLLS, *Kaiser/Submarine*

TORTILLAS—*see* **BREADS,**
Other Breads

WAFFLES—*see* **PANCAKES/WAFFLES**

CEREALS

Cereals naturally contain a small amount of fat, and the manufacturer can make them higher in fat in two ways—by adding nuts, coconut or seeds or by spraying them with a fat-based coating to retain crispness. You can help keep down the fat level by using skim milk or 1% low-fat milk.

Products listed in this book vary in sodium content. Use the values appearing on the following pages to help plan a daily intake providing no more than 3,000 milligrams of sodium.

Most of the foods in this book are brand name products; however, when a brand name is not specified, it means that most brands of that product provide about the same amount of fat, saturated fat and cholesterol and that these amounts do not exceed AHA criteria.

You can use those generic entries and the tables below to evaluate products introduced since this book went to press.

AHA Criteria for Cereals*

	Tot. Fat (g)	Sat. Fat (g)	Chol. (mg)
All cooked and ready-to-eat cereals	3	<0.5	<2

* Per serving.

Cereal Not Recommended for Frequent Consumption

A type of cereal that is usually too high in fat and/or saturated fat to be recommended for frequent consumption is shown in the table below. Values that exceed AHA criteria are followed by asterisks. The AHA does not have criteria for sodium.

You can use the values in the table to compare this type of cereal with more-healthful alternatives listed on the following pages.

Cereal High in Fat and/or Saturated Fat

	Tot. Fat (g)	Sat. Fat (g)	Chol. (mg)	Sod. (mg)	Cal.
100% natural cereal (granola), plain (¼ cup)	6.1*	4.1*	(0)	12	133

Adapted from USDA Handbook No. 8 series.

* These values exceed AHA criteria for cereals.

	Tot. Fat (g)	Sat. Fat (g)	Chol. (mg)	Sod. (mg)	Cal.

COOKED CEREALS

Bran/Fiber Cereals

	Tot. Fat (g)	Sat. Fat (g)	Chol. (mg)	Sod. (mg)	Cal.
Elam's Cereal, Miller's Bran, dry (.4 oz)	<1.0	(0.0)	0	2	16
Ralston Cereal, High Fiber Hot Cereal, dry (1 oz = 1/3 cup)	1.0	(0.2)	0	0	90

Buckwheat Groats—see Other Cooked Cereals, Buckwheat groats (kasha)

Fiber Cereals—see Bran/Fiber Cereals

Grits

	Tot. Fat (g)	Sat. Fat (g)	Chol. (mg)	Sod. (mg)	Cal.
Albers Hominy Quick Grits, dry (.7 oz = 1/4 cup)	0.0	0.0	0	0	150
Arrowhead Mills Corn Grits, White or Yellow, dry (2 oz)	1.0	(0.1)	0	1	200
Aunt Jemima Enriched Hominy Grits, Regular or Quick, White, dry (1 oz = 3 tbsp)	0.2	0.0	(0)	0	101
Corn grits, regular and quick, cooked (1 cup)	0.5	0.1	0	0	146
Quaker Grits, Enriched Hominy Grits, Quick or Regular, White or Yellow, dry (1 oz = 3 tbsp)	0.2	0.0	(0)	0	101
Quaker Instant Grits, dry (1 pkt)	0.1	0.0	(0)	440	79
with Imitation Bacon Bits, dry (1 pkt)	0.4	0.0	(0)	590	101
with Imitation Ham Bits, dry (1 pkt)	0.3	0.0	0	800	99
Tone's Grits, dry (1 1/2 oz)	0.4	0.1	0	0	142

Kasha—see Other Cooked Cereals, Buckwheat groats (kasha)

	Tot. Fat (g)	Sat. Fat (g)	Chol. (mg)	Sod. (mg)	Cal.
Multigrain Cereals					
Arrowhead Mills Cereal					
Four Grain, dry (2 oz)	1.0	(0.2)	0	1	94
Seven Grain, dry (1 oz)	1.0	(0.2)	0	1	100
Pritikin Cereal, Multigrain, dry					
(1.57 oz)	1.3	0.2	0	2	140
Oat Cereals					
Arrowhead Mills Cereal, Oat Bran, dry					
(1 oz)	1.0	(0.2)	0	2	110
Arrowhead Mills Oatmeal					
Instant Regular, dry (1 oz)	2.0	(0.3)	0	0	100
Steel Cut, dry (2 oz)	4.0	(0.6)	0	1	220
Elam's Oatmeal					
Steel Cut, dry (1.6 oz)	3.0	(0.5)	0	3	180
Stone Ground or Scotch Style, dry					
(1 oz)	2.0	(0.3)	0	3	110
Erewhon Cereal, Oat Bran with					
Toasted Wheat Germ (1 oz =					
1/3 cup dry)	2.0	(0.4)	0	15	115
Malt-O-Meal Cereal, 40% Oat Bran					
Plus, dry (1.3 oz)	1.7	(0.3)	(0)	1	128
Mother's Cereal, Oat Bran, cooked					
(1 oz dry = 2/3 cup cooked)	2.1	0.2	0	1	92
Oat bran, cooked (1/2 cup)	1.0	0.2	0	1	44
Oatmeal, regular, cooked (1 cup)	2.4	0.4	0	1	145
Quaker Cereal					
Oat Bran, dry (1 oz dry = 1/3 cup)	2.0	<1.0	0	0	90
Oats, Old Fashioned and Quick (1 oz)	2.0	0.0	0	0	100
Quaker Instant Oatmeal					
Apple, Raisin & Walnut (1.3 oz = 1					
pkt)	2.0	0.3	0	150	130
Apples & Cinnamon (1.25 oz = 1 pkt)	2.0	(0.3)	0	100	120
Cinnamon & Spice (1.6 oz = 1 pkt)	2.0	(0.3)	0	260	160
Cinnamon Toast (1.25 oz = 1 pkt)	2.0	0.3	0	160	120
Maple & Brown Sugar (1.5 oz = 1					
pkt)	2.0	0.0	0	240	140
Raisin Date Walnut (1.3 oz = 1 pkt)	2.0	0.3	0	230	130
Regular (1 oz = 1 pkt)	2.0	(0.3)	0	160	100

	Tot. Fat (g)	Sat. Fat (g)	Chol. (mg)	Sod. (mg)	Cal.
Quaker Toasted Oatmeal, Original (1 oz)	1.0	0.0	0	160	100
Roman Meal Cereal					
Oats, Wheat, Dates, Raisins and Almonds, dry (1.3 oz)	1.7	0.3	0	3	129
Original with Oats, dry (1.2 oz)	1.4	0.2	0	1	108

Rice Cereals

	Tot. Fat (g)	Sat. Fat (g)	Chol. (mg)	Sod. (mg)	Cal.
Erewhon Cereal, Organic Brown Rice Cream (1 oz = 1/3 cup dry)	1.0	(0.3)	(0)	20	110
Nabisco† Cream of Rice, dry (1 oz = 2 1/2 tbsp)	0.0	0.0	0	0	100
Perky's Cereal, Quick 'N Creamy Hot Rice, dry (1 oz)	(<1.0)	(0.0)	(0)	<2	100

Wheat Cereals/Wheat Germ

	Tot. Fat (g)	Sat. Fat (g)	Chol. (mg)	Sod. (mg)	Cal.
Arrowhead Mills Cereal					
Bulgur Wheat, dry (2 oz)	1.0	(0.2)	0	0	200
Cracked Wheat, dry (2 oz)	1.0	(0.2)	0	2	180
Elam's Cereal					
Cracked Wheat, dry (1.3 oz)	<1.0	(0.0)	0	4	130
Wheat Germ, dry (.5 oz)	1.0	(0.2)	0	3	60
Farina, cooked (1 cup)	0.2	0.0	0	1	116
General Mills Cereal, Wheat Hearts, dry (1 oz = 3 1/3 tbsp)	1.0	(0.2)	0	0	110
Malt-O-Meal Cereal					
Chocolate Flavored, dry (1 oz)	0.3	0.1	0	0	99
Quick, dry (1 oz)	0.4	0.1	0	1	100
Mother's Cereal, Whole Wheat Natural, cooked (2/3 cup)	0.6	0.1	0	1	92
Nabisco† Cream of Wheat, Regular, dry (1 oz = 2 1/2 tbsp)	0.0	0.0	0	0	100
Nabisco† Mix 'n Eat Cream of Wheat					
Apple and Cinnamon, dry (1 1/4 oz = 1 pkt)	0.0	0.0	0	250	130
Brown Sugar Cinnamon, dry (1 1/4 oz = 1 pkt)	0.0	0.0	0	230	130
Maple Brown Sugar, dry (1 1/4 oz = 1 pkt)	0.0	0.0	0	180	130

	Tot. Fat (g)	Sat. Fat (g)	Chol. (mg)	Sod. (mg)	Cal.
Original, dry (1¼ oz = 1 pkt)	0.0	0.0	0	170	100
Pillsbury Farina, cooked, made with water (⅔ cup)	<1.0	(0.0)	(0)	270	80
Quaker Cereal, Whole Wheat Hot Natural Cereal, dry (1 oz dry = ⅔ cup cooked)	0.6	0.1	0	1	92

Other Cooked Cereals

	Tot. Fat (g)	Sat. Fat (g)	Chol. (mg)	Sod. (mg)	Cal.
Arrowhead Mills Cereal, Bear Mush, dry (1 oz)	0.0	0.0	0	1	100
Buckwheat groats (kasha), roasted, cooked, made with water (¼ cup)	0.6	(0.1)	(0)	4	91
Erewhon Cereal, Organic Barley Plus (1 oz = ⅓ cup dry)	1.0	(0.2)	0	0	110
Pritikin Cereal, Apple/Raisin/Spice, dry (1.64 oz)	2.0	0.3	0	2	160
Roman Meal Cereal					
Apple Cinnamon, dry (1 oz)	2.0	0.3	0	6	105
Cream of Rye, dry (1.3 oz)	0.9	0.1	0	2	111
Original, dry (1 oz)	0.7	0.1	0	0	83

READY-TO-EAT CEREALS

Bran/Fiber Cereals

	Tot. Fat (g)	Sat. Fat (g)	Chol. (mg)	Sod. (mg)	Cal.
Arrowhead Mills Cereal					
Bran Flakes (1 oz)	1.0	(0.2)	0	4	100
Wheat Bran (2 oz)	2.0	(0.3)	0	5	50
General Mills Cereal					
Fiber One (1 oz = ½ cup)	1.0	(0.2)	0	140	60
Ripple Crisp, Honey Bran (1 oz = ⅔ cup)	<1.0	0.0	0	280	100
Health Valley Cereal					
Fat-Free 10 Bran, Almond Flavor O's (1 oz = ½ cup)	<1.0	0.0	0	5	90
Fat-Free 10 Bran, Apple Cinnamon O's (1 oz = ½ cup)	<1.0	0.0	0	5	90
Fat-Free 10 Bran, High Fiber O's (1 oz = ½ cup)	<1.0	0.0	0	5	90
Fiber 7 Flakes (1 oz = ½ cup)	<1.0	(0.0)	0	0	90

	Tot. Fat (g)	Sat. Fat (g)	Chol. (mg)	Sod. (mg)	Cal.
Kellogg's Cereal					
All-Bran (1 oz = 1/3 cup)	1.0	0.0	0	260	70
All-Bran with Extra Fiber (1 oz = 1/2 cup)	0.0	0.0	0	140	50
Bran Buds (1 oz = 1/3 cup)	1.0	0.0	0	170	70
Complete Bran Flakes (1 oz = 2/3 cup)	0.0	0.0	0	220	90
Fiberwise (1 oz = 2/3 cup)	1.0	0.0	0	140	90
Frosted Bran (1 oz = 2/3 cup)	0.0	0.0	0	190	100
Fruitful Bran (1 oz = 2/3 cup)	0.0	0.0	0	240	120
Kretschmer Cereal, Toasted Wheat					
Bran (1 oz = 1/3 cup)	2.3	0.2	0	2	57
Malt-O-Meal Cereal, Bran Flakes					
(1 oz = 2/3 cup)	0.9	0.1	0	205	93
Nabisco† Cereal, 100% Bran (1 oz =					
1/2 cup)	1.0	0.0	0	180	70
Post Cereal					
Bran Flakes (1 oz)	0.0	0.0	0	210	90
Grape-Nuts Cereal (1 oz)	0.0	0.0	0	170	110
Grape-Nuts Flakes (1 oz)	1.0	(0.2)	0	130	100
Grape-Nuts, Raisin (1 oz)	0.0	0.0	0	150	100
Quaker Cereal					
Crunchy Bran (1 oz = 2/3 cup)	1.3	0.4	(0)	316	89
Unprocessed Bran (1/4 oz = 2 tbsp)	0.2	0.0	(0)	0	8
Ralston Cereal					
Bran News, Cinnamon (1 oz = 3/4 cup)	0.0	0.0	0	160	100
Chex, Multi-Bran (1 oz = 2/3 cup)	0.0	0.0	0	200	90
Corn Cereals					
Appletree* Cereal, Corn Flakes					
(1 oz = 1 cup)	1.0	(0.1)	(0)	310	110
Arrowhead Mills Cereal					
Apple Corns (1 oz)	1.0	(0.2)	0	70	100
Corn Flakes (1 oz)	1.0	(0.1)	0	15	110
Maple Corns (1 oz)	1.0	(0.2)	0	75	100

* Appletree products are also marketed under Best Yet, Fine Fare, Food Lion, Hyde Park, Hy-Top, Parade, Piggly-Wiggly, Red & White, Roundy's, Schwegmann, Scot Lad and Tops brand names.

CEREALS

	Tot. Fat (g)	Sat. Fat (g)	Chol. (mg)	Sod. (mg)	Cal.
Puffed Corn (½ oz)	0.0	0.0	0	1	50
Barbara's Bakery Cereal, Corn Flakes					
(1 oz)	0.0	0.0	0	70	110
Erewhon Cereal, Aztec (1 oz = 1 cup)	0.0	0.0	0	85	100
General Mills Cereal					
Country Corn Flakes (1 oz = 1 cup)	1.0	0.0	0	270	110
Ripple Crisp, Golden Corn (1 oz =					
¾ cup)	<1.0	0.0	0	280	110
Total Corn Flakes (1 oz = 1 cup)	<1.0	(0.1)	0	200	110
Grainfield's Cereal, Corn Flakes					
(1 oz = 1¼ cups)	0.1	(0.0)	0	2	110
Health Valley Cereal, Blue Corn Flakes					
(1 oz = ½ cup)	<1.0	(0.0)	0	10	90
Kellogg's Cereal					
Corn Flakes (1 oz = 1 cup)	0.0	0.0	0	290	100
Corn Pops (1 oz = 1 cup)	0.0	0.0	0	90	110
Frosted Flakes (1 oz = ¾ cup)	0.0	0.0	0	200	110
Malt-O-Meal Cereal					
Corn Flakes (1 oz)	0.2	0.0	0	268	106
Sugar Frosted Corn Flakes (1 oz =					
¾ cup)	0.2	0.0	0	186	109
Post Cereal, Toasties Corn Flakes					
(1 oz)	0.0	0.0	0	280	110
Ralston Cereal, Chex, Corn (1 oz =					
1 cup)	0.0	0.0	0	310	110

Fiber Cereals—see
Bran/Fiber Cereals

Fruit Cereals

	Tot. Fat (g)	Sat. Fat (g)	Chol. (mg)	Sod. (mg)	Cal.
Erewhon Cereal					
Apple Stroodles (1 oz = 1 cup)	0.0	0.0	0	15	90
Banana-O's (1 oz)	0.0	0.0	(0)	15	110
General Mills Cereal					
Berry Berry Kix (1 oz = 1 cup)	1.0	0.0	0	160	110
Body Buddies, Natural Fruit (1 oz =					
1 cup)	1.0	(0.2)	0	280	110
Booberry (1 oz = 1 cup)	1.0	(0.2)	0	210	110
Frankenberry (1 oz = 1 cup)	1.0	(0.2)	0	210	110
Lucky Charms (1 oz = 1 cup)	1.0	(0.2)	0	180	110

	Tot. Fat (g)	Sat. Fat (g)	Chol. (mg)	Sod. (mg)	Cal.
Kellogg's Cereal					
Apple Jacks (1 oz = 1 cup)	0.0	0.0	0	125	110
Apple Raisin Crisp (1 oz = ^{2}/$_3$ cup)	0.0	0.0	0	230	130
Froot Loops (1 oz = 1 cup)	1.0	0.0	0	125	110
Just Right Fruit and Nut (1 oz = ^{3}/$_4$ cup)	1.0	0.0	0	190	140
Nutri-Grain, Almond Raisin (1 oz = ^{2}/$_3$ cup)	2.0	0.0	0	220	140
Squares					
Apple Cinnamon (1 oz = ^{1}/$_2$ cup)	0.0	0.0	0	5	90
Blueberry (1 oz = ^{1}/$_2$ cup)	0.0	0.0	0	5	90
Raisin (1 oz = ^{1}/$_2$ cup)	<1.0	0.0	0	0	90
Strawberry (1 oz = ^{1}/$_2$ cup)	0.0	0.0	0	5	90
Malt-O-Meal Cereal, Tootie Fruities (1 oz = 1 cup)	1.1	0.2	0	121	113
Nabisco[†] Cereal, Fruit Wheats, Apple (1 oz = ^{1}/$_2$ cup)	0.0	0.0	0	15	90
Post Cereal					
Fruit & Fibre					
Dates, Raisins & Walnuts (1.25 oz)	2.0	(0.3)	0	160	120
Peaches, Raisins & Almonds (1.25 oz)	2.0	(0.3)	0	160	120
Granola Cereals					
Health Valley Fat-Free Granola					
Date & Almond (1 oz = ^{1}/$_4$ cup)	<1.0	(0.0)	0	20	90
Raisin Cinnamon (1 oz = ^{1}/$_4$ cup)	<1.0	(0.0)	0	20	90
Tropical Fruit (1 oz = ^{1}/$_4$ cup)	<1.0	0.0	0	20	90
Multigrain Cereals					
General Mills Cereal					
Kix (1 oz = 1^1/$_2$ cups)	<1.0	(0.6)	0	260	110
Trix (1 oz = 1 cup)	1.0	(0.2)	0	135	110
Kellogg's Cereal					
Just Right Crunchy Nugget (1 oz = ^{2}/$_3$ cup)	1.0	0.0	0	170	110
Mueslix, Crispy Blend (1 oz = ^{2}/$_3$ cup)	2.0	0.0	0	150	160

	Tot. Fat (g)	Sat. Fat (g)	Chol. (mg)	Sod. (mg)	Cal.
Ralston Cereal					
Chex, Double (1 oz = ⅔ cup)	0.0	0.0	0	190	100
Sunflakes Multi-Grain (1 oz = 1 cup)	1.0	(0.2)	0	240	100
Oat Cereals					
Arrowhead Mills Cereal					
Nature O's (1 oz)	1.0	(0.2)	0	14	110
Oat Bran Flakes (1 oz)	2.0	(0.4)	0	30	110
Oat Flakes (2 oz = 1⅓ cups)	4.0	(0.7)	0	1	220
Barbara's Bakery Cereal, Breakfast O's					
(1 oz)	2.0	(0.4)	0	90	120
Erewhon Cereal, Super-O's (1 oz =					
¾ cup)	0.0	0.0	0	5	110
General Mills Cereal					
Cheerios (1 oz = 1¼ cups)	2.0	(0.4)	0	290	110
Cheerios, Apple Cinnamon (1 oz =					
¾ cup)	2.0	(0.4)	0	180	110
Cheerios, Multigrain (1 oz = 1 cup)	1.0	0.0	0	230	100
Oatmeal Crisp with Apples (1 oz =					
½ cup)	1.0	0.0	0	180	110
Oatmeal Crisp with Raisins (1 oz =					
1 cup)	2.0	(0.4)	0	160	130
Health Valley Cereal					
Oat Bran Flakes (1 oz = ½ cup)	<1.0	(0.0)	0	0	90
Oat Bran Flakes, Almonds and Dates					
(1 oz = ½ cup)	1.0	(0.1)	0	0	90
Oat Bran Flakes, Raisins (1 oz =					
½ cup)	<1.0	(0.0)	0	0	90
Oat Bran O's (1 oz = ½ cup)	<1.0	(0.0)	0	0	90
Oat Bran O's, Fruit & Nut (1 oz =					
¾ cup)	3.0	(0.3)	0	3	110
Kellogg's Cereal					
Common Sense Oat Bran (1 oz =					
¾ cup)	1.0	0.0	0	250	100
Common Sense Oat Bran with					
Raisins (1 oz = ¾ cup)	1.0	0.0	0	250	130
Malt-O-Meal Cereal					
Honey & Nut Toasty O's (1 oz =					
¾ cup)	1.2	0.2	0	172	107

	Tot. Fat (g)	Sat. Fat (g)	Chol. (mg)	Sod. (mg)	Cal.
Toasty O's (1 oz = 1¼ cups)	2.0	0.3	0	236	107
Post Cereal					
Honey Bunches of Oats, Honey Roasted (1 oz)	2.0	(0.4)	0	160	110
Honey Bunches of Oats, with Almonds (1 oz)	2.0	(0.4)	0	150	110
Oat Flakes (1 oz)	1.0	(0.2)	0	130	110
Quaker Cereal					
Oat Bran (1 oz = ¾ cup)	2.0	0.0	0	105	100
Oat Squares (1 oz = ½ cup)	1.0	0.0	0	135	100
Ralston Cereal, Options, Oat Bran (1.5 oz = ¾ cup)	1.0	(0.2)	0	150	130
Skinner's Cereal, Toasted Oat Rings (1 oz = 1 cup)	1.0	(0.2)	0	290	90

Raisin Bran Cereals

	Tot. Fat (g)	Sat. Fat (g)	Chol. (mg)	Sod. (mg)	Cal.
Barbara's Bakery Cereal, Raisin Bran (1.5 oz)	1.0	(0.2)	0	80	170
Erewhon Cereal, Raisin Bran (1 oz = ½ cup)	0.0	0.0	0	80	100
General Mills Cereal					
Raisin Nut Bran (1 oz = 1 cup)	2.0	0.0	0	140	100
Total Raisin Bran (1.5 oz = 1 cup)	1.0	(0.2)	0	190	140
Grainfield's Cereal, Raisin Bran (1 oz = ⅔ cup)	0.4	(0.1)	0	4	90
Health Valley Cereal, Raisin Bran Flakes (1 oz = ½ cup)	<1.0	(0.0)	0	5	90
Kellogg's Cereal					
Nutri-Grain, Raisin Bran (1 oz = 1 cup)	1.0	(0.2)	0	200	130
Raisin Bran (1 oz = ¾ cup)	1.0	0.0	0	210	120
Malt-O-Meal Cereal, Raisin Bran (1.4 oz = ¾ cup)	1.7	(0.3)	0	199	129
Post Cereal, Raisin Bran (1.4 oz)	1.0	(0.4)	0	200	120

Rice Cereals

	Tot. Fat (g)	Sat. Fat (g)	Chol. (mg)	Sod. (mg)	Cal.
Arrowhead Mills Cereal, Puffed Rice (½ oz)	0.0	0.0	0	1	50

	Tot. Fat (g)	Sat. Fat (g)	Chol. (mg)	Sod. (mg)	Cal.
Barbara's Bakery Cereal, Brown Rice					
Crisps (1.1 oz)	1.0	(0.1)	0	105	120
Erewhon Cereal					
Crispy Brown Rice (1 oz = 1 cup)	1.0	(0.1)	0	185	110
Crispy Brown Rice, Low Sodium					
(1 oz = 1 cup)	1.0	(0.1)	0	5	110
Poppets (1 oz = 1 cup)	1.0	(0.1)	0	10	110
Grainfield's Cereal					
Brown Rice (1 oz)	0.5	(0.1)	0	4	110
Crisp Rice (1 oz)	0.1	(0.0)	0	3	112
Kellogg's Cereal					
Frosted Krispies (1 oz = ¾ cup)	0.0	0.0	0	220	110
Fruity Marshmallow Krispies (1 oz =					
1¼ cups)	0.0	0.0	0	210	140
Kenmei Rice Bran (1 oz = ¾ cup)	1.0	0.0	0	230	110
Rice Krispies (1 oz = 1 cup)	0.0	0.0	0	290	110
Malt-O-Meal Cereal					
Crisp 'n Crackling Rice (1 oz = 1 cup)	0.3	0.1	0	252	108
Puffed Rice (½ oz = 1 cup)	0.2	0.0	0	0	54
Puffed Rice, Unfortified (½ oz =					
1 cup)	0.2	(0.0)	0	0	54
Perky's Cereal, Nutty Rice, Original					
(1 oz = ¼ cup)	0.1	(0.0)	(0)	56	110
Quaker Cereal, Puffed Rice (½ oz =					
1 cup)	0.1	0.0	0	1	54
Ralston Cereal, Chex, Rice (1 oz =					
1⅛ cups)	0.0	0.0	0	280	110

Wheat Cereals/Wheat Germ

	Tot. Fat (g)	Sat. Fat (g)	Chol. (mg)	Sod. (mg)	Cal.
Arrowhead Mills Cereal					
Puffed Wheat (½ oz)	0.0	0.0	0	1	50
Wheat Flakes (1 oz)	1.0	(0.2)	0	15	110
Barbara's Bakery Cereal, Shredded					
Wheat (2 biscuits)	1.0	(0.2)	0	0	140
Erewhon Cereal					
Fruit'n Wheat (1 oz = ½ cup)	1.0	(0.2)	0	75	100
Wheat Flakes (1 oz = ½ cup)	0.0	0.0	0	75	110

	Tot. Fat (g)	Sat. Fat (g)	Chol. (mg)	Sod. (mg)	Cal.
General Mills Cereal					
Crispy Wheats 'n Raisins (1 oz = ¾ cup)	1.0	(0.2)	0	140	100
Golden Grahams (1 oz = ¾ cup)	1.0	(0.2)	0	270	110
S'more Grahams (1 oz)	2.0	0.0	0	230	120
Wheaties (1 oz = 1 cup)	<1.0	(0.1)	0	200	100
Wheaties Honey Gold (1 oz = ¾ cup)	<1.0	0.0	0	200	110
Grainfield's Cereal, Wheat Flakes					
(1 oz = 1 cup)	0.6	(0.1)	0	2	100
Kellogg's Cereal					
Frosted Mini Wheats (1 oz = 4 biscuits)	0.0	0.0	0	0	100
Frosted Mini Wheats Bite Size (1 oz = ½ cup)	0.0	0.0	0	0	100
Nutri-Grain, Wheat (1 oz = ⅔ cup)	0.0	0.0	0	170	90
Smacks (1 oz = ¾ cup)	1.0	0.0	0	70	110
Kretschmer Wheat Germ					
Honey Crunch (1 oz = 3 tbsp)	3.0	0.0	0	0	110
Original Toasted (1 oz = 3 tbsp)	3.0	1.0	0	0	100
Malt-O-Meal Cereal					
Puffed Wheat (½ oz = 1 cup)	0.4	0.1	0	0	53
Puffed Wheat, Unfortified (½ oz = 1 cup)	0.4	(0.0)	0	0	49
Sugar Puffs (1 oz = 1 cup)	0.4	0.1	0	23	109
Nabisco† Cereal					
Shredded Wheat (⅚ oz = 1 biscuit)	1.0	0.0	0	0	80
Shredded Wheat 'n Bran (1 oz = ⅔ cup)	0.0	0.0	0	0	90
Shredded Wheat with Oat Bran (1 oz = ⅔ cup)	1.0	0.0	0	0	100
Spoon Size Shredded Wheat (1 oz = ⅔ cup)	1.0	0.0	0	0	90
Quaker Cereal					
Puffed Wheat (½ oz = 1 cup)	0.2	0.0	0	1	50
Shredded Wheat (1.4 oz = 2 biscuits)	0.6	(0.0)	(0)	1	132
Ralston Cereal, Chex, Wheat (1 oz = ⅔ cup)	0.0	0.0	0	230	100
Sunshine Cereal					
Shredded Wheat (1 biscuit)	<1.0	(0.1)	0	0	60

	Tot. Fat (g)	Sat. Fat (g)	Chol. (mg)	Sod. (mg)	Cal.
Shredded Wheat, Bite Size (1 oz = ²/₃ cup)	<1.0	(0.2)	0	0	90
Uncle Sam Cereal (1 oz = ¹/₂ cup dry)	1.0	(0.1)	0	65	110
Wheat germ, plain, toasted (1 oz)	3.0	0.5	0	1	108
Wheatabix (1.2 oz = 2 biscuits)	0.6	(0.1)	0	106	100

Wheat Germ—see
Wheat Cereals/Wheat Germ

Other Ready-to-Eat Cereals

	Tot. Fat (g)	Sat. Fat (g)	Chol. (mg)	Sod. (mg)	Cal.
Arrowhead Mills Cereal					
Barley Flakes (2 oz = 1¹/₄ cups)	1.0	(0.2)	0	1	200
Puffed Millet (¹/₂ oz)	0.0	0.0	0	1	50
Rye Flakes (2 oz = 1 cup)	1.0	(0.2)	0	1	190
Erewhon Cereal					
Kamut Flakes (1 oz)	0.0	0.0	(0)	60	90
Right Start (1 oz = ¹/₃ cup)	0.0	0.0	0	80	90
Right Start with Raisins (1 oz = ¹/₃ cup)	0.0	0.0	0	80	90
General Mills Cereal					
Basic Four (1.3 oz = ³/₄ cup)	2.0	0.0	0	210	130
Clusters (1 oz = 1 cup)	2.0	0.0	0	140	110
Cocoa Puffs (1 oz = 1 cup)	1.0	(0.2)	0	180	110
Count Chocula (1 oz = 1 cup)	1.0	(0.2)	0	180	110
Kaboom (1 oz = 1 cup)	1.0	(0.2)	0	270	100
Total (1 oz = 1 cup)	1.0	(0.2)	0	190	100
Triples (1 oz = 1 cup)	1.0	0.0	0	200	110
Kashi cereal, lightly puffed (³/₄ oz = 1 cup)	0.5	(0.1)	0	0	70
Kellogg's Cereal					
Cocoa Krispies (1 oz = ³/₄ cup)	0.0	0.0	0	190	110
Crispix (1 oz = 1 cup)	0.0	0.0	0	220	110
Nut & Honey Crunch (1 oz = ²/₃ cup)	1.0	0.0	0	200	110
Nut & Honey Crunch O's (1 oz = ²/₃ cup)	1.0	0.0	0	180	110
Product 19 (1 oz = 1 cup)	0.0	0.0	0	320	100
Special K (1 oz = 1 cup)	0.0	0.0	0	230	110
Nabisco† Cereal, Team Flakes (1 oz = 1 cup)	1.0	(0.0)	0	180	110

CEREALS

53

	Tot. Fat (g)	Sat. Fat (g)	Chol. (mg)	Sod. (mg)	Cal.
Post Cereal					
Alpha-Bits (1 oz)	1.0	(0.2)	0	180	110
Alpha-Bits, Marshmallow (1 oz)	1.0	(0.2)	0	150	110
Golden Crisp (1 oz)	0.0	0.0	0	45	100
Honeycomb (1 oz)	0.0	0.0	0	180	110
Quaker Cereal					
King Vitamin (1 oz = 1½ cups)	1.0	0.0	(0)	280	110
Life (1 oz = ⅔ cup)	1.7	(0.0)	(0)	186	101
Life, Cinnamon (1 oz = ⅔ cup)	1.7	(0.0)	(0)	182	101
Ralston Cereal					
Bill & Ted's Excellent Sweetened Cereal (1 oz = 1 cup)	1.0	0.2	0	160	110
Teenage Mutant Ninja Turtles (1 oz = 1 cup)	0.0	0.0	0	190	110
The Jetsons Sweetened Cereal (1 oz = ¾ cup)	1.0	0.2	0	160	110

† = tobacco company, corporate subsidiary or parent

CONDIMENTS, GRAVIES AND SAUCES

Most condiments are low in calories and contain little or no fat and cholesterol. Olives, however, do contain fat and are listed in the "Fats, Oils, Seeds and Nuts" section on page 122. All the sauces and gravies in this book are low in fat and saturated fat as purchased or when prepared as indicated on the following pages.

Products listed in this book vary in sodium content. Use the values appearing on the following pages to help plan a daily intake providing no more than 3,000 milligrams of sodium.

Most of the foods in this book are brand name products; however, when a brand name is not specified, it means that most brands of that product provide about the same amount of fat, saturated fat and cholesterol and that these amounts do not exceed AHA criteria.

You can use those generic entries and the tables below to evaluate products introduced since this book went to press.

AHA Criteria for Condiments, Gravies and Sauces*

	Tot. Fat (g)	Sat. Fat (g)	Chol. (mg)
Bacon bits substitutes, gravies and all sauces, except those listed below	3	<0.5	<2
Chili peppers, horseradish, hot sauce, ketchup, marinade, mustard, soy sauce, steak sauce, teriyaki sauce, Worcestershire sauce	<0.5	<0.5	<2
Pickle relishes and pickles	3	1	20

* Per serving.

Sauces Not Recommended for Frequent Consumption

Some types of sauce that are usually too high in fat, saturated fat and/or cholesterol to be recommended for frequent consumption are shown in the table below. Values that exceed AHA criteria are followed by asterisks. The AHA does not have criteria for sodium.

You can use the values in the table to compare these sauces with more-healthful alternatives listed on the following pages.

Sauces High in Fat, Saturated Fat and/or Cholesterol

	Tot. Fat (g)	Sat. Fat (g)	Chol. (mg)	Sod. (mg)	Cal.
Bernaise sauce, made from mix with whole milk and butter (1/4 cup)	17.1*	10.4*	47*	316	175
Cheese sauce, made from mix with whole milk (1/4 cup)	4.3*	2.3*	13*	392	77
White sauce, made from mix with whole milk (1/4 cup)	3.4	1.6*	9*	199	60

Adapted from USDA Handbook No. 8 series.

* These values exceed AHA criteria for sauces.

	Tot. Fat (g)	Sat. Fat (g)	Chol. (mg)	Sod. (mg)	Cal.
BACON BITS SUBSTITUTES					
McCormick					
Bac'n Chips (¼ tsp)	0.1	(0.0)	(0)	51	7
Bac'n Pieces Chips (¼ tsp)	0.1	(0.0)	0	51	7
Tone's Bacon Bits (1 tsp)	0.3	0.0	0	59	7
BARBECUE SAUCES					
Bovril Sauce Mix, B.B.Q., made as directed (½ cup)	0.6	(0.1)	(0)	n/a	57
Hain Bar-B-Que Sauce, Honey (1 tbsp)	1.0	(0.1)	0	120	14
Healthy Choice Barbecue Sauce					
Hickory (2 tbsp)	0.0	0.0	0	290	30
Hot'n Spicy (2 tbsp)	0.0	0.0	0	290	30
Original (2 tbsp)	0.0	0.0	0	290	30
Hunt's Barbecue Sauce					
Country Style (½ oz)	<1.0	(0.0)	0	140	20
Hickory (½ oz)	<1.0	(0.0)	0	160	20
Homestyle (½ oz)	<1.0	(0.0)	0	170	20
Kansas City (½ oz)	<1.0	(0.0)	0	85	20
New Orleans (½ oz)	<1.0	(0.0)	0	150	20
Original (½ oz)	<1.0	(0.0)	0	160	20
Southern Style (½ oz)	<1.0	(0.0)	0	170	20
Texas (½ oz)	<1.0	(0.0)	0	150	25
Western (½ oz)	<1.0	(0.0)	0	170	20
Kraft† Barbecue Sauce (2 tbsp)	1.0	0.0	0	460	45
Garlic (2 tbsp)	0.0	0.0	0	420	40
Hickory Smoke (2 tbsp)	1.0	0.0	0	440	45
Hickory Smoke Onion Bits (2 tbsp)	1.0	0.0	0	340	50
Hot (2 tbsp)	1.0	0.0	0	520	45
Hot Hickory Smoke (2 tbsp)	1.0	0.0	0	360	45
Italian Seasonings (2 tbsp)	1.0	0.0	0	280	50
Kansas City Style (2 tbsp)	1.0	0.0	0	270	50
Mesquite Smoke (2 tbsp)	1.0	0.0	0	410	45
Onion Bits (2 tbsp)	1.0	0.0	0	340	50
Kraft† Thick'n Spicy Barbecue Sauce					
Chunky (2 tbsp)	1.0	0.0	0	420	60
Hickory Smoke (2 tbsp)	1.0	0.0	0	430	50

	Tot. Fat (g)	Sat. Fat (g)	Chol. (mg)	Sod. (mg)	Cal.
Kansas City Style (2 tbsp)	1.0	0.0	0	270	60
Mesquite Smoke (2 tbsp)	1.0	0.0	0	430	50
Original (2 tbsp)	1.0	0.0	0	430	50
With Honey (2 tbsp)	1.0	0.0	0	340	60
Lawry's Barbecue Sauce					
Dijon & Honey (¼ cup)	1.2	0.3	0	1768	203
Fajitas Barbecue (1 oz)	1.0	0.1	0	534	38
Stir Fry Oriental Style (¼ cup)	3.8	0.5	0	1128	120
Teriyaki Barbecue (1 oz)	0.4	0.1	0	568	63

CHILI/COCKTAIL SAUCES

	Tot. Fat (g)	Sat. Fat (g)	Chol. (mg)	Sod. (mg)	Cal.
El Molino Chile Sauce, Mild Green (2 tbsp)	0.0	0.0	0	210	10
Kraft† Sauceworks, Cocktail Sauce (1 tbsp)	0.0	0.0	0	170	14

COCKTAIL SAUCES—see CHILI/COCKTAIL SAUCES

COOKING SAUCES

	Tot. Fat (g)	Sat. Fat (g)	Chol. (mg)	Sod. (mg)	Cal.
Angostura Worcestershire Sauce, Low Sodium (1 tsp)	0.0	0.0	(0)	19	4
Bovril Sauce Mix					
Beef, made as directed (½ cup)	0.7	(0.4)	(tr)	n/a	51
Chicken, made as directed (½ cup)	0.8	(0.3)	(1)	n/a	46
3 Pepper, made as directed (½ cup)	0.8	(0.3)	(0)	n/a	56
Gebhardt Chili Hot Dog Sauce (2 tbsp)	1.0	0.4	3	180	30
Hunt's Manwich Sauce					
Chili Fixins (sauce only) (5.3 oz)	<1.0	(0.0)	0	900	110
Extra Thick and Chunky (sauce only) (2.5 oz)	<1.0	(0.0)	0	640	60
Mexican (sauce only) (2.5 oz)	1.0	(<1.0)	0	460	35
Sloppy Joe (sauce only) (2.5 oz)	<1.0	(0.0)	0	390	40
Just Rite Hot Dog Sauce (2 oz)	3.0	1.1	7	220	60
Knorr Grilling and Broiling Sauce					
Chardonnay (1.6 oz)	4.0	(1.2)	(<1)	630	50
Spicy Plum (1.7 oz)	2.0	(0.6)	(0)	790	60
Tequila Lime (1.6 oz)	3.0	(0.9)	(<1)	690	50

CONDIMENTS, GRAVIES AND SAUCES

	Tot. Fat (g)	Sat. Fat (g)	Chol. (mg)	Sod. (mg)	Cal.
Tuscan Herb (1.6 oz)	4.0	(1.2)	(0)	600	50
Knorr Microwave Sauce, Vera Cruz (3.3 oz)	3.0	(0.4)	(0)	580	70
Knorr Sauce Mix					
Demi-Glace, made with water (2 fl oz = ¼ cup)	1.0	(0.2)	(<1)	310	30
Hunter, made with water (2 fl oz = ¼ cup)	<1.0	(0.0)	(0)	340	25
Lyonnaise, made with water (2 fl oz = ¼ cup)	<1.0	(0.0)	(0)	360	20
Napoli, made with tomato puree and oil (4 fl oz = ½ cup)	3.0	(0.4)	(2)	960	100
Pepper, made with water (2 fl oz = ¼ cup)	1.0	(<1.0)	(0)	380	20
Maggie Gin's Canton Noodle Sauce (1 tbsp)	0.0	0.0	0	305	18
Progresso Sauce, Sicilian (½ cup)	2.5	<1.0	0	660	30
Ragu Chicken Tonight Light Sauces					
Cajun Chicken (4 oz)	<1.0	(0.0)	0	520	50
Honey Mustard Chicken (4 oz)	<1.0	(0.0)	0	420	50
Italian Primavera Chicken (4 oz)	<1.0	(0.0)	0	540	50
Sweet & Spicy Chicken (4 oz)	<1.0	(0.0)	0	390	50
Ragu Chicken Tonight Sauces					
Chicken Cacciatore (4 oz)	2.0	(0.3)	0	490	70
Oriental Chicken (4 oz)	1.0	(0.2)	0	580	70
Salsa Chicken (4 oz)	0.0	0.0	0	680	35
Spanish Chicken (4 oz)	2.0	(0.3)	0	640	70
Sweet & Sour Chicken (4 oz)	0.0	0.0	0	280	80
Ragu Italian Cooking Sauce (4 oz)	2.0	(0.3)	0	540	70
Wolf Brand Chili Hot Dog Sauce (⅙ cup)	2.0	(0.9)	(0)	200	40

ENCHILADA SAUCES

	Tot. Fat (g)	Sat. Fat (g)	Chol. (mg)	Sod. (mg)	Cal.
La Victoria Enchilada Sauce (½ cup)	2.0	(0.7)	0	710	40
Old El Paso Enchilada Sauce, Green (2 tbsp)	0.0	0.0	0	200	11
Rosarita Enchilada Sauce					
Hot (3 tbsp)	<1.0	(0.0)	0	150	15
Mild (3 tbsp)	<1.0	0.0	0	150	15

GRAVIES

	Tot. Fat (g)	Sat. Fat (g)	Chol. (mg)	Sod. (mg)	Cal.
Appletree* Gravy Mix, Brown, made with water (¼ cup)	<1.0	(0.0)	tr	370	20
Franco-American Gravies					
Au Jus (2 oz = ¼ cup)	0.0	0.0	(tr)	330	10
Mushroom (2 oz)	1.0	(0.1)	(0)	290	25
Hain Seasoning and Gravy Mix, Brown Gravy (¼ pkg)	0.0	0.0	0	600	16
Heinz Home Style Gravy					
Brown (2 oz)	1.0	0.0	0	300	25
Chicken (2 oz)	1.5	0.0	0	340	30
Mushroom (2 oz)	0.5	0.0	(0)	340	25
Turkey (2 oz)	1.0	0.0	0	360	25
Knorr Sauce Mix, Au Jus, made with water (2 fl oz = ¼ cup)	<1.0	(0.0)	(tr)	160	8
McCormick Gravy Mix					
Au Jus, made as directed (¼ cup)	0.3	(0.1)	(tr)	786	20
Brown, made as directed (¼ cup)	0.8	(0.4)	(tr)	313	23
Chicken, made as directed (¼ cup)	0.4	(0.1)	(1)	300	22
Herb, made as directed (¼ cup)	0.5	(0.2)	(tr)	312	20
Homestyle, made as directed (¼ cup)	0.8	(0.4)	(tr)	295	24
Lite Chicken, made as directed (¼ cup)	1.0	(0.3)	(1)	450	12
Mushroom, made as directed (¼ cup)	0.5	(0.3)	(tr)	270	19
Onion, made as directed (¼ cup)	0.6	(0.4)	(tr)	337	22
Pork, made as directed (¼ cup)	0.6	(0.2)	(1)	297	20
Turkey, made as directed (¼ cup)	0.5	(0.1)	(1)	353	22
Pepperidge Farm Gravies					
Golden Chicken (2 oz = ¼ cup)	1.0	(0.3)	(1)	240	25
Seasoned Turkey (2 oz = ¼ cup)	1.0	(0.3)	(1)	320	30
Pillsbury Gravy Mix					
Brown, made with water (¼ cup)	0.0	0.0	0	180	16

* Appletree products are also marketed under Best Yet, Fine Fare, Food Lion, Hyde Park, Hy-Top, Parade, Piggly-Wiggly, Red & White, Roundy's, Schwegmann, Scot Lad and Tops brand names.

CONDIMENTS, GRAVIES AND SAUCES

	Tot. Fat (g)	Sat. Fat (g)	Chol. (mg)	Sod. (mg)	Cal.
Chicken, made with water and 2% milk (¼ cup)	0.0	0.0	0	170	18
Homestyle, made with water (¼ cup)	0.0	0.0	0	240	16

HORSERADISH

Beaver* Horseradish (1 oz)	0.9	0.1	1	173	22
Kraft† Cream Style Prepared Horseradish (1 tbsp)	1.0	0.0	0	85	12
Kraft† Prepared Horseradish (1 tbsp)	0.0	0.0	0	140	10

HOT SAUCES/PEPPERS

Gebhardt Hot Sauce (½ tsp)	(0.0)	(0.0)	0	55	<1.0
Gedney Banana Peppers					
Hot (½ oz)	0.0	0.0	(0)	170	2
Mild (½ oz)	0.0	0.0	(0)	170	2
Gedney Cherry Peppers					
Hot (½ oz)	0.0	0.0	(0)	200	4
Sweet (½ oz)	0.0	0.0	(0)	200	4
Gedney Pepper Rings					
Hot (½ oz)	0.0	0.0	(0)	170	2
Mild (½ oz)	0.0	0.0	(0)	170	2
Hot chili peppers					
Canned (1 pepper)	0.1	0.0	0	(3)	18
Raw (1 pepper)	0.1	0.0	0	3	18
Jalapeño peppers, canned (½ cup)	0.4	0.0	0	995	17
Progresso Tuscan Peppers (½ cup)	0.0	0.0	0	5	20
Tabasco Brand Pepper Sauce (¼ tsp)	0.0	0.0	0	9	<1.0
Vlasic Peppers					
Hot Banana Pepper Rings or Chunks (1 oz)	0.0	0.0	(0)	480	4
Hot Cherry Peppers (1 oz)	0.0	0.0	(0)	480	8
Mexican Hot Chili Peppers (1 oz)	0.0	0.0	(0)	470	8
Mild Banana Pepper Chunks or Rings (1 oz)	0.0	0.0	(0)	480	4
Mild Cherry Peppers (1 oz)	0.0	0.0	(0)	480	8

* Beaver products are also marketed under Ingelhoffer and Old Spice brand names.

CONDIMENTS, GRAVIES AND SAUCES

	Tot. Fat (g)	Sat. Fat (g)	Chol. (mg)	Sod. (mg)	Cal.
Pepperoncini Salad Peppers (1 oz)	0.0	0.0	(0)	440	4
Sweet Banana Pepper Rings (1 oz)	0.0	0.0	(0)	170	4

KETCHUP/STEAK SAUCE

	Tot. Fat (g)	Sat. Fat (g)	Chol. (mg)	Sod. (mg)	Cal.
Healthy Choice Ketchup (1 tbsp)	0.0	0.0	0	110	10
Ketchup					
Low sodium (1 tbsp)	0.1	0.0	0	3	16
Regular (1 tbsp)	0.1	0.0	0	156	16
Mrs. Dash Steak Sauce (1 tbsp)	0.1	(0.0)	0	10	(17)

MARINARA/PASTA/SPAGHETTI SAUCES

	Tot. Fat (g)	Sat. Fat (g)	Chol. (mg)	Sod. (mg)	Cal.
Appletree* All Natural Spaghetti Sauce, Plain (4 oz)	3.0	(0.4)	(0)	740	80
Aunt Millie's Family Style Spaghetti Sauce					
Chunky Tomato and Italian Spices (4 oz)	<1.0	0.0	0	600	80
Chunky Tomato and Sliced Mushrooms (4 oz)	<1.0	0.0	0	480	80
Aunt Millie's Old Fashioned Cooking Sauce, Italian Style Marinara (4 oz)	2.0	0.0	0	320	60
Aunt Millie's Old Fashioned Spaghetti Sauce, Traditional Meatless (4 oz)	2.0	0.0	0	290	60
Classico Pasta Sauce					
Di Roma Arrabbiata Spicy Red Pepper (4 oz)	2.0	0.0	0	250	50
Di Sicilia Ripe Olives and Mushrooms (4 oz)	2.0	0.0	0	470	50
Contadina Fresh Marinara Sauce (7½ oz)	4.0	(0.6)	0	700	100
Contadina Light Sauce, Garden Vegetable (5 oz)	0.0	0.0	0	620	50

* Appletree products are also marketed under Best Yet, Fine Fare, Food Lion, Hyde Park, Hy-Top, Parade, Piggly-Wiggly, Red & White, Roundy's, Schwegmann, Scot Lad and Tops brand names.

	Tot. Fat (g)	Sat. Fat (g)	Chol. (mg)	Sod. (mg)	Cal.
Contadina Spaghetti Sauce					
Marinara (4 oz)	3.0	0.4	0	630	70
Meatless (4 oz)	2.0	0.3	0	680	60
Mushroom (4 oz)	2.0	0.3	0	660	60
Eden Organic Spaghetti Sauce, No Salt Added (4 oz)	2.0	(0.3)	(0)	0	80
Enrico's All Natural Spaghetti Sauce					
Mushrooms and Green Peppers (4 oz)	1.0	(0.1)	(0)	(770)	60
No Salt Added (4 oz)	1.0	(0.1)	(0)	30	60
Plain (4 oz)	1.0	(0.1)	(0)	(770)	60
Healthy Choice Chunky Pasta Sauce					
Garlic & Onions (4 oz)	0.0	0.0	0	350	40
Italian Style Vegetables (4 oz)	0.0	0.0	0	350	40
With Mushrooms (4 oz)	0.0	0.0	0	350	45
Hunt's Classic Italian Spaghetti Sauce					
with Parmesan (4 oz)	2.0	(0.2)	0	550	60
Hunt's Spaghetti Sauce					
Chunky (4 oz)	<1.0	(0.0)	0	470	50
Homestyle (4 oz)	2.0	0.3	0	530	60
Homestyle with Mushrooms (4 oz)	1.0	0.2	0	530	50
Mushrooms (4 oz)	2.0	0.3	0	560	70
Traditional (4 oz)	2.0	0.3	0	530	70
Newman's Own Spaghetti Sauce					
(4 oz)	2.0	(0.3)	0	560	70
Sockarooni (4 oz)	2.0	(0.3)	0	560	70
with Mushrooms (4 oz)	2.0	(0.3)	0	560	70
Prego Extra Chunky Spaghetti Sauce					
Garden Combination (4 oz)	2.0	(0.3)	(0)	420	80
Mushroom and Diced Tomato (4 oz)	3.0	(0.4)	(0)	480	100
Mushroom and Green Pepper (4 oz)	3.0	(0.4)	(0)	410	90
Mushroom with Extra Spice (4 oz)	3.0	(0.4)	(0)	450	100
Prego Spaghetti Sauce					
Three Cheese (4 oz)	2.0	(0.3)	(0)	410	100
Tomato and Basil (4 oz)	2.0	(0.3)	(0)	370	100
Pritikin Spaghetti Sauce (4 oz = 1/2 cup)	0.6	0.1	0	35	60
Chunky Garden Style (4 oz = 1/2 cup)	0.4	0.1	0	30	50
Ragu Fino Italian Pasta Sauce					
Garden Medley (4 oz)	3.0	(0.4)	0	490	80
Garlic & Basil (4 oz)	3.0	(0.4)	0	490	80

	Tot. Fat (g)	Sat. Fat (g)	Chol. (mg)	Sod. (mg)	Cal.
Mushroom (4 oz)	3.0	(0.4)	0	490	80
Tomato and Herbs (4 oz)	3.0	(0.4)	0	490	90
Zesty Tomato (4 oz)	3.0	(0.4)	0	490	70
Ragu Thick and Hearty Pasta Sauce, Plain or Mushroom (4 oz)	3.0	(0.4)	0	460	100
Ragu Today's Recipe 100% Natural Pasta Sauce					
Chunky Mushroom (4 oz)	1.0	0.0	0	370	50
Garden Harvest (4 oz)	1.0	0.0	0	370	50
Tomato Herb (4 oz)	1.0	0.0	0	370	50
Tree of Life Pasta Sauce					
Calabrese (4 oz)	3.0	(0.4)	(0)	190	70
No Salt Added (4 oz)	3.0	(0.4)	(0)	10	65
Regular (4 oz)	3.0	(0.4)	(0)	290	66
Weight Watchers Spaghetti Sauce Flavored with Mushrooms (1/3 cup)	0.0	0.0	0	300	35

MAYONNAISE—see "SALAD DRESSINGS AND SANDWICH SPREADS," MAYONNAISE/MAYONNAISE-TYPE DRESSINGS, page 205

MUSTARDS

	Tot. Fat (g)	Sat. Fat (g)	Chol. (mg)	Sod. (mg)	Cal.
Beaver* Mustard					
Chinese (1 oz)	1.8	0.1	0	230	43
Gold Honey (1 oz)	1.4	0.1	0	154	80
Hot (1 oz)	2.0	0.1	0	292	51
Lemon Dill (1 oz)	1.7	0.1	0	130	57
Orange 'N' Honey (1 oz)	1.6	0.1	0	104	52
Raspberry (1 oz)	1.3	0.1	0	101	60
Russian (1 oz)	1.4	0.1	0	262	64
Sweet Hot (1 oz)	2.3	0.2	1	166	69
Escoffier Sauce, Diable (1 tbsp)	0.0	0.0	(0)	160	20
Featherweight Mustard (1 tsp)	0.0	0.0	0	0	5

* Beaver products are also marketed under Ingelhoffer and Old Spice brand names.

CONDIMENTS, GRAVIES AND SAUCES

	Tot. Fat (g)	Sat. Fat (g)	Chol. (mg)	Sod. (mg)	Cal.
Grey Poupon† Mustard					
Country Dijon (1 tsp)	0.0	0.0	0	120	6
Parisian (1 tsp)	0.0	0.0	0	55	6
Hain Stone Ground Mustard (1 tbsp)	1.0	(0.0)	0	185	14
No Salt Added (1 tbsp)	1.0	(0.0)	0	10	14
Kraft† Horseradish Mustard (1 tbsp)	1.0	0.0	0	135	14
Mustard					
Chinese (1 tsp)	0.2	0.0	0	63	4
Horseradish (1 tsp)	tr	0.0	0	5	2
Regular (1 tsp)	0.2	0.0	0	63	4

OLIVES—*see* **"FATS, OILS, SEEDS AND NUTS," OLIVES,** *page 131*

ORIENTAL/SWEET AND SOUR SAUCES

	Tot. Fat (g)	Sat. Fat (g)	Chol. (mg)	Sod. (mg)	Cal.
Contadina International Sauces, Sweet 'n Sour (4 oz)	3.0	1.0	0	430	150
Kikkoman Sweet & Sour Sauce (1 tbsp)	0.0	0.0	0	97	19
Kraft† Sauceworks, Sweet'N Sour Sauce (1 tbsp)	0.0	0.0	0	50	25
La Choy Bead Molasses (1/2 tsp)	<1.0	(0.0)	0	1	7
La Choy Sauce					
Hot & Spicy Szechwan (1 tbsp)	<1.0	(0.0)	0	70	25
Mandarin Orange (1 tbsp)	<1.0	(0.0)	0	40	25
Plum (2 tbsp)	0.0	0.0	0	8	40
Sweet and Sour (1 tbsp)	<1.0	(0.0)	0	190	25
Sweet & Sour Duck Sauce (1 tbsp)	<1.0	(0.0)	0	40	25
Tangy Plum (1 tbsp)	<1.0	(0.0)	0	10	25
Maggie Gin's Sweet and Sour Sauce (1 tbsp)	0.0	0.0	0	58	27

PASTA SAUCES—*see* **MARINARA/PASTA/SPAGHETTI SAUCES**

PEPPERS—*see* **HOT SAUCES/PEPPERS**

CONDIMENTS, GRAVIES AND SAUCES

	Tot. Fat (g)	Sat. Fat (g)	Chol. (mg)	Sod. (mg)	Cal.
PICANTE/SALSA/TACO SAUCES					
El Molino Taco Sauce, Mild Red					
(2 tbsp)	0.0	0.0	0	170	10
Frito-Lay's Chunky Salsa Dip					
Hot (1 oz)	0.0	0.0	0	180	12
Medium (1 oz)	0.0	0.0	0	150	12
Mild (1 oz)	0.0	0.0	0	200	12
Guiltless Gourmet Salsa					
Hot (1 oz = 2 tbsp)	0.0	0.0	0	150	5
Medium (1 oz = 2 tbsp)	0.0	0.0	0	150	5
Mild (1 oz = 2 tbsp)	0.0	0.0	0	150	5
Hain Salsa					
Hot (¼ cup)	0.0	0.0	0	480	22
Mild (¼ cup)	0.0	0.0	(0)	410	20
Hain Taco Dip and Sauce (4 tbsp)	1.0	(<1.0)	5	350	25
La Victoria Salsa					
Brava (2 tbsp)	<1.0	(0.0)	0	170	8
Green Chili (2 tbsp)	<1.0	(0.0)	0	140	4
Jalapeña, Green (2 tbsp)	<1.0	(0.0)	0	190	4
Jalapeña, Red (2 tbsp)	<1.0	(0.0)	0	170	6
Picante (1 tbsp)	<1.0	0.0	0	180	6
Picante, Mild (2 tbsp)	<1.0	(0.0)	0	160	6
Ranchera (2 tbsp)	<1.0	(0.0)	0	140	4
Suprema (2 tbsp)	<1.0	(0.0)	0	180	4
Victoria (2 tbsp)	<1.0	(0.0)	0	160	4
La Victoria Taco Sauce					
Green (2 tbsp)	<1.0	(0.0)	(0)	180	4
Red (2 tbsp)	<1.0	(0.0)	(0)	160	6
Newman's Own Bandito Salsa					
Hot (1 tbsp)	<1.0	(0.0)	0	120	6
Medium (1 tbsp)	<1.0	(0.0)	0	45	6
Mild (1 tbsp)	<1.0	(0.0)	0	40	6
Old El Paso Sauce					
Chunky Picante (2 tbsp)	0.0	0.0	0	270	7
Picante (2 tbsp)	<1.0	(0.0)	0	310	8
Picante Salsa (2 tbsp)	<1.0	(0.0)	0	160	10
Taco (can) (2 tbsp)	0.0	0.0	0	300	15
Taco (jar), Mild, Medium, or Hot					
(2 tbsp)	<1.0	(0.0)	0	130	10

	Tot. Fat (g)	Sat. Fat (g)	Chol. (mg)	Sod. (mg)	Cal.
Old El Paso Thick 'n Chunky Salsa					
Green Chili (2 tbsp)	0.0	0.0	0	270	3
Mild, Medium, or Hot (2 tbsp)	<1.0	(0.0)	0	170	6
Verde (2 tbsp)	<1.0	0.0	0	135	10
Ortega† Green Chili Salsa					
Hot (½ oz = 1 tbsp)	0.0	0.0	0	190	6
Medium (½ oz = 1 tbsp)	0.0	0.0	0	190	6
Mild (½ oz = 1 tbsp)	0.0	0.0	0	190	8
Ortega† Thick and Smooth Taco Sauce					
Hot (½ oz = 1 tbsp)	0.0	0.0	0	105	8
Medium (½ oz = 1 tbsp)	0.0	0.0	0	105	8
Mild (½ oz = 1 tbsp)	0.0	0.0	0	115	8
Pace					
Picante Sauce (2 tsp)	<1.0	(0.0)	(0)	111	3
Thick & Chunky Salsa (2 tsp)	<1.0	(0.0)	(0)	102	4
Rosarita Chunky Salsa Dip					
Hot (3 tbsp)	<1.0	(0.0)	0	300	25
Medium (3 tbsp)	<1.0	(0.0)	0	350	25
Mild (3 tbsp)	<1.0	(0.0)	0	340	25
Rosarita Picante Sauce					
Hot Chunky (3 tbsp)	<1.0	(0.0)	0	515	18
Medium Chunky (3 tbsp)	<1.0	(0.0)	0	650	16
Mild Chunky (3 tbsp)	<1.0	(0.0)	0	630	25
Rosarita Taco Sauce					
Medium Chunky (3 tbsp)	<1.0	(0.0)	0	310	25
Mild (3 tbsp)	<1.0	(0.0)	0	310	15
Mild Chunky (3 tbsp)	<1.0	(0.0)	0	300	25
Tree of Life Salsa, Medium (1 oz)	0.0	0.0	0	30	8
Western Salsa, Medium (2 tsp)	0.0	0.0	0	100	4
Wise Picante Sauce (2 tbsp)	0.0	0.0	(0)	130	12

PICKLED VEGETABLES/PICKLES

	Tot. Fat (g)	Sat. Fat (g)	Chol. (mg)	Sod. (mg)	Cal.
Bread and butter pickles (2 slices)	tr	0.0	0	101	11
Dill pickles (1 large = 3¾" long)	0.1	0.0	0	833	12
Low sodium (1 large = 3¾" long)	0.1	0.0	0	12	12
Low sodium (1 slice)	0.0	0.0	0	tr	1
Featherweight Pickles, Sweet, sliced (3-4 slices)	0.0	0.0	0	5	24

	Tot. Fat (g)	Sat. Fat (g)	Chol. (mg)	Sod. (mg)	Cal.
Gedney Pickles					
Dill (1 oz)	0.0	0.0	(0)	280	4
Sweet Pantry (1 oz)	0.0	0.0	(0)	170	25
Pickled cocktail onions (1 onion)	0.0	0.0	0	5	12
Pickled sweet peppers (1 med)	0.0	0.0	0	26	8
Sour pickles (1 med = 3¾" long)	0.0	0.0	0	423	4
Low sodium (1 med = 3¾" long)	0.0	0.0	0	6	4
Sweet gherkins (1 med)	0.0	0.0	0	141	18
Talk O' Texas Crisp Okra Pickles (2 pods)	<0.1	(0.0)	0	244	4
Hot (2 pods)	<0.1	(0.0)	0	244	4
Vlasic Bread & Butter Pickles					
Chips (1 oz)	0.0	0.0	(0)	170	25
Old Fashioned (1 oz)	0.0	0.0	(0)	170	25
Old Fashioned Chunks (1 oz)	0.0	0.0	(0)	135	24
Stixs (1 oz)	0.0	0.0	(0)	130	20
Zesty Chips (1 oz)	0.0	0.0	(0)	220	45
Vlasic Dill Pickles					
Polish Snack Chunks, Polish Spears, Zesty Baby Dills, Zesty Crunchy Dills, Zesty Dill Spears or Zesty Snack Chunks (1 oz)	0.0	0.0	(0)	280	4
Vlasic Dills, Original and Original Hamburger Chips (1 oz)	0.0	0.0	(0)	390	4
Vlasic Half-the-Salt Pickles					
Hamburger Dill Chips (1 oz)	0.0	0.0	(0)	180	4
Kosher Crunchy Dills (1 oz)	0.0	0.0	(0)	110	4
Kosher Dill Spears (1 oz)	0.0	0.0	(0)	110	4
Sweet Butter Chips (1 oz)	0.0	0.0	(0)	85	30
Vlasic Hot & Spicy Vegetables					
Cauliflower (1 oz)	0.0	0.0	(0)	450	4
Garden Mix (1 oz)	0.0	0.0	(0)	480	4
Vlasic Kosher Pickles					
Baby Dills (1 oz)	0.0	0.0	(0)	220	4
Crunchy Dills (1 oz)	0.0	0.0	(0)	390	4
Dill Spears (1 oz)	0.0	0.0	(0)	220	4
Hamburger Dill Chips (1 oz)	0.0	0.0	(0)	180	4
Snack Chunks (1 oz)	0.0	0.0	(0)	220	4
Vlasic Lightly Spiced Cocktail Onions (1 oz)	0.0	0.0	(0)	410	4

	Tot. Fat (g)	Sat. Fat (g)	Chol. (mg)	Sod. (mg)	Cal.
Vlasic No Garlic Pickles, Crunchy Dills (1 oz)	0.0	0.0	(0)	220	4
Vlasic Pickles					
Kosher Dill Gherkins (1 oz)	0.0	0.0	(0)	220	4
No Garlic Dill Spears (1 oz)	0.0	0.0	(0)	220	4
Sweet Chips, Sweet Gherkins or Sweet Pickles (1 oz)	0.0	0.0	(0)	170	45
Sweet Midgets (1 oz)	0.0	0.0	(0)	220	45
Vlasic Refrigerated Pickles					
Deli Hearty Garlic Halves (1 oz)	0.0	0.0	(0)	300	4
Deli Hearty Garlic Wholes, Deli Kosher Dill Halves or Wholes, or Deli Miniature Kosher Dills (1 oz)	0.0	0.0	(0)	310	4
Vlasic Relishes, Dill (1 oz)	0.0	0.0	(0)	450	2
Vlasic Sweet Cauliflower (1 oz)	0.0	0.0	0	260	35
Vlasic Vegetables, Cocktail Onions (1/2 oz)	0.0	0.0	(0)	420	4
Watermelon rind pickles (1 piece)	0.1	0.0	0	214	44

PICKLES—*see* **PICKLED VEGETABLES/PICKLES**

PIZZA SAUCES

	Tot. Fat (g)	Sat. Fat (g)	Chol. (mg)	Sod. (mg)	Cal.
Contadina Pizza Sauce					
Italian Cheeses (1/4 cup)	1.0	0.2	<1	380	30
Original Quick and Easy (1/4 cup)	1.0	(0.1)	(0)	330	30
Pepperoni (1/4 cup)	2.0	0.4	0	390	40
Pizza Squeeze (1/4 cup)	1.0	(0.1)	(0)	330	30
Ragu Pizza Quick Sauce					
Cheese (1.7 oz = 3 tbsp)	2.0	(0.3)	0	330	35
Garlic & Basil (1.7 oz = 3 tbsp)	2.0	(0.3)	0	330	35
Mushroom (1.7 oz = 3 tbsp)	2.0	(0.3)	0	330	35
Traditional (1.7 oz = 3 tbsp)	2.0	(0.3)	0	330	35
Ragu Pizza Sauce (1.6 oz)	1.0	(0.1)	0	200	25

CONDIMENTS, GRAVIES AND SAUCES

	Tot. Fat (g)	Sat. Fat (g)	Chol. (mg)	Sod. (mg)	Cal.
RELISHES					
Chow chow					
Sour (1 tbsp)	0.2	0.0	0	201	4
Sweet (1 tbsp)	0.1	0.0	0	81	18
Chutney (1 tbsp)	0.1	0.0	0	9	21
Corn relish (1 tbsp)	0.5	0.0	0	135	20
Dromedary Pimientos, all types (1 oz)	0.0	0.0	(0)	5	10
Hot dog relish (1 tbsp)	0.1	0.0	0	164	14
Old El Paso Jalapeño Relish (2 tbsp)	0.0	0.0	0	100	16
Pickle relish (1 tbsp)	0.0	0.0	0	164	19
Sour (1 tbsp)	0.0	0.0	0	192	3
Sweet (1 tbsp)	0.1	0.0	0	122	19
Vlasic Relish					
Green Tomato Piccalilli (1 oz)	0.0	0.0	(0)	180	35
Hamburger or Sweet Relish (1 oz)	0.0	0.0	(0)	260	35
Hot Dog (1 oz)	0.0	0.0	(0)	260	35
Hot Piccalilli (1 oz)	0.0	0.0	(0)	180	35
India (1 oz)	0.0	0.0	(0)	260	30

SALAD DRESSINGS—see "SALAD DRESSINGS AND SANDWICH SPREADS," *page 201*

SALSA—see **PICANTE/SALSA/TACO SAUCES**

SANDWICH SPREADS—see "SALAD DRESSINGS AND SANDWICH SPREADS," *page 208*

SOY SAUCES

	Tot. Fat (g)	Sat. Fat (g)	Chol. (mg)	Sod. (mg)	Cal.
Angostura Soy Sauce, Low Sodium (1 tsp)	0.0	0.0	(0)	130	2
Eden Soy Sauce					
Naturally Brewed Tamari, Wheat Free (½ tsp)	0.0	0.0	0	160	2
Organic, Reduced Sodium (½ tsp)	0.0	0.0	0	80	2

	Tot. Fat (g)	Sat. Fat (g)	Chol. (mg)	Sod. (mg)	Cal.
Organic Shoyu, Traditional Japanese (1/2 tsp)	0.0	0.0	0	140	2
Shoyu, Naturally Brewed (1/2 tsp)	0.0	0.0	0	160	2
Shoyu, Traditional Japanese (1/2 tsp)	0.0	0.0	0	140	2
Kikkoman Soy Sauce (1 tbsp)	0.0	0.0	0	938	12
Lite (1 tbsp)	0.0	0.0	0	564	13
La Choy Soy Sauce (1/2 tsp)	<1.0	(0.0)	0	230	2
Lite (1/2 tsp)	<1.0	(0.0)	0	110	1

SPAGHETTI SAUCES—*see*
**MARINARA/PASTA/SPAGHETTI
SAUCES**

STEAK SAUCES—*see*
KETCHUP/STEAK SAUCE

STIR-FRY SAUCES

	Tot. Fat (g)	Sat. Fat (g)	Chol. (mg)	Sod. (mg)	Cal.
Kikkoman Stir-Fry Sauce (1 tbsp)	0.0	0.0	1	369	16
Maggie Gin's Stir-Fry Sauce					
Mandarin (1 tbsp)	tr	0.0	0	59	22
Traditional (1 tbsp)	0.2	(0.1)	tr	304	27

SWEET AND SOUR SAUCES—*see*
**ORIENTAL/SWEET AND SOUR
SAUCES**

TACO SAUCES—*see*
PICANTE/SALSA/TACO SAUCES

TERIYAKI SAUCES

	Tot. Fat (g)	Sat. Fat (g)	Chol. (mg)	Sod. (mg)	Cal.
Angostura Teriyaki Sauce, Low Sodium (1 tsp)	0.0	0.0	(0)	85	4
Kikkoman Teriyaki Baste & Glaze (1 tbsp)	0.0	0.0	(0)	310	24
Kikkoman Teriyaki Sauce (1 tbsp)	0.0	0.0	0	626	15
Lite (1 tbsp)	0.1	(0.0)	(0)	298	14
Maggie Gin's Lite and Low Teriyaki and Stir-Fry (1 tbsp)	0.0	0.0	0	245	20

	Tot. Fat (g)	Sat. Fat (g)	Chol. (mg)	Sod. (mg)	Cal.
TOMATO SAUCES					
Contadina Fresh Sauces, Plum Tomato with Basil (7½ oz)	4.0	(0.5)	5	700	100
Contadina Tomato Sauce					
Italian Style (½ cup)	<1.0	(0.0)	(0)	670	30
Thick & Zesty (½ cup)	<1.0	(0.0)	(0)	650	40
Hunt's Tomato Sauce					
Garlic (4 oz)	2.0	0.3	0	480	70
Herb Flavored (4 oz)	2.0	0.6	<1	470	70
Italian (4 oz)	2.0	0.5	<1	460	60
Meatloaf Fixings (2 oz)	<1.0	(0.0)	0	580	20
Mushrooms (4 oz)	<1.0	(0.0)	0	710	25
No Salt Added (4 oz)	<1.0	(0.0)	0	20	35
Onions (4 oz)	<1.0	(0.0)	0	650	40
Special (4 oz)	<1.0	(0.0)	0	280	35
Tomato Bits (4 oz)	<1.0	(0.0)	0	620	30
Rokeach Tomato Sauce					
Italian Style (3 oz)	2.0	(0.3)	0	243	60
Low Sodium (3 oz)	2.0	(0.3)	0	124	60
Marinara Style (3 oz)	2.0	(0.3)	0	257	60

WORCESTERSHIRE SAUCES—*see* **COOKING SAUCES**

† = tobacco company, corporate subsidiary or parent

CRACKERS

The crackers in this section are low in fat, saturated fat and cholesterol.

Products listed in this book vary in sodium content. Use the values appearing on the following pages to help plan a daily intake providing no more than 3,000 milligrams of sodium.

You can use the tables below to evaluate products introduced since this book went to press.

AHA Criteria for Crackers*

	Tot. Fat (g)	Sat. Fat (g)	Chol. (mg)
Crackers not used as snacks, such as saltines, oyster crackers and melba toast	3	<0.5	<2
Crackers usually used as snacks	3	1	<2

* Per serving.

Crackers Not Recommended for Frequent Consumption

Some types of cracker that are usually too high in fat, saturated fat and/or cholesterol to be recommended for frequent consumption are shown in the table below. Values that exceed AHA criteria are followed by asterisks. The AHA does not have criteria for sodium.

You can use the values in the table to compare these crackers with more-healthful alternatives listed on the following pages.

Crackers High in Fat, Saturated Fat and/or Cholesterol

	Tot. Fat (g)	Sat. Fat (g)	Chol. (mg)	Sod. (mg)	Cal.
Cheese cracker (1 ounce)	7.2*	2.7*	4*	282	142
Rye cracker sandwich with cheese filling (1 ounce or sandwiches)	6.4*	1.6*	2*	296	136
Wheat cracker sandwich with peanut butter filling (1 ounce or 4 sandwiches)	7.6*	1.6*	0	228	140

Adapted from USDA Handbook No. 8 series.

* These values exceed AHA criteria for crackers.

	Tot. Fat (g)	Sat. Fat (g)	Chol. (mg)	Sod. (mg)	Cal.
BREADSTICKS, HARD—*see* "BREADS AND BREAD PRODUCTS," **BREADSTICKS,** *page 31*					
CRACKERS					
Cheese Crackers					
Health Valley Fat-Free Crackers, Organic Wheat with Cheese (¹/₂ oz = 6 crackers)	<1.0	(0.0)	0	80	40
Nabisco† SnackWell's Crackers, Cheese (¹/₂ oz = 18 crackers)	1.0	<0.5	0	160	60
Crackerbreads/Crispbreads					
Crispini					
Seeds and Spice (1 oz)	1.0	(0.5)	0	120	100
Sesame (1 oz)	1.0	(0.5)	0	140	100
Sesame with Garlic (1 oz)	1.0	(0.5)	0	140	100
Stoned Ground Wheat (1 oz)	1.0	(0.5)	0	140	100
Finn Crisp Bread Cracker					
Dark (.4 oz = 2 slices)	0.0	0.0	(0)	130	38
Dark with Caraway (.4 oz = 2 slices)	0.0	0.0	(0)	130	38
Grissol Hors d'oeuvre Petite Biscotte Ronde					
Aux Legumes (Vegetable Round Rusk) (10 slices)	1.6	0.3	0	(72)	126
Reguliere (Regular Round Rusk) (10 slices)	1.7	0.4	0	(72)	127
Ideal Norwegian Crispbread					
Extra Thins (3 slices)	0.0	0.0	(0)	191	49
Fiber Thins (2 slices)	0.5	(0.1)	(0)	175	41
J. J. Flats Breadflats					
Flavorall (1 slice)	1.2	0.3	0	130	55
Garlic (1 slice)	0.8	0.2	0	135	55
Oat Bran (1 slice)	0.7	0.2	0	75	50
Onion (1 slice)	0.8	0.2	0	130	55
Plain (1 slice)	0.8	0.2	0	140	55
Poppy (1 slice)	1.1	0.3	0	130	55

	Tot. Fat (g)	Sat. Fat (g)	Chol. (mg)	Sod. (mg)	Cal.
Sesame (1 slice)	1.2	0.3	0	130	55
Kavli Crispbread					
All Natural Whole Grain (1 slice)	<1.0	(0.0)	0	10	15
Muesli (1 slice)	0.0	0.0	0	30	30
Rye Bran (1 slice)	0.2	(0.0)	(0)	35	30
Kavli Norwegian Crispbread, Thin Style (2 wafers)	0.3	(0.0)	(0)	32	40
LaVosh Hawaii Flatbread, Ten-Grain (4 pieces)	1.6	0.3	0	120	59
Master Old Country Zwieback Toast, Cinnamon (.5 oz = 1 slice)	1.0	(<1.0)	0	65	60
Nejaime's Lavasch Crisp Sesame Wafer Bread					
Dill & Garlic (1/2 oz)	1.1	(0.5)	(0)	57	58
Garlic (1/2 oz)	1.1	(0.5)	(0)	57	58
Nejaime's Lavasch Crisp Wafer Bread					
Combo (1/2 oz)	1.1	(0.5)	0	57	58
Onion (1/2 oz)	1.1	(0.5)	0	57	58
Poppy (1/2 oz)	1.1	(0.5)	(0)	57	58
Sesame (1/2 oz)	1.1	(0.2)	(0)	57	5
Old London Cracker Bread, Wheat (1/2 oz = 3 slices)	<1.0	(0.0)	0	70	50
Olof Sweden Crisp Rolls					
Four Grain (1 crisp)	<1.0	0.0	0	35	43
Oat Bran (1 crisp)	1.2	0.2	0	32	44
Whole Grain (1 crisp)	<1.0	0.0	0	75	42
Pepperidge Farm Crunchy Baked Wheat Crispbread					
Cinnamon Sugar (1/2 oz)	1.0	0.0	0	100	60
Poppy (1/2 oz)	1.0	0.0	0	80	20
Pogen Krisprolls Original Swedish Toast (.4 oz = 1 toast)	1.0	(0.4)	0	(50)	38
Ryvita Crisp Bread					
Dark Rye (1 cracker)	<1.0	0.0	0	35	26
High Fiber (1 cracker)	<1.0	0.0	0	10	23
Light Rye (1 cracker)	<1.0	0.0	0	20	26
Toasted Sesame Rye (1 cracker)	<1.0	0.0	0	10	31
Tuscany Toast					
Pepato (1 oz)	2.0	(0.3)	0	400	90
Plain (1 oz)	2.0	(0.3)	0	390	100

	Tot. Fat (g)	Sat. Fat (g)	Chol. (mg)	Sod. (mg)	Cal.
Tomato-Onion (1 oz)	2.0	(0.3)	0	380	100
Venus Crackers					
Cracker Bread (1/2 oz = 5 crackers)	1.0	0.2	0	90	60
Parak, A Crisp Lavash Wafer Bread, Original (1/2 oz = 2 1/2 wafers)	1.0	0.2	0	90	60
Parak, A Crisp Lavash Wafer Bread, Sesame (1/2 oz = 2 wafers)	1.3	0.2	0	70	60
Wasa Crisp Bread					
Falu-Rye (1 slice)	0.0	0.0	0	50	30
Fiber-Plus (1 slice)	1.0	(0.3)	0	60	35
Golden Rye (1 slice)	0.0	0.0	0	50	30
Hearty Rye (1 slice)	0.0	0.0	0	75	50
Light Rye (1 slice)	0.0	0.0	0	40	25
Toasted Wheat (1/2 oz = 1 slice)	1.0	(0.4)	0	70	50
Weight Watchers Crispbread					
Garlic (2 wafers)	0.0	0.0	0	55	30
Golden Wheat (2 wafers)	0.0	0.0	0	55	30
Harvest Rice (2 wafers)	0.0	0.0	0	55	30

Crispbreads—see
Crackerbreads/Crispbreads

Graham Crackers—see
"DESSERTS," COOKIES,
page 108

Matzos

	Tot. Fat (g)	Sat. Fat (g)	Chol. (mg)	Sod. (mg)	Cal.
Manischewitz Matzo Crackers					
Dietetic Matzo Thins (1 board)	0.4	0.0	0	0	91
Miniatures (10 crackers)	<1.0	0.0	0	<10	90
Passover (1 board)	0.4	0.0	0	<5	129
Thin Salted Matzos (1 board)	0.3	0.0	0	n/a	100
Thin Tea Matzos (Daily) (1 board)	0.3	0.0	0	1	103
Unsalted Matzos (Daily) (1 board)	0.3	0.0	0	1	110
Whole Wheat Matzos with Bran (1 board)	0.6	0.0	0	1	110

	Tot. Fat (g)	Sat. Fat (g)	Chol. (mg)	Sod. (mg)	Cal.

Melba Toast/Rounds

Delicious Snack Crackers

	Tot. Fat (g)	Sat. Fat (g)	Chol. (mg)	Sod. (mg)	Cal.
Melba Toasts, Sesame (.3 oz = 2 slices)	<1.0	(0.0)	(0)	35	35
Unsalted (.3 oz = 2 slices)	<1.0	(0.0)	(0)	5	30
Whole Wheat (.3 oz = 2 slices)	<1.0	(0.0)	(0)	50	30

Devonsheer Melba Rounds

Garlic (½ oz = 5 rounds)	1.2	(0.3)	0	132	56
Honey Bran (½ oz = 5 rounds)	0.9	(0.1)	0	98	52
Onion (½ oz = 5 rounds)	0.6	(0.3)	0	120	51
Plain (½ oz = 5 rounds)	0.6	(0.1)	0	111	53
Plain, Unsalted (½ oz = 5 rounds)	0.6	(0.1)	0	<5	52
Rye (½ oz = 5 rounds)	0.6	(0.3)	0	130	53

Grissol Melba Toast

Double Fiber (7 slices)	1.1	0.2	0	(194)	120
No Salt Added (7 slices)	1.1	0.2	0	11	140
Regular (7 slices)	1.2	0.2	0	(194)	138
Rye (7 slices)	1.3	0.3	0	(194)	138
Sesame (7 slices)	2.1	0.4	0	(117)	140
60% Whole Wheat (7 slices)	1.4	0.1	0	(194)	137

Lance Crackers, Melba Toast, Oblong

(2 slices)	0.0	0.0	0	50	30

Nabisco† Crackers, Rounds, Plain (2

rounds)	0.2	(0.0)	0	37	20

Old London Melba Snacks

Bacon (½ oz = approx 5 rounds)	1.6	0.4	0	75	60
Cheese (½ oz = approx 5 rounds)	0.7	0.0	0	150	45
Garlic (½ oz = approx 5 rounds)	1.0	0.0	0	105	50
Onion (½ oz = approx 5 rounds)	1.4	0.3	0	130	50
Rye (½ oz = approx 5 rounds)	1.4	0.3	0	210	50
White (½ oz = approx 5 rounds)	1.5	0.4	0	100	60
Whole Grain (½ oz = approx 5 rounds)	1.0	0.0	0	110	50

Old London Melba Toast

Onion (½ oz = 3 slices)	0.4	0.0	0	140	50
Rye (½ oz = 3 slices)	0.4	0.0	0	100	50
Sesame (½ oz = 3 slices)	1.3	0.3	0	135	50
Sesame, Unsalted (½ oz = 3 slices)	1.3	0.3	0	0	60
Wheat (½ oz = 3 slices)	<1.0	0.0	0	120	50

	Tot. Fat (g)	Sat. Fat (g)	Chol. (mg)	Sod. (mg)	Cal.
White (1/2 oz = 3 slices)	0.4	0.0	0	105	50
Whole Grain (1/2 oz = 3 slices)	<1.0	(0.0)	(0)	130	50
Whole Grain, Unsalted (1/2 oz = 3 slices)	0.4	0.0	0	0	50
Old London Rounds, Garlic (1/2 oz = 5 crackers)	1.5	0.3	0	100	60

Oyster Crackers/Saltines

Appletree* Saltines (1/2 oz = 5 crackers)	<1.0	(0.6)	(0)	200	60
Delicious Crackers					
Oyster (.5 oz)	1.0	(0.4)	0	180	60
Saltines, Unsalted Tops (.5 oz)	2.0	0.0	0	120	60
Lance Crackers, Saltines, Slug Pack (1/3 oz = 4 crackers)	1.0	0.0	0	130	50
Nabisco† Crackers, Premium Saltine, Fat Free (1/2 oz = 5 crackers)	0.0	0.0	0	115	50
O.T.C. (Original Trenton Cracker) Crackers, Soup, Chowder and Oyster Crackers (10 g)	1.0	(0.1)	0	5	40

Saltines—see Oyster Crackers/Saltines

Wafers

Bremner Wafers, Plain (.5 oz = 6–7 crackers)	1.7	(0.7)	0	83	60
Lance Crackers					
Captain Wafers (1/2 oz = 2 crackers)	1.0	0.0	0	60	30
Wheatswafer (1/2 oz = 2 crackers)	1.0	0.0	0	50	30
Venus Crackers, Bite Size Wafers, Stoned Wheat (1/2 oz = 7 wafers)	1.4	0.3	0	180	60
Venus Crackers, Wafers Bran, Salt Free (1/2 oz = 5 wafers)	1.0	0.2	0	0	60

* Appletree products are also marketed under Best Yet, Fine Fare, Food Lion, Hyde Park, Hy-Top, Parade, Piggly Wiggly, Red & White, Roundy's, Schwegmann, Scot Lad and Tops brand names.

CRACKERS

	Tot. Fat (g)	Sat. Fat (g)	Chol. (mg)	Sod. (mg)	Cal.
Corn Bran, Salt Free (½ oz = 5 wafers)	1.2	(0.3)	0	0	50
Corn Bran with Salt (½ oz = 5 wafers)	1.2	(0.3)	0	60	50
Corn, Salt Free (½ oz = 5 wafers)	1.3	0.2	0	0	60
Cracked Wheat, Salt Free (½ oz = 5 wafers)	1.3	0.3	0	0	60
Oat Bran (½ oz = 5 wafers)	1.4	0.3	0	105	60
Oat Bran, Salt Free (½ oz = 5 wafers)	1.2	0.3	0	0	60
Rice Bran, Salt Free (½ oz = 5 wafers)	1.6	(0.4)	0	0	50
Rice Bran with Salt (½ oz = 5 wafers)	1.6	(0.4)	0	70	50
Rye, Low Salt (½ oz = 5 wafers)	1.0	0.3	0	110	60
Rye, Salt Free (½ oz = 5 wafers)	0.7	(0.3)	0	0	60
Stoned Wheat (½ oz = 5 wafers)	1.4	0.3	0	180	60
Wheat (½ oz = 5 wafers)	1.5	(0.4)	0	120	60
Wheat, Salt Free (½ oz = 5 wafers)	1.2	(0.3)	0	0	60

Wheat Crackers

	Tot. Fat (g)	Sat. Fat (g)	Chol. (mg)	Sod. (mg)	Cal.
Health Valley Fat-Free Crackers					
Organic Wheat with Herbs (½ oz = 6 crackers)	<1.0	(0.0)	0	80	40
Organic Wheat with Onion (½ oz = 6 crackers)	<1.0	(0.0)	0	80	40
Organic Wheat with Vegetables (½ oz = 6 crackers)	<1.0	(0.0)	0	80	40
Whole Wheat (½ oz = 6 crackers)	<1.0	(0.0)	0	80	40
Lance Crackers, Twins, Wheat (½ oz = 2 crackers)	1.0	0.0	0	70	30
Nabisco† SnackWell's Crackers, Wheat (½ oz = 5 crackers)	0.0	0.0	0	160	50
R.W. Frookie Fat Free! Gourmet Crackers, Whole Wheat (4 crackers)	0.0	0.0	0	60	35

	Tot. Fat (g)	Sat. Fat (g)	Chol. (mg)	Sod. (mg)	Cal.

Other Crackers

	Tot. Fat (g)	Sat. Fat (g)	Chol. (mg)	Sod. (mg)	Cal.
Jacobs Crackers, Choice Grain (1 cracker)	0.9	(0.1)	(0)	72	13
Lance Crackers					
Twins, Rye (1/2 oz = 2 crackers)	1.0	0.0	0	65	30
Twins, Sesame (1/2 oz = 2 crackers)	1.0	0.0	0	65	40
O.T.C. (Original Trenton Cracker) Crackers, Wine Crackers (1/2 oz)	1.5	(0.2)	0	25	60
Pepperidge Farm Distinctive Crackers, English Water Biscuit (4 crackers)	1.0	0.0	0	100	70
R.W. Frookie Fat Free! Gourmet Crackers					
Cracked Pepper (4 crackers)	0.0	0.0	0	40	35
Garlic & Herb (4 crackers)	0.0	0.0	0	120	35
Water (4 crackers)	0.0	0.0	0	60	35
Rickburn Pita Crisps, Plain (1 oz)	1.0	(0.1)	0	320	90
Rykrisp Crackers					
Natural (1/2 oz = 2 triple crackers)	0.0	0.0	0	75	40
Seasoned Crackers (1/2 oz = 2 triple crackers)	1.0	(0.5)	0	105	45
Seasoned Twindividuals Snack Crackers (1/2 oz = 2 triple crackers)	1.0	(0.5)	0	105	45
Valley Lahvosh Crackers					
Hearts (1/4 oz = 2 hearts)	0.4	(0.1)	(0)	40	28
Rounds, 3" (1/4 oz = 1 cracker)	0.3	0.1	0	40	28
Rounds, 5" (.6 oz = 1 cracker)	0.8	0.2	0	100	70
Venus Crackers					
Armenian Cracker Bread (1/2 oz = 5 wafers)	<1.0	(0.0)	0	90	60
Armenian Thin Bread (.9 oz = 2 thin breads)	1.3	0.3	0	165	100
Corn, Salt Free (1/2 oz = 5 wafers)	1.2	(0.2)	0	0	50
Fat Free Water Crackers (1/2 oz = 5 crackers)	0.0	0.0	0	70	55

GRAIN CAKES—see
RICE/POPCORN/GRAIN CAKES

CRACKERS

	Tot. Fat (g)	Sat. Fat (g)	Chol. (mg)	Sod. (mg)	Cal.
ICE CREAM CONES—see "FROZEN DESSERTS," ICE CREAM CONES, *page 144*					
POPCORN CAKES—see RICE/POPCORN/GRAIN CAKES					
RICE/POPCORN/GRAIN CAKES					
Chico San Mini Rice Cakes					
Apple Cinnamon (1/2 oz = 4 cakes)	1.0	(<1.0)	0	20	60
Cinnamon Sugar (1/2 oz = 5 cakes)	0.0	0.0	0	0	50
Honey Nut (1/2 oz = 4 cakes)	1.0	(<1.0)	0	35	60
Sesame, Sodium Free (1/2 oz = 6 cakes)	0.0	0.0	0	0	50
Chico San Popcorn Cakes					
Lightly Salted (1/8 oz = 1 cake)	0.0	0.0	0	45	40
Natural Butter Flavor (1 cake)	0.0	0.0	0	45	40
Chico San Rice Cakes					
Sesame, Sodium Free (1 cake)	0.0	0.0	0	30	35
Sesame, Very Low Sodium (.3 oz = 1 cake)	0.0	0.0	0	30	35
Hain Mini Rice Cakes					
Apple Cinnamon (1/2 oz)	<1.0	(0.0)	0	10	60
Honey Nut (1/2 oz)	<1.0	(0.0)	0	30	60
Plain (1/2 oz)	<1.0	(0.0)	0	20	60
Plain, No Salt Added (1/2 oz)	<1.0	(0.0)	0	5	60
Teriyaki (1/2 oz)	<1.0	(0.0)	0	75	50
Hain Rice Cakes					
5-Grain (1 cake)	<1.0	(0.0)	0	10	40
Plain (1 cake)	<1.0	(0.0)	0	10	40
Plain, No Salt Added (1 cake)	<1.0	(0.0)	0	<5	40
Sesame (1 cake)	<1.0	(0.0)	0	10	40
Sesame, No Salt Added (1 cake)	<1.0	(0.0)	0	<5	40
Heart Lovers Rice Cakes					
Plain, Lightly Salted (1 cake)	0.0	0.0	0	30	35
Sesame, Lightly Salted (1 cake)	0.0	0.0	0	30	35
Mother's Rice Cakes					
Barley & Oats (1 cake)	0.3	0.1	0	41	34
Buckwheat (unsalted) (1 cake)	0.3	0.1	0	0	35

	Tot. Fat (g)	Sat. Fat (g)	Chol. (mg)	Sod. (mg)	Cal.
Pacific Grain Crispy Cakes					
Apple Cinnamon (1 cake)	0.4	(0.1)	0	20	35
Cheddar (1 cake)	0.5	(0.1)	0	50	35
Natural (1 cake)	0.2	(0.0)	0	20	30
Pizza (1 cake)	0.5	(0.1)	0	50	35
Ranch (1 cake)	0.5	(0.1)	0	60	35
Toasted Brown Rice (1 cake)	0.4	(0.0)	0	50	35
Vegetable (1 cake)	0.5	(0.1)	0	50	35
Pacific Grain Mini Crispys Rice Cake Snacks					
Apple Spice (1/4 oz)	<1.0	(0.0)	0	10	30
Barbecue (1/4 oz)	<1.0	(0.0)	0	10	30
Honey Almond (1/4 oz)	<1.0	(0.0)	0	10	30
Honey Sesame (1/4 oz)	<1.0	(0.0)	0	10	30
Teriyaki (1/4 oz)	<1.0	(0.0)	0	10	30
Pritikin Rice Cakes					
Multi-Grain (1 cake)	0.4	0.1	(0)	29	35
Multi-Grain, Salt-Free (1 cake)	0.4	0.1	0	0	35
Plain (1 cake)	0.3	0.1	0	36	35
Plain, Unsalted (1 cake)	0.3	0.1	0	0	35
Sesame (1 cake)	0.3	0.1	0	36	35
Sesame, Salt-Free (1 cake)	0.0	0.1	0	1	35
Quaker Corn Cakes, Caramel Corn (1/2 oz = 1 cake)	0.0	0.0	0	30	50
Quaker Grain Cakes					
Corn (1 cake)	0.2	(0.0)	(0)	53	35
Rye (1 cake)	0.3	0.0	0	52	35
Wheat (1 cake)	0.3	0.1	0	52	34
Quaker Rice Cakes					
Corn (1 cake)	0.3	0.1	0	31	35
Multigrain (1 cake)	0.4	0.1	(0)	29	34
Multigrain (unsalted) (1 cake)	0.4	0.1	0	0	35
Plain (1 cake)	0.3	0.1	0	36	35
Plain (unsalted) (1 cake)	0.3	0.1	0	0	35
Rye (1 cake)	0.4	0.1	0	12	34
Sesame (1 cake)	0.3	0.1	0	36	35
Sesame (unsalted) (1 cake)	0.3	0.1	0	1	35

CRACKERS

† = tobacco company, corporate subsidiary or parent

DAIRY PRODUCTS AND DAIRY SUBSTITUTES

D airy products provide much of the calcium in our diet. However, regular dairy products are high in fat and saturated fat. Fortunately, many nonfat and low-fat dairy products are now available that are as high in calcium as regular dairy products.

Products listed in this book vary in sodium content. Use the values appearing on the following pages to help plan a daily intake providing no more than 3,000 milligrams of sodium.

Most of the foods in this book are brand name products; however, when a brand is not specified, it means that most brands of that product provide about the same amount of fat, saturated fat and cholesterol and that these amounts do not exceed AHA criteria.

You can use those generic entries and the tables below to evaluate products introduced since this book went to press.

AHA Criteria for Dairy Products and Dairy Substitutes*

	Tot. Fat (g)	Sat. Fat (g)	Chol. (mg)
Buttermilk, cheese (except as listed below), milk, milk-based products, sour cream and yogurt	3	2	20
Coffee creamers, liquid and powdered	3	<0.5	<2
Condensed or evaporated milk, undiluted, and whipped toppings	<0.5	<0.5	<2
Hard cheeses, grated, such as parmesan and romano	3	1	20

* Per serving.

Dairy Products Not Recommended for Frequent Consumption

Some types of dairy product that are usually too high in fat, saturated fat and/or cholesterol to be recommended for frequent consumption are shown in the table below. Values that exceed AHA criteria are followed by asterisks. The AHA does not have criteria for sodium.

You can use the values in the table to compare these dairy products with more-healthful alternatives listed on the following pages.

Dairy Products High in Fat, Saturated Fat and/or Cholesterol

	Tot. Fat (g)	Sat. Fat (g)	Chol. (mg)	Sod. (mg)	Cal.
Cheddar cheese (1 ounce)	9.5*	6.1*	30*	178	115
Coffee cream (1 tablespoon)	2.9	1.8*	10*	6	29
Creamed cottage cheese (½ cup)	5.1*	3.2*	17	457	117
Cultured sour cream (1 ounce or about 2½ tablespoons)	5.9*	3.7*	12	14	61
Evaporated whole milk (2 tablespoons)	2.4*	1.5*	9*	33	42
Pimiento pasteurized process cheese (1 ounce)	8.8*	5.6*	27*	405	106
Swiss cheese (1 ounce)	7.8*	5.0*	26*	74	107
Whole milk (1 cup)	8.2*	5.1*	33*	120	150

Adapted from USDA Handbook No. 8 series.

* These values exceed AHA criteria for dairy products.

BUTTERMILK—*see*
MILK/BUTTERMILK

CHEESES

American Cheese

	Tot. Fat (g)	Sat. Fat (g)	Chol. (mg)	Sod. (mg)	Cal.
Alpine Lace Free N' Lean Pasteurized Process Cheese, American (1 oz)	0.0	0.0	5	290	40
Borden Fat Free Pasteurized Process Cheese Product Singles, American (1 oz)	0.0	0.0	5	380	40
Borden Lite-Line Pasteurized Process Cheese Product Singles					
American (1 oz)	2.0	(1.3)	10	430	50
American, Low Sodium (2/3 oz)	2.0	(1.3)	5	90	35
American, Low Sodium (1 oz)	2.0	(1.3)	10	140	50
American Flavor, Yellow and White (2/3 oz)	2.0	(1.3)	5	280	35
Count Down Imitation Cheese (1 oz)	<1.0	(<1.0)	2	(439)	40
Healthy Choice Cheese					
Singles (1 oz)	0.0	0.0	5	390	40
Two Pound Loaf (1 oz)	0.0	0.0	5	390	30
Two Pound Loaf, Mexican (1 oz)	0.0	0.0	5	390	30
Heart's D'Lite Cheese (1 oz)	0.0	0.0	0	190	45
Kraft† Free Singles Nonfat Pasteurized Process Cheese Product (1 oz)	0.0	0.0	5	420	45
Kraft† Healthy Favorites					
Process Cheese Slices, American Flavored (colored and white slices) (2/3 oz)	2.0	1.0	10	260	45
Processed Cheese Spread (1 oz)	3.0	2.0	10	450	60
Smart Beat Cheese					
Fat Free American, slices (2/3 oz)	0.0	0.0	0	180	30
Low Sodium, slices (2/3 oz)	2.0	<1.0	0	90	35
Tasty-Lo Cheese, American (1 oz)	2.0	0.8	10	200	50
Weight Watchers Cheese					
American, White or Yellow, slices (.8 oz)	2.0	1.0	10	310	50

	Tot. Fat (g)	Sat. Fat (g)	Chol. (mg)	Sod. (mg)	Cal.
American, White or Yellow, Low Sodium, slices (.8 oz)	2.0	1.0	5	110	50
American Flavor, slices (.8 oz)	2.0	1.0	10	310	50

Cheddar Cheese

	Tot. Fat (g)	Sat. Fat (g)	Chol. (mg)	Sod. (mg)	Cal.
Alpine Lace Free N' Lean Cheese, Cheddar (1 oz)	0.0	0.0	5	290	40
Alpine Lace Free N' Lean Pasteurized Process Cheese Spread					
Cheddar Cheese (1 oz)	0.0	0.0	5	180	30
Cheddar Cheese with Jalapeño (1 oz)	0.0	0.0	5	210	30
Borden Fat Free Pasteurized Process Cheese Product Singles, Sharp (1 oz)	0.0	0.0	<5	380	40
Borden Lite-Line Pasteurized Process Cheese Product Singles					
Mild Cheddar (1 oz)	2.0	(1.3)	10	445	50
Mild Cheddar Flavor (2/3 oz)	2.0	(1.3)	5	300	35
Sharp Cheddar (1 oz)	2.0	(1.3)	10	450	50
Sharp Cheddar Flavor (2/3 oz)	2.0	(1.3)	5	300	35
County Line Advantage Cheese, Cheddar (1 oz)	3.0	1.9	13	50	70
Healthy Choice Cheese, Cheddar					
Chunk (1 oz)	0.0	0.0	5	200	40
Fancy, Shredded (1 oz)	0.0	0.0	5	200	40
Shredded (1 oz)	0.0	0.0	5	200	40
Hickory Farms Light Cold Pack Cheese Product, Sharp (1 oz)	3.0	2.0	15	190	70
Lifetime Fat Free Cheese					
Cheddar (1 oz)	<1.0	0.0	3	200	40
Sharp Cheddar (1 oz)	<1.0	(<1.0)	3	200	40
Lifetime Natural Cheese, Mild Cheddar (1 oz)	3.0	(2.0)	9	60	70
Mrs. Margareten's Parvemage Cheese Alternative, Cheddar (1 oz)	3.0	<1.0	0	120	60
Smart Beat Cheese					
Fat Free Mellow Cheddar, slices (2/3 oz)	0.0	0.0	0	180	30

	Tot. Fat (g)	Sat. Fat (g)	Chol. (mg)	Sod. (mg)	Cal.
Fat Free Sharp Cheddar Cheese					
Flavor, slices (2/3 oz)	0.0	0.0	0	230	30
Weight Watchers Cheese Cup					
Sharp Cheddar (1 oz)	3.0	2.0	10	190	70
Sharp Cheddar, slices (.8 oz)	2.0	1.0	10	310	50
White Wave Fat Free Soy A Melt,					
Cheddar Style (1 oz)	<1.0	(0.0)	0	370	40

Colby Cheese

Borden Lite-Line Pasteurized Process					
Cheese Product Singles					
Colby (2/3 oz)	2.0	(1.3)	5	240	35
Colby (1 oz)	2.0	(1.3)	10	350	50
County Line Advantage Cheese, Colby					
(1 oz)	3.0	(1.9)	13	50	70

Cottage Cheese

Alta Dena Cottage Cheese					
Lowfat (1/2 cup)	2.0	(1.4)	7	340	100
Nonfat (1/2 cup)	<1.0	(0.0)	<5	360	80
Borden Cottage Cheese, Dry Curd					
0.5% Milkfat (1/2 cup)	1.0	(0.6)	(8)	20	80
Borden Lite-Line Cottage Cheese					
Lowfat 1½% Milkfat (1/2 cup)	2.0	(1.3)	(7)	400	90
Nonfat (1/2 cup)	0.0	0.0	5	430	70
Breakstone's Cottage Cheese, Dry					
Curd (4 oz)	0.0	0.0	10	65	90
Cottage cheese					
Dry curd (1/2 cup)	0.3	0.2	5	10	62
1% fat (1/2 cup)	1.2	0.7	5	459	82
2% fat (1/2 cup)	2.2	1.4	9	459	101
Friendship Lowfat 1% Milk Fat					
Cottage Cheese (4 oz)	1.0	(0.6)	5	350	90
Lactose Reduced (4 oz)	1.0	(0.6)	5	350	90
No Salt Added (4 oz)	1.0	(0.6)	5	31	90
No Salt-Added, with Pineapple (4 oz)	1.0	(0.6)	5	300	110
Friendship Lowfat 2% Milk Fat					
Cottage Cheese, Large Curd Pot					
Style (4 oz)	2.0	(1.3)	9	405	100

	Tot. Fat (g)	Sat. Fat (g)	Chol. (mg)	Sod. (mg)	Cal.
Friendship Nonfat Cottage Cheese (1/2 cup)	0.0	0.0	0	350	70
Kemps Cottage Cheese					
Lite (4 oz)	1.0	(0.6)	5	490	90
Nonfat (4 oz)	<0.5	(<0.3)	5	500	80
Knudsen Cottage Cheese, Nonfat (4 oz)	0.0	0.0	5	420	70
Knudsen Lowfat 2% Milkfat Cottage Cheese					
with Fruit Cocktail (4 oz)	2.0	2.0	10	330	130
with Mandarin Orange (4 oz)	2.0	2.0	10	320	110
with Peach (6 oz)	2.0	2.0	15	270	170
with Pear (4 oz)	2.0	2.0	10	320	110
with Pineapple (6 oz)	2.0	2.0	15	300	170
with Spiced Apple (6 oz)	2.0	2.0	15	280	180
with Strawberry (6 oz)	2.0	2.0	15	320	170
Light N' Lively Lowfat 1% Milkfat Cottage Cheese (4 oz)	2.0	1.0	10	370	80
Garden Salad (4 oz)	2.0	1.0	10	350	80
with Peach and Pineapple (4 oz)	1.0	1.0	10	320	100
Light N' Lively Nonfat Cottage Cheese, Free (4 oz)	0.0	0.0	10	400	90
Nancy's Cottage Cheese, Lowfat (4 oz)	1.0	(0.6)	5	353	82
Viva Cottage Cheese, Nonfat (1/2 cup)	0.0	0.0	5	430	70
Wells' Blue Bunny Cottage Cheese					
Dry Curd (1/2 cup)	<1.0	<1.0	5	10	60
Lite 1% fat (1/2 cup)	1.0	<1.0	5	300	90
Lowfat 2% fat (1/2 cup)	2.0	2.0	10	430	100

Cream Cheese

	Tot. Fat (g)	Sat. Fat (g)	Chol. (mg)	Sod. (mg)	Cal.
Alpine Lace Free N' Lean Cream Cheese Spread					
Garlic and Herb Party Spread (1 oz)	0.0	0.0	5	180	30
Plain (1 oz)	0.0	0.0	5	180	30
with Chives (1 oz)	0.0	0.0	5	180	30
Healthy Choice Cream Cheese					
Box (1 oz)	0.0	0.0	5	200	30
Cup (1 oz)	0.0	0.0	5	200	30

	Tot. Fat (g)	Sat. Fat (g)	Chol. (mg)	Sod. (mg)	Cal.
Herb and Spice (1 oz)	0.0	0.0	5	200	30
Strawberry (1 oz)	0.0	0.0	5	200	30
Mrs. Margareten's Parvemage Cream Cheese (1 oz)	3.0	<1.0	0	120	60
Weight Watchers Creamed Cheese (1 oz)	2.0	1.0	10	40	35

Monterey Jack Cheese

	Tot. Fat (g)	Sat. Fat (g)	Chol. (mg)	Sod. (mg)	Cal.
Borden Lite-Line Pasteurized Process Cheese Product Singles					
Monterey Jack (2/3 oz)	2.0	(1.3)	5	245	35
Monterey Jack (1 oz)	2.0	(1.3)	10	370	50
County Line Advantage Cheese, Monterey Jack (1 oz)	3.0	1.9	13	50	70
Healthy Choice Cheese, Monterey Jack, Chunk (1 oz)	0.0	0.0	5	200	40
Lifetime Fat Free Cheese, Monterey Jack (1 oz)	<1.0	(<1.0)	3	200	40
Lifetime Natural Cheese, Monterey Jack (1 oz)	3.0	(1.9)	9	60	70
Mrs. Margareten's Parvemage Cheese Alternative, Monterey Jack (1 oz)	3.0	<1.0	0	120	60

Mozzarella Cheese

	Tot. Fat (g)	Sat. Fat (g)	Chol. (mg)	Sod. (mg)	Cal.
Alpine Lace Free N' Lean Cheese Mozzarella (1 oz)	0.0	0.0	5	290	40
Natural Mozzarella Squares (1 oz)	0.0	0.0	5	180	40
Borden Lite-Line Pasteurized Process Cheese Product Singles					
Mozzarella (2/3 oz)	2.0	(1.2)	10	230	35
Mozzarella (1 oz)	2.0	(1.3)	10	340	50
County Line Advantage Cheese, Mozzarella (1 oz)	2.0	1.3	8	70	60
County Line Light Reduced Fat/Sodium Cheese, Mozzarella (1 oz)	3.0	1.0	10	70	70
Frigo Truly Lite Cheese, Reduced Fat Low Moisture Part Skim Mozzarella (1 oz)	2.0	2.0	8	140	60

	Tot. Fat (g)	Sat. Fat (g)	Chol. (mg)	Sod. (mg)	Cal.
Healthy Choice Cheese, Mozzarella					
Ball (1 oz)	0.0	0.0	5	200	40
Chunk (1 oz)	0.0	0.0	5	200	40
Fancy, Shredded (1 oz)	0.0	0.0	5	200	40
Shredded (1 oz)	0.0	0.0	5	200	40
Kraft† Healthy Favorites, Natural Reduced Fat Cheese, Mozzarella, chunk or shredded (1 oz)	3.0	2.0	10	220	70
Lifetime Natural Cheese, Mozzarella (1 oz)	2.0	(1.3)	7	50	60
Mrs. Margareten's Parvemage Cheese Alternative, Mozzarella (1 oz)	3.0	<1.0	0	120	60
Polly-O, Free Natural Nonfat Cheese Lite Mozzarella (1 oz)	3.0	2.0	10	240	60
Mozzarella or Shredded Mozzarella (1 oz)	0.0	0.0	5	240	40
Sargento Preferred Light Fancy Shredded Reduced Fat Mozzarella (1 oz)	3.0	1.9	10	150	60
Sliced Mozzarella (1 oz)	3.0	(1.9)	10	150	60
White Wave Fat Free Soy A Melt, Mozzarella Style (1 oz)	<1.0	(0.0)	0	370	40

Muenster Cheese

	Tot. Fat (g)	Sat. Fat (g)	Chol. (mg)	Sod. (mg)	Cal.
Borden Lite-Line Pasteurized Process Cheese Product Singles					
Muenster (²/₃ oz)	2.0	(1.3)	5	245	35
Muenster (1 oz)	2.0	(1.3)	10	370	50
Healthy Choice Cheese, Muenster, Chunk (1 oz)	0.0	0.0	5	200	40

Parmesan/Romano Cheese

	Tot. Fat (g)	Sat. Fat (g)	Chol. (mg)	Sod. (mg)	Cal.
Alpine Lace Free N' Lean Cheese, Grated Italian (1 oz)	0.0	0.0	5	420	45
Weight Watchers Country Cottage Farms Cheese, Grated Parmesan Italian Topping (1 tbsp)	0.0	0.0	0	60	14

	Tot. Fat (g)	Sat. Fat (g)	Chol. (mg)	Sod. (mg)	Cal.
Ricotta Cheese					
Crystal Farm's Cheese, No Fat Ricotta (1 oz)	0.0	<1.0	0	20	20
Frigo Truly Lite Cheese					
Fat Free Ricotta (1 oz)	0.0	0.0	3	15	20
Low Fat-Low Salt Ricotta (1 oz)	1.0	1.0	5	10	30
No Fat Ricotta (1 oz)	1.0	0.0	3	15	20
Maggio Cheese, Ricotta, Non Fat (1 oz)	<0.5	<0.2	<2	50	20
Miceli Cheese, Ricotta, Natural Lite (1 oz)	1.0	(0.6)	14	20	25
Polly-O Free Natural Nonfat Cheese, Ricotta (1 oz)	0.0	0.0	0	35	25
Ricotta, part skim milk (1 oz)	2.2	1.4	9	35	39
Sargento Cheese, Ricotta Light (1 oz)	1.0	(0.5)	5	30	25
Romano Cheese—*see* ***Parmesan/Romano Cheese***					
String Cheese					
Frigo Truly Lite Cheese, Reduced Fat String Cheese, Low Moisture Part Skim Milk Mozzarella (1 oz)	2.0	2.0	8	140	60
Healthy Choice String Cheese (1 oz)	0.0	0.0	5	200	40
Mexican (1 oz)	0.0	0.0	5	200	40
Pizza (1 oz)	0.0	0.0	5	200	40
Sargento Cheese, MooTown Snackers Light String Cheese, Mozzarella (1 oz)	2.0	(1.3)	10	130	50
Swiss Cheese					
Borden Fat Free Pasteurized Process Cheese Product Singles, Swiss (1 oz)	0.0	0.0	<5	380	40
Borden Lite-Line Pasteurized Process Cheese Product, Singles					
Swiss (1 oz)	2.0	(1.3)	10	380	50
Swiss, Low Sodium (1 oz)	2.0	(1.3)	5	80	40

	Tot. Fat (g)	Sat. Fat (g)	Chol. (mg)	Sod. (mg)	Cal.
County Line Advantage Cheese, Swiss (1 oz)	3.0	1.9	12	8	80
Hickory Farms Light Cold Pack Cheese Product, Creamy Swiss (1 oz)	3.0	2.0	15	180	70
Lifetime Fat Free Cheese, Swiss (1 oz)	<1.0	(<1.0)	3	200	40
Mrs. Margareten's Parvemage Cheese Alternative, Swiss (1 oz)	3.0	<1.0	0	120	60
Swiss Knight Light (1 oz)	2.0	1.5	10	280	40
Weight Watchers Country Cottage Farms Cheese, Swiss, slices (.8 oz = 1 slice)	2.0	1.0	10	310	50

Other Cheeses

	Tot. Fat (g)	Sat. Fat (g)	Chol. (mg)	Sod. (mg)	Cal.
Borden Lite-Line Pasteurized Process Cheese Product Singles					
Hot Jalapeño (1 oz)	2.0	(1.3)	10	410	50
Mild Jalapeño (1 oz)	2.0	(1.3)	10	410	50
Healthy Choice Cheese					
Mexican, Shredded (1 oz)	0.0	0.0	5	200	40
Pepper Jack, Chunk (1 oz)	0.0	0.0	5	200	40
Pizza, Fancy, Shredded (1 oz)	0.0	0.0	5	200	40
Hickory Farms Light Cold Pack Cheese Product, Port Wine (1 oz)	3.0	2.0	15	190	70
Koched Kase High Protein Dairy Spread					
Caraway (1 oz)	0.0	0.0	0	260	25
Plain (1 oz)	0.0	0.0	0	260	25
Laughing Cow Cheese, Lite Soft Cheese Spread					
Original Flavor (1 oz)	3.0	2.0	10	370	50
Reduced Calorie Cheesebits (⅙ oz)	0.4	(0.2)	(2)	55	8
Reduced Calorie Wedges (1 oz)	3.0	(1.9)	10	370	50
Lifetime Fat Free Cheese					
Garden Vegetable (1 oz)	<1.0	0.0	3	200	40
Mild Mexican (1 oz)	<1.0	(<1.0)	3	200	40
Mrs. Margareten's Parvemage Cheese Alternative, Jalapeño (1 oz)	3.0	<1.0	0	120	60
Price Light Pimiento Spread (1 oz)	3.0	1.0	10	230	50
Sargento Cheese, Pot Cheese (1 oz)	0.2	(0.1)	0	1	26

DAIRY PRODUCTS AND DAIRY SUBSTITUTES

	Tot. Fat (g)	Sat. Fat (g)	Chol. (mg)	Sod. (mg)	Cal.
Tasty-Lo Cheese					
Dill (1 oz)	2.0	0.8	10	200	50
Garlic (1 oz)	2.0	0.8	10	200	50
Onion (1 oz)	2.0	0.8	10	200	50
Pepper (1 oz)	2.0	0.8	10	200	50
Tupper Pot Cheese Diet Dairy Spread					
(1 oz)	0.0	0.0	0	185	25
Weight Watchers Cheese Cup, Port					
Wine (1 oz)	3.0	2.0	10	190	70

COFFEE CREAMERS

Liquid Coffee Creamers

	Tot. Fat (g)	Sat. Fat (g)	Chol. (mg)	Sod. (mg)	Cal.
Carnation Coffee-Mate Non-Dairy					
Creamer (1 tbsp)	1.0	0.3	0	5	16
Lite (1 tbsp)	<1.0	0.0	0	10	10
Farm Rich Light Creamer (1/2 fl oz)	0.9	0.1	0	5	10
Mocha Mix Non-Dairy Creamer					
Light (1/2 fl oz = 1 tbsp)	<1.0	0.0	0	0	10
Regular (1/2 fl oz = 1 tbsp)	2.0	0.0	0	5	20
Morning Blend Non-Dairy Creamer					
(2 tbsp)	3.0	0.0	0	10	30
Swiss Miss N'Rich Coffee Cream					
(1 tsp)	<1.0	0.3	0	0	10

Powdered Coffee Creamers

	Tot. Fat (g)	Sat. Fat (g)	Chol. (mg)	Sod. (mg)	Cal.
Carnation Coffee-Mate Lite Non-Dairy					
Creamer, Powder (1 tsp)	<1.0	0.0	0	0	8
Cremora Non-Dairy Creamer					
Lite (1 tsp)	<1.0	0.0	0	<5	8
Regular (1 tsp)	<1.0	(0.0)	0	5	10
Weight Watchers Dairy Creamer					
Instant Non-Fat Dry Milk (1 pkt)	0.0	0.0	0	15	10

FROZEN DAIRY DESSERTS—see
"FROZEN DESSERTS," FROZEN
DAIRY DESSERTS/ICE MILK, *page 136*

DAIRY PRODUCTS AND DAIRY SUBSTITUTES

	Tot. Fat (g)	Sat. Fat (g)	Chol. (mg)	Sod. (mg)	Cal.
MILK/BUTTERMILK					
Borden Lowfat Milk, 1% Milkfat with L. Acidophilus Culture Added (1 cup)	2.0	(1.2)	(10)	130	100
Buttermilk, cultured (1 cup)	2.2	1.3	9	257	99
Carnation Instant Nonfat Dry Milk, dry (5 tbsp)	0.2	0.1	5	125	80
Evaporated skim milk, canned (½ cup)	0.3	0.2	5	147	99
Kemps Chocolate Milk					
Skim (8 fl oz)	1.0	(0.6)	5	230	150
Swiss Style (8 fl oz)	3.0	(1.8)	3	230	170
Lactaid Lactose Reduced Nonfat Milk (1 cup)	0.0	0.0	(4)	125	90
Mayfield 1% Milkfat Lowfat Milk, Nu*trish a/B with Vitamin A & D and Acidophilus & Bifidum Cultures (1 cup)	2.0	(1.2)	10	125	100
Milk					
½% fat (1 cup)	1.0	1.0	7	125	94
1% fat (1 cup)	2.6	1.6	10	123	102
Skim or nonfat (1 cup)	0.4	0.3	4	126	86
Wells' Blue Bunny Chocolate Milk					
Lite Nonfat (1 cup)	1.0	<1.0	<5	210	90
Skim (1 cup)	1.0	<1.0	<5	210	150
MILK SUBSTITUTES					
Edensoy Natural Soy Beverage, Vanilla (8.45 fl oz)	3.0	0.4	0	140	150
SOUR CREAM					
Alta Dena Light Sour Cream (1 oz)	2.0	(1.4)	7	35	35
Borden Lite-Line Lowfat Sour Cream, 9% (1 oz = 2 tbsp)	2.0	(1.2)	10	30	40
Friendship Light Sour Cream (1 oz)	2.0	(1.3)	8	25	35
Kemps Lite					
Sour Cream (1 oz = 2 tbsp)	2.0	(1.2)	8	35	30
Tator Topper (1 oz)	2.0	(1.2)	8	105	30

	Tot. Fat (g)	Sat. Fat (g)	Chol. (mg)	Sod. (mg)	Cal.
King Cholesterol Free Non-Butterfat Sour Cream Alternative (1 oz)	3.0	0.1	0	20	40
King Sour Non-Butterfat Sour Dressing (1 oz)	3.0	(<1.0)	0	15	40
Knudsen Light N' Lively Light Sour Cream (1 oz)	3.0	2.0	10	20	40
Land O'Lakes Sour Cream, Light Chives (2 tbsp)	2.0	1.0	5	150	40
No Fat (2 tbsp)	0.0	0.0	0	40	30
Plain (2 tbsp)	2.0	1.0	5	35	40
Light N' Lively Nonfat Sour Cream Alternative (½ oz = 1 tbsp)	0.0	0.0	0	10	10
Neilson Light Sour Cream (2 tbsp)	1.7	1.1	5	(25)	32
Sour Lean (2 tbsp)	2.0	(1.2)	(10)	16	40
Viva Lite Lowfat Sour Cream, 9% (1 oz = 2 tbsp)	2.0	(1.2)	10	30	40
Weight Watchers Light Sour Cream (2 tbsp = 1 oz)	2.0	1.0	5	40	35
Wells' Blue Bunny Lite Sour Cream (2 tbsp)	2.0	1.0	5	50	30

WHIPPED TOPPING

	Tot. Fat (g)	Sat. Fat (g)	Chol. (mg)	Sod. (mg)	Cal.
Dream Whip Whipped Topping Mix, made with whole milk (1 tbsp)	0.0	0.0	0	0	10
Featherweight Whipped Topping (1 tbsp)	0.0	0.0	0	5	4

YOGURT

	Tot. Fat (g)	Sat. Fat (g)	Chol. (mg)	Sod. (mg)	Cal.
Alta Dena Nonfat Liquid Yogurt Drink Black Cherry, Peach, Raspberry, Strawberry or Strawberry-Banana (1 cup)	<1.0	(0.0)	<5	120	170
Alta Dena Nonfat Yogurt					
Black Cherry or Strawberry (1 cup)	<1.0	(0.0)	(0)	128	190
Mixed Berries (1 cup)	<1.0	(0.0)	(0)	128	200
Plain (1 cup)	<1.0	(0.0)	(0)	160	100
Vanilla (1 cup)	<1.0	(0.0)	(0)	140	170

	Tot. Fat (g)	Sat. Fat (g)	Chol. (mg)	Sod. (mg)	Cal.
Borden Lite-Line Lowfat Yogurt					
Cherry Vanilla or Strawberry (1 cup)	2.0	(1.2)	(10)	150	240
Peach (1 cup)	2.0	(1.2)	(10)	150	230
Breyer's 1% Milkfat Lowfat Yogurt					
Black Cherry, Blueberry, Mixed Berry, Peach, Pineapple, Red Raspberry, Strawberry or Strawberry-Banana (8 oz)	3.0	1.0	10	120	260
Breyer's 1.5% Milkfat Lowfat Yogurt,					
Vanilla Bean (8 oz)	3.0	2.0	20	150	230
Colombo Nonfat Yogurt					
Fruit on the Bottom, all flavors (8 oz)	<1.0	<1.0	5	140	190
Lite Minipack, all flavors (4 oz)	<1.0	<1.0	<5	65-75	100
Lite Vanilla (8 oz)	<1.0	<1.0	5	140	160
Continental Light Nonfat Yogurt with Nutrasweet					
Peach, Strawberry, Strawberry-Banana or Wild Berry (7 oz)	0.0	0.0	0	100	80
Dannon Blended Fat Free Yogurt					
Blueberry, Peach, Raspberry, Strawberry or Strawberry-Banana (6 oz)	0.0	0.0	<5	110	150
Dannon Lowfat Fruit on Bottom Yogurt, Mini-6 Pack (1% Milkfat)					
Banana, Blueberry, Boysenberry, Cherry, Dutch Apple, Exotic Fruit, Mixed Berries, Peach, Pina-Colada, Raspberry, Strawberry or Strawberry-Banana (8 oz)	3.0	(1.9)	10	120	240
Blueberry/Raspberry, Strawberry-Banana/Cherry, Strawberry/Blueberry or Strawberry/Mixed Berries (4.4 oz)	1.0	(0.6)	5	65	120
Dannon Lowfat Yogurt					
Coffee, Lemon or Vanilla (8 oz)	3.0	(1.9)	10	120	200
Dannon Nonfat Blended Yogurt					
Blueberry, Peach, Raspberry, Strawberry or Strawberry-Banana (6 oz)	0.0	0.0	<5	105	140

	Tot. Fat (g)	Sat. Fat (g)	Chol. (mg)	Sod. (mg)	Cal.
Dannon Nonfat Light Yogurt with Aspartame					
Blueberry, Cherry Vanilla, Peach, Raspberry, Strawberry, Strawberry Fruit Cup, Strawberry-Banana or Vanilla (8 oz)	0.0	0.0	<5	130	100
Danone Fresh Flavors Yogurt					
Banana, Cafe Au Lait, Lemon or Vanilla (6.2 oz)	2.6	(1.7)	7	103	160
Danone Yogurt					
Lowfat (6.2 oz)	2.6	(1.7)	7	134	105
Nofat (6.2 oz)	0.3	(0.1)	1	136	85
Horizon Organic Fat Free Yogurt					
Blueberry or Cherry (6 oz)	0.0	0.0	5	115	130
Cappuccino (6 oz)	0.0	0.0	5	125	110
Peach (6 oz)	0.0	0.0	5	110	130
Plain (6 oz)	0.0	0.0	5	115	80
Raspberry (6 oz)	0.0	0.0	5	115	120
Strawberry (6 oz)	0.0	0.0	5	105	120
Vanilla (6 oz)	0.0	0.0	5	125	120
Kemps Yogurt					
Lite Nonfat (6 oz)	<0.5	(<0.3)	0	110	80
Yogurt Jr.'s (4 oz)	1.0	(0.6)	4	110	130
Knudsen Cal 70 Nonfat Yogurt with Aspartame Sweetener					
Black Cherry or Strawberry Fruit Basket (6 oz)	0.0	0.0	5	75	70
Blueberry, Red Raspberry or Strawberry Banana (6 oz)	0.0	0.0	5	80	70
Lemon or Pineapple (6 oz)	0.0	0.0	0	125	70
Peach (6 oz)	0.0	0.0	0	95	70
Strawberry (6 oz)	0.0	0.0	0	85	70
Vanilla (6 oz)	0.0	0.0	0	90	70
Light N' Lively 1% Milkfat Lowfat Yogurt					
Banana Berry (4.4 oz)	1.0	1.0	10	75	130
Black Cherry (8 oz)	2.0	1.0	15	125	230
Blueberry or Red Raspberry (4.4 oz)	1.0	1.0	5	70	130
Blueberry (8 oz)	2.0	1.0	10	130	240

	Tot. Fat (g)	Sat. Fat (g)	Chol. (mg)	Sod. (mg)	Cal.
Cherry or Wild Berry (4.4 oz)	1.0	1.0	5	70	140
Grape or Strawberry (4.4 oz)	1.0	1.0	10	70	130
Peach (4.4 oz)	1.0	1.0	10	65	130
Peach or Strawberry Banana (8 oz)	2.0	1.0	15	120	240
Pineapple (4.4 oz)	1.0	1.0	5	65	130
Pineapple (8 oz)	2.0	1.0	10	120	230
Red Raspberry (8 oz)	2.0	1.0	10	130	230
Strawberry (8 oz)	2.0	2.0	15	130	240
Strawberry Banana (4.4 oz)	1.0	1.0	5	65	140
Strawberry Fruit Cup (8 oz)	2.0	2.0	15	120	240
Light N' Lively 100 Calorie Nonfat Yogurt with Aspartame Sweetener					
Black Cherry (8 oz)	0.0	0.0	0	100	100
Blueberry (8 oz)	0.0	0.0	0	110	90
Lemon (8 oz)	0.0	0.0	5	150	100
Peach (8 oz)	0.0	0.0	5	115	100
Red Raspberry (8 oz)	0.0	0.0	0	105	90
Strawberry (8 oz)	0.0	0.0	5	105	90
Strawberry Banana (8 oz)	0.0	0.0	0	105	100
Strawberry Fruit Cup (8 oz)	0.0	0.0	0	100	90
Light N' Lively Free Nonfat Yogurt with Aspartame Sweetener					
Blueberry, Red Raspberry, Strawberry or Strawberry Banana (4.4 oz)	0.0	0.0	0	60	50
Strawberry Fruit Cup (4.4 oz)	0.0	0.0	0	55	50
Nancy's					
Lowfat Yogurt, Maple (8 oz)	3.0	(1.9)	(10)	148	200
Nonfat Yogurt (8 oz)	<1.0	<1.0	5	174	130
Nancy's Nonfat Yogurt—to Drink					
Blueberry (8 oz)	<1.0	(<1.0)	5	147	179
Boysenberry or Raspberry (8 oz)	<1.0	(<1.0)	5	145	176
Cherry (8 oz)	<1.0	(<1.0)	5	145	185
Strawberry (8 oz)	<1.0	(<1.0)	5	145	168
Weight Watchers Yogurt					
Nonfat Fruited (8 oz = 1 cup)	0.0	<1.0	5	120	90
Ultimate 90 (8 oz = 1 cup)	0.0	<1.0	5	135	90

DAIRY PRODUCTS AND DAIRY SUBSTITUTES

	Tot. Fat (g)	Sat. Fat (g)	Chol. (mg)	Sod. (mg)	Cal.
Well's Blue Bunny Lite 85 Nonfat Yogurt					
Black Cherry, Blueberry, Cherry Vanilla, Mixed Berry, Peach, Pina-Colada, Pineapple, Plain, Raspberry, Strawberry, Strawberry Banana or Vanilla (6 oz)	0.0	0.0	0	110	80
Orange (6 oz)	<1.0	0.0	0	110	80
White Mountain Nonfat Bulgarian Yogurt with Live Acidophilus (8 oz)	0.4	(0.3)	5	138	93
White Wave Dairyless					
Apricot Mango, Blueberry, Peach, Raspberry, Strawberry or Vanilla (6 oz)	2.0	(0.3)	0	25	150
Yoplait Crunch n Yogurt with Granola Peach, Strawberry or Vanilla Nonfat Yogurt (7 oz)	2.0	1.0	<5	125	220
Strawberry Nonfat Yogurt with Crunchy Cereal Nuggets (7 oz)	<1.0	0.0	<5	170	210
Vanilla Nonfat Yogurt with Chocolate Flavor Crunchies (7 oz)	2.0	1.0	<5	180	220
Yoplait Fat Free Fruit on the Bottom Cherry, Peach, Raspberry or Strawberry (6 oz)	0.0	0.0	5	105	160
Yoplait Fat Free Yogurt, Fruit Flavors (6 oz)	0.0	0.0	<5	100	170
Yoplait Light Yogurt					
Fruit Flavors (4 oz)	0.0	0.0	<5	50	60
Fruit Flavors (6 oz)	0.0	0.0	<5	70	90
Yoplait Nonfat Yogurt					
Plain (8 oz)	0.0	0.0	10	170	120
Vanilla (8 oz)	0.0	0.0	10	160	180
Yoplait Original 99% Fat Free, Fruit Flavors (6 oz)	2.0	1.0	<5	130	180

† = tobacco company, corporate subsidiary or parent

DESSERTS

The desserts listed in this section allow you to satisfy your sweet tooth more healthfully. As purchased, when prepared according to package directions or when prepared with skim milk, as indicated on the following pages, they are low enough in fat, saturated fat and cholesterol to meet AHA criteria.

Even if package directions do not say so, prepare mixes by substituting skim or 1% low-fat milk for whole milk and using egg whites or egg substitute instead of whole eggs.

Products listed in this book vary in sodium content. Use the values appearing on the following pages to help plan a daily intake providing no more than 3,000 milligrams of sodium.

Most of the foods in this book are brand name products; however, when a brand name is not specified, it means that most brands of that product provide about the same amount of fat, saturated fat and cholesterol and that these amounts do not exceed AHA criteria.

You can use those generic entries and the tables below to evaluate products introduced since this book went to press.

AHA Criteria for Desserts*

	Tot. Fat (g)	Sat. Fat (g)	Chol. (mg)
Brownies, cakes and cupcakes, cookies, graham crackers, pies, and quick-type sweet breads, such as muffins, sweet rolls and coffee cake	3	1	<2
Custard, gelatin, mousse and pudding, prepared	3	1	20
Frosting	<0.5	<0.5	<2

* Per serving.

Desserts Not Recommended for Frequent Consumption

Some types of dessert that are usually too high in fat, saturated fat and/or cholesterol to be recommended for frequent consumption are shown in the table below. Values that exceed AHA criteria are followed by asterisks. The AHA does not have criteria for sodium.

You can use the values in the table to compare these desserts with more-healthful alternatives listed on the following pages.

Desserts High in Fat, Saturated Fat and/or Cholesterol

	Tot. Fat (g)	Sat. Fat (g)	Chol. (mg)	Sod. (mg)	Cal.
Almond Danish pastry (2 ounces or about 3⅞ inches in diameter)	14.2*	3.1*	26*	206	244
Brownie from mix, made with oil and egg (about 2 inches by 2½ inches)	7.9*	1.6*	11*	100	167

	Tot. Fat (g)	Sat. Fat (g)	Chol. (mg)	Sod. (mg)	Cal.
Cheesecake, made from no-bake mix with whole milk; graham cracker crust made with butter (about 1/6 of 8-inch cheesecake)	15.9*	8.8*	(39)*	475	341
Cherry fried pie (about 5 inches by 3¾ inches)	20.7*	3.1*	(13)*	479	404
Chocolate chip cookie (3 2¼ inch in diameter)	6.9*	2.3*	(0)	96	144
Coconut cream pie, made from no-bake mix with whole milk; crust made with butter (1/6 of 9-inch pie)	22.0*	12.8*	(148)*	412	345
Creme-filled sponge snack cake (2.8 ounces or about 2 cakes)	9.2*	2.2*	13*	291	291
Fudge cake, made from mix with egg, without frosting (1/10 of 9-inch cake)	9.3*	2.1*	43*	455	244
Glazed cake doughnut (about 3⅜ inches in diameter)	12.6*	2.9*	17*	221	235
Peanut butter cookie (1 ounce or about 2 cookies)	6.7*	1.5*	(0)	118	135
Pecan shortbread cookie (1 ounce or about 2 cookies)	9.2*	2.0*	9*	80	154

Adapted from USDA Handbook No. 8 series.
* These values exceed AHA criteria for desserts.

	Tot. Fat (g)	Sat. Fat (g)	Chol. (mg)	Sod. (mg)	Cal.
BROWNIES					
Betty Crocker Light Fudge Brownie Mix, made with water ($^1/_{24}$ of a recipe)	1.0	<1.0	0	90	100
Healthy Greenfield Foods Fat Free Brownie (1 oz)	0.0	0.0	0	40	90
CAKE FROSTING—see **FROSTING**					
CAKES/CUPCAKES					
Angel food cake, plain or flavored ($^1/_{12}$ of a cake)	0.0	0.0	0	77	137
Betty Crocker Angel Food Cake Mix					
Confetti ($^1/_{12}$ of a cake)	0.0	0.0	0	300	150
Lemon Custard ($^1/_{12}$ of a cake)	0.0	0.0	0	300	150
Traditional ($^1/_{12}$ of a cake)	0.0	0.0	0	170	130
White ($^1/_{12}$ of a cake)	0.0	0.0	0	280	140
Betty Crocker Supermoist Light Cake Mix					
Devils Food, made with egg whites or egg substitute ($^1/_{12}$ of a cake)	3.0	1.0	0	370	180
White Cake, made with egg whites and water ($^1/_{12}$ of a cake)	3.0	1.0	0	330	180
Yellow Cake, made with egg whites ($^1/_{12}$ of a cake)	3.0	1.0	0	330	190
Entenmann's Fat Free and Cholesterol Free Cakes					
Apple Spice (1 oz)	0.0	0.0	0	80	80
Banana Crunch (1 oz)	0.0	0.0	0	90	80
Banana Loaf (1.3 oz)	0.0	0.0	0	125	90
Blueberry Crunch (1 oz)	0.0	0.0	0	85	70
Chocolate Crunch (1 oz)	0.0	0.0	0	130	70
Chocolate Loaf (1 oz)	0.0	0.0	0	130	70
Fudge Iced Chocolate (1.3 oz)	0.0	0.0	0	125	90
Fudge Iced Golden (1.3 oz)	0.0	0.0	0	100	90
Golden Loaf (1 oz)	0.0	0.0	0	100	70
Louisiana Crunch (1 oz)	0.0	0.0	0	100	80

	Tot. Fat (g)	Sat. Fat (g)	Chol. (mg)	Sod. (mg)	Cal.
Marble Loaf (1 oz)	0.0	0.0	0	115	70
Pineapple Crunch (1 oz)	0.0	0.0	0	105	70
Hostess Snack Cakes					
Light Chocolate Cupcakes with Vanilla Pudding (1 cake)	1.0	<1.0	0	180	130
Light Twinkies (1 cake)	2.0	<1.0	0	160	110
Hostess Snack Cakes, Grizzly Chomps					
Chocolate (1¼ oz = 1 cake)	1.0	<1.0	0	140	110
Vanilla (1¼ oz = 1 cake)	1.0	<1.0	0	140	110
Pepperidge Farm Fat Free Pound Cake					
Chocolate (1 oz)	1.0	(0.4)	0	85	70
Golden (1 oz)	0.0	0.0	0	80	70
Sara Lee Free and Light					
Chocolate Cake (⅛ of a cake)	0.0	0.0	0	140	110
Pound Cake (1/10 of a cake)	0.0	0.0	0	90	70

COFFEE CAKES—*see*
SWEET ROLLS/COFFEE CAKES

COOKIES

Chocolate/Chocolate Chip Cookies

	Tot. Fat (g)	Sat. Fat (g)	Chol. (mg)	Sod. (mg)	Cal.
Nabisco† Cookies, Devil's Food Cakes (¾ oz = 1 cookie)	1.0	<1.0	0	40	70
Nabisco† SnackWell's Cookies					
Chocolate Chip (½ oz = 6 cookies)	1.0	0.5	0	85	60
Devil's Food Cookie Cakes (½ oz = 1 cake)	0.0	0.0	0	30	60
Trolley Cakes					
Devil's Food (2 cookies)	2.0	(0.7)	(0)	80	120
Snow Drop Devil's Food (1 oz = 2 cookies)	1.0	<1.0	0	70	100
Weight Watchers Cookies					
Chocolate (3 cookies)	3.0	1.0	0	70	80
Chocolate Chip (2 cookies)	2.0	1.0	0	65	90

Fruit Cookies

	Tot. Fat (g)	Sat. Fat (g)	Chol. (mg)	Sod. (mg)	Cal.
A Whale of a Snack Fruit Bars					
Apple (2 oz = 1 bar)	4.0	(1.6)	0	80	210
Blueberry (2 oz = 1 bar)	3.0	(1.2)	0	90	210
Fig (2 oz = 1 bar)	4.0	(1.4)	0	160	210
Barbara's Bakery Cookies, Fruit & Nut					
(1 oz)	2.0	(0.3)	0	55	125
Delicious Cookies, Fig Bars (1.5 oz)	2.0	(0.5)	0	80	150
Entenmann's Fat Free and Cholesterol Free Cookies					
Fruit and Honey (2 cookies)	0.0	0.0	0	110	80
Homestyle Apple (2 cookies)	0.0	0.0	0	125	70
Raisin (2 cookies)	0.0	0.0	0	100	70
Health Valley Fat-Free Cookies					
Apple Spice (1.18 oz = 3 cookies)	<1.0	(0.0)	0	40	75
Apricot Delight (1.18 oz = 3 cookies)	<1.0	(0.0)	0	40	75
Date Delight (1.18 oz = 3 cookies)	<1.0	(0.0)	0	40	75
Hawaiian Fruit (1.18 oz = 3 cookies)	<1.0	(0.0)	0	40	75
Health Valley Fat-Free Fruit Bars					
Apple (1.5 oz = 1 bar)	<1.0	(0.0)	0	10	140
Apricot (1.5 oz = 1 bar)	<1.0	(0.0)	0	10	140
Date (1.5 oz = 1 bar)	<1.0	(0.0)	0	10	140
Raisin (1.5 oz = 1 bar)	<1.0	(0.0)	0	10	140
Health Valley Fat-Free Jumbo Fruit Cookies					
Apple Raisin (1 cookie)	<1.0	(0.0)	0	35	70
Raisin Raisin (1 cookie)	<1.0	(0.0)	0	35	70
Raspberry (1 cookie)	<1.0	(0.0)	0	35	70
Health Valley Fruit & Nut Jumbo Fruit					
Bars, Oat Bran (1.5 oz = 1 bar)	2.0	(0.2)	0	10	140
Lance Cookies					
Fig Bar (1½ oz = 1 pkg)	2.0	1.0	0	85	150
Fig Cake (2⅛ oz = 1 pkg)	3.0	1.0	0	90	210
Little Debbie Figaroos (1.5 oz)	4.0	1.0	<2	105	160
Mother's Fig Bars					
Regular (1 oz = 1.6 bars)	2.0	(0.7)	<2	75	100
Whole Wheat (1 oz = 1.6 bars)	2.0	(0.7)	<2	80	90
Nabisco† Cookies, Newtons					
Apple (¾ oz = 1 cookie)	2.0	<1.0	0	70	70

	Tot. Fat (g)	Sat. Fat (g)	Chol. (mg)	Sod. (mg)	Cal.
Raspberry (¾ oz = 1 cookie)	2.0	<1.0	0	70	70
Strawberry (¾ oz = 1 cookie)	2.0	<1.0	0	70	70
Variety Pack (1¼ oz = 1 cookie)	3.0	1.0	0	110	120
Pepperidge Farm Wholesome Choice Cookies, Raspberry Tart (.55 oz = 1 cookie)	1.0	0.0	0	35	60
R.W. Frookie Fat Free Cookies					
Apple Spice (.52 oz = 1 cookie)	0.0	0.0	0	80	50
Banana (.5 oz = 1 cookie)	0.0	0.0	0	90	45
Cranberry Orange (.5 oz = 1 cookie)	0.0	0.0	0	75	45
R.W. Frookie Fat Free Fruitins					
Fig (1 oz = 2 cookies)	0.0	0.0	0	75	90
Raspberry (1 oz = 2 cookies)	0.0	0.0	0	75	90
Tom's Cookies, Fig Bar (2 oz = 1 pkg)	2.0	1.0	0	180	200
Weight Watchers Cookies					
Apple Raisin Bar (1 oz = 1 bar)	3.0	<1.0	(0)	115	100
Fruit Filled Apple (1 cookie)	<1.0	0.0	0	35	80
Fruit Filled Raspberry (1 cookie)	<1.0	0.0	0	45	80

Graham Crackers

	Tot. Fat (g)	Sat. Fat (g)	Chol. (mg)	Sod. (mg)	Cal.
Mother's Mini Dinosaur Grrrahams, Original (½ oz = 7 cookies)	1.0	(0.4)	0	40	60
Nabisco† SnackWell's Cookies, Cinnamon Graham Snacks (½ oz = 9 cookies)	0.0	0.0	0	50	50

Oatmeal/Oatmeal and Fruit Cookies

	Tot. Fat (g)	Sat. Fat (g)	Chol. (mg)	Sod. (mg)	Cal.
Archway Cookies, Oatmeal Raisin Bran (1 cookie)	3.0	1.0	0	85	110
Barbara's Bakery Cookies, Oatmeal Raisin (1 oz)	2.0	(0.8)	0	48	102
Delicious Cookies, Oatmeal (.9 oz = 1 cookie)	<1.0	<1.0	0	135	120
Entenmann's Fat Free and Cholesterol Free Cookies, Oatmeal Raisin (2 cookies)	0.0	0.0	0	120	80
Health Valley Fat-Free Cookies, Raisin Oatmeal (1.18 oz = 3 cookies)	<1.0	(0.0)	0	40	75

	Tot. Fat (g)	Sat. Fat (g)	Chol. (mg)	Sod. (mg)	Cal.
Healthy Greenfield Foods Fat Free Cookie, Oatmeal Raisin (1 oz = 1 cookie)	<1.0	(0.0)	0	30	95
Nabisco† SnackWell's Cookies, Oatmeal Raisin (½ oz = 6 cookies)	1.0	<0.5	0	65	60
Pepperidge Farm Wholesome Choice Cookies, Oatmeal Raisin (.55 oz = 1 cookie)	1.0	0.0	0	50	60
R.W. Frookie Fat Free Cookies, Oatmeal Raisin (.52 oz = 1 cookie)	0.0	0.0	0	75	50
Weight Watchers Cookies, Oatmeal Spice (1 pkt = 3 cookies)	2.0	<1.0	(0)	75	80

Other Cookies

	Tot. Fat (g)	Sat. Fat (g)	Chol. (mg)	Sod. (mg)	Cal.
Delicious Cookies					
Animal Crackers (2 oz)	3.0	2.0	0	240	250
Sugar (.9 oz = 1 cookie)	1.0	1.0	0	115	130
Grandma's Big Cookies, Old Time Molasses (2.75 oz = 2 cookies)	9.0	(3.3)	5	520	320
Healthy Greenfield Foods Fat Free Cookie, Lemon (1 oz = 1 cookie)	<1.0	(0.0)	0	34	95
La Choy Fortune Cookies (1 cookie)	?0.1	(0.0)	0	1	15
Pepperidge Farm Wholesome Choice Cookies, Carrot Walnut (.55 oz = 1 cookie)	1.0	0.0	0	45	60
Tom's Cookies, Animal Crackers (2.5 oz = 1 pkg)	7.0	(1.7)	(0)	350	300
Weight Watchers Cookies, Shortbread (1 pkt = 3 cookies)	2.0	1.0	(0)	95	80

CREAM PIE FILLINGS/PUDDINGS

Banana

	Tot. Fat (g)	Sat. Fat (g)	Chol. (mg)	Sod. (mg)	Cal.
Jello-O Instant Pudding and Pie Filling, Banana Cream, made with skim milk (½ cup)	0.2	0.1	2	413	133
Jell-O Pudding and Pie Filling, Banana Cream, made with skim milk (½ cup)	0.2	0.1	2	183	93

	Tot. Fat (g)	Sat. Fat (g)	Chol. (mg)	Sod. (mg)	Cal.
Jell-O Sugar Free Instant Pudding and Pie Filling, Banana, made with skim milk (1/2 cup)	0.2	0.1	2	393	68
Royal† Instant Pudding and Pie Filling, Banana Cream, made with skim milk (1/2 cup)	0.2	0.1	2	453	133
Royal† Pudding and Pie Filling, Banana Cream, made with skim milk (1/2 cup)	0.2	0.1	2	173	123

Butterscotch

	Tot. Fat (g)	Sat. Fat (g)	Chol. (mg)	Sod. (mg)	Cal.
D-Zerta Reduced Calorie Pudding, made with skim milk (1/2 cup)	0.0	0.0	0	65	70
Jell-O Instant Pudding and Pie Filling, made with skim milk (1/2 cup)	0.2	0.1	2	453	133
Jell-O Pudding and Pie Filling, made with skim milk (1/2 cup)	0.2	0.1	2	193	133
Jell-O Sugar Free Instant Pudding and Pie Filling, made with skim milk (1/2 cup)	0.2	0.1	2	393	68
My-T-Fine† Pudding, made with skim milk (1/2 cup)	0.2	0.1	2	253	133
Royal† Instant Pudding and Pie Filling, made with skim milk (1/2 cup)	0.2	0.1	2	463	133
Royal† Pudding and Pie Filling, made with skim milk (1/2 cup)	0.2	0.1	2	243	133
Ultra Slim-Fast Pudding (4 oz)	<1.0	(0.0)	0	230	100

Chocolate

	Tot. Fat (g)	Sat. Fat (g)	Chol. (mg)	Sod. (mg)	Cal.
D-Zerta Reduced Calorie Pudding, made with skim milk (1/2 cup)	0.0	0.0	0	70	60
Del Monte† Light Snack Cups (4.25 oz)	1.0	0.0	0	85	100
Hunt's Snack Pack Lite Pudding (4 oz)	2.0	0.3	1	120	100
Jell-O Free Pudding Snacks					
Chocolate (4 oz cup)	0.0	0.0	0	200	100
Chocolate/Mint Swirl (4 oz cup)	0.0	0.0	0	220	100
Chocolate/Vanilla Swirl (4 oz cup)	0.0	0.0	0	220	100

	Tot. Fat (g)	Sat. Fat (g)	Chol. (mg)	Sod. (mg)	Cal.
Jell-O Instant Pudding and Pie Filling					
Chocolate, made with skim milk (1/2 cup)	0.2	0.1	2	483	143
Chocolate Fudge, made with skim milk (1/2 cup)	1.2	(0.4)	2	443	143
Milk Chocolate, made with skim milk (1/2 cup)	1.2	(0.4)	2	473	143
Jell-O Pudding and Pie Filling					
Chocolate, made with skim milk (1/2 cup)	0.2	0.1	2	173	133
Chocolate Fudge, made with skim milk (1/2 cup)	0.2	0.1	2	173	133
Milk Chocolate, made with skim milk (1/2 cup)	0.2	0.1	2	178	133
Jell-O Sugar Free Instant Pudding and Pie Filling					
Chocolate, made with skim milk (1/2 cup)	1.2	(0.4)	2	383	83
Chocolate Fudge, made with skim milk (1/2 cup)	1.2	(0.4)	2	333	83
Jell-O Sugar Free Pudding and Pie Filling, made with skim milk (1/2 cup)	0.2	0.1	2	163	73
My-T-Fine† Pudding					
Chocolate, made with skim milk (1/2 cup)	0.2	0.1	2	198	143
Chocolate Almond, made with skim milk (1/2 cup)	1.2	(0.4)	2	198	143
Chocolate Fudge, made with skim milk (1/2 cup)	0.2	0.1	2	203	143
Royal† Dark 'N' Sweet Pudding and Pie Filling, made with skim milk (1/2 cup)	0.2	0.1	2	158	133
Royal† Instant Pudding and Pie Filling					
Chocolate, made with skim milk (1/2 cup)	0.2	0.1	2	513	153
Chocolate Almond, made with skim milk (1/2 cup)	1.2	(0.4)	2	503	163
Chocolate Chocolate Chip, made with skim milk (1/2 cup)	1.2	(0.4)	2	453	153

	Tot. Fat (g)	Sat. Fat (g)	Chol. (mg)	Sod. (mg)	Cal.
Chocolate Peanut Butter Chip, made with skim milk (1/2 cup)	1.2	(0.4)	2	543	153
Royal† Pudding and Pie Filling, made with skim milk (1/2 cup)	0.2	0.1	2	153	133
Royal† Sugar Free Instant Pudding and Pie Filling, made with skim milk (1/2 cup)	0.2	0.1	2	483	93
Swiss Miss Light Pudding					
Chocolate (4 oz)	1.0	0.3	1	120	100
Chocolate Fudge (4 oz)	1.0	0.3	1	120	100
Ultra Slim-Fast Pudding (4 oz)	<1.0	(0.0)	0	240	100
Weight Watchers Pudding Mix, made with skim milk (1/2 cup)	1.0	<1.0	5	420	90

Custard

	Tot. Fat (g)	Sat. Fat (g)	Chol. (mg)	Sod. (mg)	Cal.
Jell-O Americana Pudding & Custard Mix, Golden Egg Custard, made with skim milk (1/2 cup)	0.2	0.1	2	193	123
Royal† Dessert Mix, Custard, made with skim milk (1/2 cup)	0.2	0.1	2	138	103
Royal† Flan Caramel Custard, made with skim milk (1/2 cup)	0.2	0.1	2	118	103
Sweet N Low Custard Mix					
Chocolate, made with skim milk (1/2 cup)	<1.0	0.0	5	115	70
Lemon or Vanilla, made with skim milk (1/2 cup)	<1.0	0.0	5	145	70

Lemon

	Tot. Fat (g)	Sat. Fat (g)	Chol. (mg)	Sod. (mg)	Cal.
Jell-O Instant Pudding and Pie Filling, made with skim milk (1/2 cup)	0.2	0.1	2	363	133
Jell-O Pudding and Pie Filling, made with skim milk (1/2 cup)	0.2	0.1	2	133	93
My-T-Fine† Pudding and Pie Filling, made with skim milk (1 serving)	0.2	0.1	2	233	133
Royal† Instant Pie Filling, made with skim milk (1/2 cup)	0.2	0.1	2	383	133
Royal† Pie Filling, made with skim milk (1 serving)	0.2	0.1	2	183	93

	Tot. Fat (g)	Sat. Fat (g)	Chol. (mg)	Sod. (mg)	Cal.

Pistachio

	Tot. Fat (g)	Sat. Fat (g)	Chol. (mg)	Sod. (mg)	Cal.
Jell-O Instant Pudding and Pie Filling, made with skim milk (½ cup)	1.2	(0.4)	2	413	143
Jell-O Sugar Free Instant Pudding and Pie Filling, made with skim milk (½ cup)	1.2	(0.4)	2	393	73
Royal† Instant Pudding and Pie Filling, made with skim milk (½ cup)	1.2	(0.4)	2	423	133

Tapioca

	Tot. Fat (g)	Sat. Fat (g)	Chol. (mg)	Sod. (mg)	Cal.
Hunt's Snack Pack Lite Pudding (4 oz)	2.0	0.4	1	105	100
Jell-O Americana Pudding Mix, Vanilla Tapioca Pudding, made with skim milk (½ cup)	0.2	0.1	0	173	123
My-T-Fine† Pudding, Vanilla Tapioca, made with skim milk (½ cup)	0.2	0.1	2	223	123

Vanilla

	Tot. Fat (g)	Sat. Fat (g)	Chol. (mg)	Sod. (mg)	Cal.
D-Zerta Reduced Calorie Pudding, made with skim milk (½ cup)	0.0	0.0	0	65	70
Del Monte† Light Snack Cups (4.25 oz)	1.0	0.0	0	200	100
Jell-O Free Pudding Snacks (4 oz cup)	0.0	0.0	0	250	100
Jell-O Instant Pudding and Pie Filling French Vanilla, made with skim milk (½ cup)	0.2	0.1	2	413	133
Vanilla, made with skim milk (½ cup)	0.2	(0.1)	2	413	133
Jell-O Pudding and Pie Filling French Vanilla, made with skim milk (½ cup)	0.2	0.1	2	188	133
Vanilla, made with skim milk (½ cup)	0.2	0.1	2	203	123
Jell-O Sugar Free Pudding and Pie Filling, made with skim milk (½ cup)	0.2	0.1	2	203	63
Jell-O Sugar Free Instant Pudding and Pie Filling, made with skim milk (½ cup)	0.2	0.1	2	393	68

	Tot. Fat (g)	Sat. Fat (g)	Chol. (mg)	Sod. (mg)	Cal.
My-T-Fine† Pudding, made with skim milk (½ cup)	0.2	0.1	2	183	133
Royal† Instant Pudding and Pie Filling Vanilla, made with skim milk (½ cup)	0.2	0.1	2	388	133
Vanilla Chocolate Chip, made with skim milk (½ cup)	1.2	(0.4)	2	413	133
Royal† Pudding and Pie Filling, made with skim milk (1 serving)	0.2	0.1	2	223	123
Swiss Miss Light Pudding Vanilla (4 oz)	1.0	0.3	<1	105	100
Vanilla/Chocolate Parfait (4 oz)	1.0	0.3	<1	110	100
Ultra Slim-Fast Pudding (4 oz)	<1.0	(0.0)	0	230	100
Weight Watchers Pudding Mix, made with skim milk (½ cup)	0.0	0.0	5	510	90

Other Cream Pie Fillings/Puddings

	Tot. Fat (g)	Sat. Fat (g)	Chol. (mg)	Sod. (mg)	Cal.
Jell-O Americana Pudding Mix, Rice Pudding, made with skim milk (½ cup)	0.2	(0.1)	2	163	143
Jell-O Instant Pudding and Pie Filling, Butter Pecan, made with skim milk (½ cup)	1.2	(0.4)	2	413	143
Jell-O Pudding and Pie Filling Coconut Cream, made with skim milk (½ cup)	2.2	(0.4)	2	163	103
Flan, made with skim milk (½ cup)	0.2	0.1	2	68	123
Royal† Instant Pudding and Pie Filling Cherry Vanilla, made with skim milk (½ cup)	0.2	0.1	2	363	133
Strawberry, made with skim milk (½ cup)	0.2	0.1	2	393	143
Toasted Coconut, made with skim milk (½ cup)	2.2	(0.7)	2	513	143
Royal† Pie Filling, Key Lime, made with skim milk (½ cup)	0.2	0.1	2	183	93

DESSERTS

114

	Tot. Fat (g)	Sat. Fat (g)	Chol. (mg)	Sod. (mg)	Cal.

CUPCAKES—see **CAKES/CUPCAKES**

FROSTING

	Tot. Fat (g)	Sat. Fat (g)	Chol. (mg)	Sod. (mg)	Cal.
Betty Crocker Fluffy Frosting Mix, White, made as directed (1/12 mix)	0.0	0.0	0	40	70
Pillsbury Frost It Hot Frosting Mix					
Chocolate (.5 oz = 1/8 of mix)	0.0	0.0	0	50	50
Fluffy White (.5 oz = 1/8 of mix)	0.0	0.0	0	50	50
Pillsbury Frosting Mix, Fluffy White (.6 oz = 1/12 mix)	0.0	0.0	0	65	60

FRUIT PIE FILLINGS

	Tot. Fat (g)	Sat. Fat (g)	Chol. (mg)	Sod. (mg)	Cal.
Apples, sweetened, sliced (1/2 cup)	0.5	0.1	0	3	68
Appletree* Pie Filling					
Apple (4 oz = 1/2 cup)	0.0	0.0	(0)	60	120
Cherry (3 1/3 oz)	0.0	0.0	(0)	40	120
Comstock Pie Filling or Topping					
Apple (1/2 cup)	0.0	0.0	(0)	15	120
Blackberry (1/2 cup)	0.0	0.0	(0)	20	130
Blueberry or Cherry (1/2 cup)	0.0	0.0	(0)	15	110
Cherry Lite (1/2 cup)	0.0	0.0	(0)	15	80
Peach or Strawberry (1/2 cup)	0.0	0.0	(0)	20	110
Pineapple (1/2 cup)	0.0	0.0	(0)	30	130
Raspberry (1/2 cup)	0.0	0.0	(0)	30	120
Libby's Pumpkin Pie Mix (1 cup)	0.3	0.0	0	440	260
Marie's Glazes					
Blueberry (2.35 oz)	0.0	0.0	0	65	90
Peach (2.35 oz)	0.0	0.0	0	110	90
Strawberry (2.35 oz)	0.0	0.0	0	70	90
Pumpkin pie mix (1/2 cup)	0.2	0.1	0	280	141

* Appletree products are also marketed under Best Yet, Fine Fare, Food Lion, Hyde Park, Hy-Top, Parade, Piggly-Wiggly, Red & White, Roundy's, Schwegmann, Scot Lad and Tops brand names.

	Tot. Fat (g)	Sat. Fat (g)	Chol. (mg)	Sod. (mg)	Cal.
GELATIN					
D-Zerta Low Calorie Gelatin, all flavors (1/2 cup)	0.0	0.0	0	0	8
Gelatin					
Sweetened with NutraSweet or saccharin, all flavors, made with water (1/2 cup)	0.0	0.0	0	(3)	8
Sweetened with sugar, all flavors, made with water (1/2 cup)	0.0	0.0	0	(61)	71
Jell-O Brand Gelatin					
Snacks, all flavors (3.5 oz cup)	0.0	0.0	0	40	80
Sugar Free, all flavors, made with water (1/2 cup)	0.0	0.0	0	50-65	8
Sugar Sweetened, all flavors, made with water (1/2 cup)	0.0	0.0	0	35-75	80
Royal[†] Gelatin Dessert					
Sugar Free, all flavors, made with water (1/2 cup)	0.0	0.0	{0}	85-100	8-10
Sugar Sweetened, all flavors, made with water (1/2 cup)	0.0	0.0	{0}	90-130	80
GRAHAM CRACKERS—*see* **COOKIES,** *Graham Crackers*					
ICING—*see* **FROSTING**					
MOUSSE					
Lite Whip Mousse Instant Dessert Mix					
Chocolate, made with skim milk (1/2 cup)	2.0	(0.7)	0	55	70
Lemon, made with skim milk (1/2 cup)	2.0	(0.9)	0	55	60
Strawberry, made with skim milk (1/2 cup)	2.0	(0.9)	0	55	60
Vanilla, made with skim milk (1/2 cup)	2.0	(0.9)	0	55	60

	Tot. Fat (g)	Sat. Fat (g)	Chol. (mg)	Sod. (mg)	Cal.
Sans Sucre de Paris Mousse Mix					
Cheesecake, made with skim milk (½ cup)	1.0	(0.4)	1	180	73
Chocolate Cheesecake, made with skim milk (½ cup)	1.0	(0.3)	1	180	73
Weight Watchers Mousse Mix, White Chocolate Almond, made with skim milk (½ cup)	3.0	1.0	5	105	70

MUFFINS

	Tot. Fat (g)	Sat. Fat (g)	Chol. (mg)	Sod. (mg)	Cal.
Betty Crocker Light Muffin Mix, Wild Blueberry, made with egg white or egg substitute and water (1 muffin)	0.5	(0.0)	0	190	120
Betty Crocker Muffin Mix					
Apple Cinnamon, made with egg white and skim milk (1 muffin)	2.5	0.5	0	200	130
Wild Blueberry, made with egg white and skim milk (1 muffin)	3.0	1.0	0	220	150
Entenmann's Fat Free and Cholesterol Free Muffins					
Blueberry (1 muffin)	0.0	0.0	0	140	150
Cinnamon Apple Raisin (1 muffin)	0.0	0.0	0	140	160
Health Valley Fat-Free Muffins					
Apple Spice (2 oz = 1 muffin)	<1.0	(0.0)	0	110	130
Banana (2 oz = 1 muffin)	<1.0	(0.0)	0	110	130
Raisin Spice (2 oz = 1 muffin)	<1.0	(0.0)	0	110	140
Health Valley Fat-Free Oat Bran Fancy Fruit Muffins					
Almonds and Dates (1 muffin)	<1.0	(0.0)	0	80	140
Blueberry (1 muffin)	<1.0	(0.0)	0	100	140
Raisin (1 muffin)	<1.0	(0.0)	0	90	140
Healthy Choice Breakfast					
Apple Spice Muffin (2.5 oz)	4.0	<1.0	0	90	190
Blueberry Muffin (2.5 oz)	4.0	<1.0	0	110	190
Hostess Breakfast Muffins					
Apple Streusel (1¼ oz = 1 muffin)	1.0	<1.0	0	160	100
Blueberry (1¼ oz)	1.0	<1.0	0	160	100

	Tot. Fat (g)	Sat. Fat (g)	Chol. (mg)	Sod. (mg)	Cal.
Pepperidge Farm Wholesome Choice Muffins					
Blueberry (1.9 oz = 1 muffin)	2.0	<1.0	0	190	130
Corn (1.9 oz = 1 muffin)	3.0	(1.0)	0	180	150
Raisin Bran (2.05 oz = 1 muffin)	2.0	(1.0)	0	260	140
Sara Lee Free and Light, Blueberry					
Muffin (1 muffin)	3.0	(1.3)	0	140	150
PIES					
Sara Lee Free and Light, Strawberry					
Yogurt Dessert (1/10 of a pie)	1.0	<1.0	0	90	120
PUDDINGS—*see* **CREAM PIE FILLINGS/PUDDINGS**					
SWEET ROLLS/COFFEE CAKES					
Entenmann's Fat Free and Cholesterol Free Danish					
Apricot Twist (1.1 oz)	0.0	0.0	0	80	90
Bavarian Creme Pastry (1.3 oz)	0.0	0.0	0	95	80
Cheese Filled Crumb Pastry (1.2 oz)	0.0	0.0	0	95	90
Cherry Cheese Pastry (1.3 oz)	0.0	0.0	0	85	90
Cherry Filled Coffee Cake (1.3 oz)	0.0	0.0	0	80	90
Cinnamon Apple Coffee Cake (1.3 oz)	0.0	0.0	0	90	90
Cinnamon Apple Twist (1.1 oz)	0.0	0.0	0	75	90
Cinnamon Ring (1 oz)	0.0	0.0	0	75	80
Cinnamon Twist (1 oz)	0.0	0.0	0	75	80
Lemon Twist (1.1 oz)	0.0	0.0	0	80	90
Orange Twist (1.1 oz)	0.0	0.0	0	70	90
Pineapple Cheese Pastry (1.3 oz)	0.0	0.0	0	85	90
Raspberry Twist (1.1 oz)	0.0	0.0	0	75	90
Hostess Snack Cakes					
Light Apple Spice (1 cake)	1.0	<1.0	0	150	130
Light Crumb Cakes (1 cake)	1.0	<1.0	0	95	80
Sara Lee Free and Light, Apple					
Danish (1/8 of a cake)	0.0	0.0	0	120	130

† = tobacco company, corporate subsidiary or parent

EGG SUBSTITUTES

Egg substitutes are manufactured to contain limited amounts of fat, saturated fat and cholesterol. In this section, you will find some egg substitutes that meet AHA criteria for such products.

Products listed in this book vary in sodium content. Use the values appearing on the following pages to help plan a daily intake providing no more than 3,000 milligrams of sodium.

You can use the tables below to evaluate products introduced since this book went to press.

AHA Criteria for Egg Substitutes*

	Tot. Fat (g)	Sat. Fat (g)	Chol. (mg)
All egg substitutes	3	1	<2

* Per serving.

Not Recommended for Frequent Consumption

As shown in the table below, whole eggs are too high in cholesterol to be recommended for frequent consumption. Values that exceed AHA criteria are followed by asterisks. The AHA does not have criteria for sodium.

You can use the values in the table to compare whole eggs with more-healthful alternatives listed on the following page.

Egg—High in Fat, Saturated Fat and Cholesterol

	Tot. Fat (g)	Sat. Fat (g)	Chol. (mg)	Sod. (mg)	Cal.
Chicken egg (1 large, raw)	5.6*	1.7*	213*	69	79

Adapted from USDA Handbook No. 8 series.
* These values exceed AHA criteria for egg substitutes.

EGG SUBSTITUTES

	Tot. Fat (g)	Sat. Fat (g)	Chol. (mg)	Sod. (mg)	Cal.
Ballas Egg Whites (2 tbsp)	<1.0	(0.0)	0	150	50
Egg white, raw (1)	0.0	0.0	0	50	16
Fleischmann's† Egg Beaters, Plain (1/4 cup)	0.0	0.0	0	80	25
Healthy Choice Cholesterol Free Egg Product (1/4 cup)	<1.0	0.0	0	90	30
Morningstar Farms Egg Substitute					
Better'n Eggs (1/4 cup)	0.0	0.0	0	100	25
Scramblers (1/4 cup)	3.0	0.0	0	125	60
Second Nature Egg Substitute, Plain (2 fl oz = 1/4 cup)	0.0	0.0	0	100	40
Sunny Fresh Free (2 fl oz = 1/4 cup = 1 egg)	0.0	0.0	0	90	30

Egg Substitute Mixtures

	Tot. Fat (g)	Sat. Fat (g)	Chol. (mg)	Sod. (mg)	Cal.
Fleischmann's† Egg Beaters, Omelette Mix, Vegetable (1/2 cup)	0.0	0.0	0	170	50
Second Nature Egg Substitute, with Garden Vegetables (2.5 oz)	0.0	0.0	0	100	40

† = tobacco company, corporate subsidiary or parent

FATS, OILS, SEEDS AND NUTS

The AHA diet includes limited amounts of unsaturated oil and margarine. Although all oils have the same number of calories and almost the same total fat content per ounce, they contain varying amounts of saturated fat. The oils, margarines and other high-fat foods on the following pages are low in saturated fat. Salad dressing, another source of unsaturated fat, is in the "Salad Dressings and Sandwich Spreads" section, which begins on page 199.

Products listed in this book vary in sodium content. Use the values appearing on the following pages to help plan a daily intake providing no more than 3,000 milligrams of sodium.

Most of the foods in this book are brand name products; however, when a brand name is not specified, it means that most brands of that product provide about the same amount of fat, saturated fat and cholesterol and that these amounts do not exceed AHA criteria.

You can use those generic entries and the tables below to evaluate products introduced since this book went to press.

AHA Criteria for Fats, Oils, Seeds and Nuts*

	Tot. Fat (g)	Sat. Fat (g)	Chol. (mg)
Avocados, butter substitutes, cooking sprays, margarine, nut and seed butters, nuts, oils, olives and seeds	**	2	<2

* Per serving.

** No criterion; these foods are naturally high in fat but low in saturated fat.

Fats, Oils and Nuts Not Recommended for Frequent Consumption

Some types of fat, oil and nut that are usually too high in saturated fat and/or cholesterol to be recommended for frequent consumption are shown in the table on the following page. Values that exceed AHA criteria are followed by asterisks. The AHA does not have criteria for sodium.

You can use the values in the table to compare these fats, oils and nuts with more-healthful alternatives listed on the following pages.

Fats, Oils and Nuts High in Fat, Saturated Fat and/or Cholesterol

	Tot. Fat (g)	Sat. Fat (g)	Chol. (mg)	Sod. (mg)	Cal.
Butter (3 pats or 1 tablespoon)	12.2	7.5*	33*	123	108
Cashew nuts, salted (1 ounce)	13.2	2.6*	0	486	163
Cottonseed oil (1 tablespoon)	13.6	8.9*	(0)	(0)	120
Oil-roasted macadamia nuts, salted (1 ounce)	21.7	3.3*	0	74	204
Peanut oil (1 tablespoon)	13.5	2.3*	(0)	0	119
Shortening, made from hydrogenated soybean and hydrogenated cottonseed oil (1 tablespoon)	12.8	3.2*	(0)	(0)	113
Stick margarine, made from hydrogenated soybean oil, corn oil and hydrogenated cottonseed oil (1 tablespoon)	11.4	2.7*	(0)	133	101
Sweetened flaked coconut, canned (½ ounce)	4.5	4.0*	0	3	63

Adapted from USDA Handbook No. 8 series.

* These values exceed AHA criteria for fats, oils and nuts.

	Tot. Fat (g)	Sat. Fat (g)	Chol. (mg)	Sod. (mg)	Cal.
AVOCADOS					
Avocado, California, raw (3 tbsp puree)	7.5	1.1	0	5	76
BUTTER SUBSTITUTES					
Butter Buds					
Mix (1 tbsp)	0.0	0.0	0	70	6
Sprinkles (1/2 tsp)	0.0	0.0	0	65	4
Molly McButter Sprinkles, Butter Flavor (1/2 tsp)	0.0	0.0	0	90	4
COOKING SPRAYS					
Baker's Joy Vegetable Oil and Flour Baking Spray (1/10 of 8-in. 2-layer cake)	<1.0	(0.0)	0	0	4
Buttery Delite Cooking Spray (.8 grams = 1-second spray)	<1.0	(0.0)	0	0	<8
Garlic-Mist Cooking Spray (.8 grams = 1-second spray)	<1.0	(0.0)	0	0	<8
Mazola No Stick Cooking Spray (2.5-second spray)	0.2	tr	0	0	2
Mesquite Mist Cooking Spray (.8 grams = 1-second spray)	<1.0	(0.0)	0	0	<8
Olive-Mist Cooking Spray (.8 grams = 1-second spray)	<1.0	(0.0)	0	0	<8
Oriental-Mist Cooking Spray (.8 grams = 1-second spray)	<1.0	(0.0)	0	0	<8
Pizza Pizazz Cooking Spray (.8 grams = 1-second spray)	<1.0	(0.0)	0	0	<8
Weight Watchers					
Buttery Spray (.28 g)	<1.0	(0.0)	(0)	0	2
Cooking Spray (.33 g)	<1.0	(0.0)	(0)	0	2
Wesson Lite Cooking Spray (.3 g)	<1.0	(0.0)	0	0	0.4

	Tot. Fat (g)	Sat. Fat (g)	Chol. (mg)	Sod. (mg)	Cal.

MARGARINES

Diet/Light Margarines

Blue Bonnet† Better Blend Spread, Soft, 76% fat (1 tbsp)	11.0	2.0	0	95	90
Canola Sunrise Spread, soft (1 tbsp)	7.0	<1.0	0	95	70
Fleischmann's† Margarine, Diet, Reduced Calorie (1 tbsp)	6.0	1.0	0	50	50
Fleischmann's† Spread					
Extra Light Corn Oil, 40% oil (1 tbsp)	6.0	1.0	0	55	50
Soft, Light Corn Oil, 60% oil (1 tbsp)	8.0	1.0	0	70	80
Stick, Light Corn Oil, 60% oil (1 tbsp)	8.0	1.0	0	70	80
Kraft† Touch of Butter Spread					
Stick (1 tbsp)	10.0	2.0	0	110	90
Tub (1 tbsp)	6.0	1.0	0	110	50
Mazola					
Margarine, Corn Oil Diet Reduced Calorie (1 tbsp)	5.5	0.9	0	130	50
Spread, Light Corn Oil (1 tbsp)	5.6	0.9	0	100	50
Nucanola Spread (1 tbsp)	7.0	<1.0	0	90	70
Parkay Margarine					
Soft Diet Reduced Calorie (1 tbsp)	6.0	1.0	0	110	50
Spread (1 tbsp)	7.0	1.0	0	110	60
Squeeze Spread (1 tbsp)	10.0	2.0	0	110	90
Smart Beat Spread (1 tbsp)	3.0	0.0	0	110	25
Weight Watchers Margarine					
Extra Light Spread, tub (1 tbsp)	4.0	1.0	(0)	75	45
Extra Light Spread, Sweet Unsalted, tub (1 tbsp)	6.0	1.0	(0)	0	50
Light Spread, stick (1 tbsp)	7.0	1.0	(0)	130	60

Light Margarines—see Diet/Light Margarines

Regular Margarines

Blue Bonnet† Margarine					
Soft (1 tbsp)	11.0	2.0	0	95	100
Stick (1 tbsp)	11.0	2.0	0	95	100

	Tot. Fat (g)	Sat. Fat (g)	Chol. (mg)	Sod. (mg)	Cal.
Canola Harvest Margarine, stick (1 tbsp)	11.0	2.0	0	110	100
Canola Sunrise Margarine, stick (1 tbsp)	11.0	1.0	0	95	100
Chiffon Margarine					
Soft, tub (1 tbsp)	10.0	1.0	0	95	90
Soft Unsalted (1 tbsp)	10.0	2.0	0	0	90
Stick (1 tbsp)	11.0	2.0	0	105	100
Fleischmann's† Margarine					
Soft (1 tbsp)	11.0	2.0	0	95	100
Soft, Sweet Unsalted (1 tbsp)	11.0	2.0	0	0	100
Stick (1 tbsp)	11.0	2.0	0	95	100
Stick, Sweet, Unsalted (1 tbsp)	11.0	2.0	0	0	100
Hain Margarine, Safflower					
Soft (1 tbsp)	11.0	2.0	0	170	100
Stick (1 tbsp)	11.0	2.0	0	170	100
Unsalted (1 tbsp)	11.0	2.0	0	<5	100
Hollywood Margarine, Safflower (1 tbsp)	11.0	2.0	0	130	100
Sweet Unsalted (1 tbsp)	11.0	2.0	0	2	100
Mazola Margarine, Corn Oil (1 tbsp)	11.2	1.9	0	100	100
Unsalted (1 tbsp)	11.0	2.0	0	0	100
Mazola Rightblend (1 tbsp)	14.0	1.0	0	0	120
Parkay† Margarine, Soft (1 tbsp)	11.0	2.0	0	105	100
Tree of Life Margarine					
Canola Soy (1 tbsp)	11.0	2.0	0	110	100
Canola Soy, Salt Free (1 tbsp)	11.0	2.0	0	<2	100
Soy (1 tbsp)	11.0	2.0	0	110	100
Soy, Salt Free (1 tbsp)	11.0	2.0	0	<2	100

Whipped Margarines

	Tot. Fat (g)	Sat. Fat (g)	Chol. (mg)	Sod. (mg)	Cal.
Blue Bonnet† Margarine					
Stick, Whipped (1 tbsp)	7.0	1.0	0	70	70
Spread, Whipped, 60% oil (1 tbsp)	8.0	1.0	0	100	80
Chiffon Margarine, Whipped (1 tbsp)	8.0	1.0	0	80	70
Fleischmann's† Margarine, Whipped					
Lightly Salted (1 tbsp)	7.0	2.0	0	60	70
Unsalted (1 tbsp)	7.0	2.0	0	0	70

	Tot. Fat (g)	Sat. Fat (g)	Chol. (mg)	Sod. (mg)	Cal.
Miracle Brand Margarine, Whipped					
Stick (1 tbsp)	7.0	1.0	0	65	70
Tub (1 tbsp)	7.0	1.0	0	70	60
Parkay† Margarine, Whipped					
Stick (1 tbsp)	7.0	1.0	0	65	70
Tub (1 tbsp)	7.0	1.0	0	70	70

NUT BUTTERS/NUTS/SEED BUTTERS/SEEDS

Nut/Seed Butters

	Tot. Fat (g)	Sat. Fat (g)	Chol. (mg)	Sod. (mg)	Cal.
Erewhon Nut Butter					
Almond Butter (1 tbsp)	8.0	(0.8)	0	18	90
Sunflower Butter (2 tbsp)	18.0	(1.9)	0	20	200
Hain Nut Butter					
Almond Butter, Natural, Raw (2 tbsp)	18.0	2.0	0	5	190
Almond Butter, Toasted, Blanched (2 tbsp)	19.0	2.0	0	5	210
Skippy Peanut Butter					
Creamy (2 tbsp)	17.0	2.0	0	150	190
Super Chunk (2 tbsp)	17.0	2.0	0	130	190

Nuts

	Tot. Fat (g)	Sat. Fat (g)	Chol. (mg)	Sod. (mg)	Cal.
Beer Nuts, Almonds (1 oz)	14.0	1.0	0	65	170
Blue Diamond Almonds					
Barbecue (1 oz)	16.0	1.0	0	220	160
Blanched, Sliced or Whole (1 oz)	13.0	1.0	0	0	150
Chili with Lemon (1 oz)	13.0	1.0	0	160	160
Chopped, Natural, Sliced, Slivered or Whole (1 oz)	13.0	1.0	0	0	150
Honey Roasted (1 oz)	12.0	1.0	0	40	140
No Salt (1 oz)	13.0	1.0	0	0	150
Roasted Salted (1 oz)	13.0	1.0	0	140	150
Smokehouse (1 oz)	14.0	1.0	0	170	150
Sour Cream and Onion (1 oz)	14.0	1.0	0	140	150
Toasted, No Salt (1 oz)	13.0	1.0	0	0	150
Chestnuts, roasted (6 tbsp)	0.5	0.2	0	2	102
Dole Almonds					
Blanched, Slivered or Whole (1 oz)	14.0	(1.3)	(0)	4	170

	Tot. Fat (g)	Sat. Fat (g)	Chol. (mg)	Sod. (mg)	Cal.
Natural, Chopped, Sliced or Whole (1 oz)	14.0	(1.3)	(0)	4	170
Dole Pistachios, Natural (1 oz)	7.0	(0.9)	(0)	250	90
Fisher Almonds, Raw (1 oz)	15.0	1.0	0	0	170
Fisher Mixed Nuts					
Cashew and Almond (1 oz)	15.0	2.0	0	95	170
Dry Roasted (1 oz)	15.0	2.0	0	125	170
Honey Roasted Peanuts and Cashews (1 oz)	13.0	2.0	0	105	150
Oil Roasted (1 oz)	16.0	2.0	0	110	170
Fisher Nut Toppings, Oil Roasted with Peanuts (1 oz)	14.0	2.0	0	115	160
Fisher Peanuts					
Dry Honey Roasted (1 oz)	13.0	2.0	0	110	150
Dry Roasted (1 oz)	14.0	2.0	0	210	160
Honey Roasted (1 oz)	13.0	2.0	0	115	150
Oil Roasted (1 oz)	14.0	2.0	0	130	160
Roasted in Shell (1 oz)	14.0	2.0	0	165	160
Fisher Pecans, Raw, Ground or Chopped (1 oz)	19.0	2.0	0	0	190
Fisher Pistachios					
Natural Tint (1 oz)	14.0	2.0	0	85	170
Red Tint (1 oz)	14.0	2.0	0	85	170
Fisher Spanish Peanuts					
Raw (1 oz)	14.0	2.0	0	(5)	160
Roasted (1 oz)	14.0	2.0	0	130	170
Fisher Walnuts					
Black (1 oz)	16.0	1.0	0	0	170
English, Raw, Chopped or Ground (1 oz)	18.0	2.0	0	0	180
Lance Nuts					
Almonds, Smoke Flavored (3/4 oz = 1 pkg)	11.0	1.0	0	130	120
Pistachios (1 1/8 oz = 1 pkg)	8.0	1.0	0	100	100

Seeds

	Tot. Fat (g)	Sat. Fat (g)	Chol. (mg)	Sod. (mg)	Cal.
Fisher Sunflower Seeds					
Dry Roasted (1 oz)	15.0	2.0	0	200	170
Dry Roasted Salted in Shell (1 oz)	15.0	1.0	0	110	170

FATS, OILS, SEEDS AND NUTS

129

	Tot. Fat (g)	Sat. Fat (g)	Chol. (mg)	Sod. (mg)	Cal.
Oil Roasted (1 oz)	16.0	2.0	0	170	170
Salted in Shell (1 oz)	14.0	1.0	0	110	170
Salted in Shell (seeds only) ($^{15}/_{16}$ oz)	14.0	1.0	0	100	160
Unsalted (1 oz)	14.0	1.0	0	0	170
Frito-Lay Sunflower Seeds (1 oz)	14.0	(1.5)	(0)	265	160

NUTS—*see*
NUT BUTTERS/NUTS/SEED BUTTERS/SEEDS

OILS

	Tot. Fat (g)	Sat. Fat (g)	Chol. (mg)	Sod. (mg)	Cal.
Canola Harvest Oil (1 tbsp)	14.0	1.0	0	0	120
Canola oil (1 tbsp)	13.6	0.8	0	0	120
Corn oil (1 tbsp)	13.6	1.7	0	0	120
Crisco Oil					
Corn-Canola (1 tbsp)	14.0	1.5	0	0	120
Puritan Canola (1 tbsp)	14.0	1.0	0	0	120
Vegetable (blend of canola, sunflower and soybean oils) (1 tbsp)	14.0	1.5	0	0	120
Eden Oil					
Hot Pepper Sesame (1 tbsp)	14.0	2.0	(0)	0	120
Toasted Sesame (1 tbsp)	14.0	2.0	(0)	0	120
Hain Oil					
Almond (1 tbsp)	14.0	1.0	0	0	120
Apricot Kernel (1 tbsp)	14.0	1.0	0	0	120
Avocado (1 tbsp)	14.0	1.0	0	0	120
Safflower, Hi-Oleic (1 tbsp)	14.0	1.0	0	0	120
Walnut (1 tbsp)	14.0	2.0	0	0	120
Mazola Corn Oil (1 tbsp)	14.0	2.0	0	0	120
Olive oil (1 tbsp)	13.5	1.8	0	0	119
Safflower oil (1 tbsp)	13.6	1.2	0	0	120
Sesame oil (1 tbsp)	13.6	1.9	0	0	120
Soybean oil (1 tbsp)	13.6	2.0	0	0	120
Sunflower oil (1 tbsp)	13.6	1.4	0	0	120

	Tot. Fat (g)	Sat. Fat (g)	Chol. (mg)	Sod. (mg)	Cal.

OLIVES

Olives
Green (5 small) 1.8   0.2   0   343   17
Ripe (2 extra large) 1.6   0.2   0   96   15
Vlasic Early California Enticing Olives,
Chopped, Pitted, Sliced or Whole
(.5 oz)... 2.0   0.0   (0)   110   18
Vlasic Early California Ripe Olives
Chopped, Chopped Jalapeño, Sliced,
Sliced Jalapeño or Whole (.5 oz)........ 2.0   0.0   (0)   110   18
Pitted (.5 oz)...................................... 2.0   0.0   (0)   110   16
Vlasic Ripe Olives, Chopped, Chopped
Jalapeño, Pitted, Sliced, Sliced
Jalapeño or Whole (.5 oz)................. 2.0   0.0   (0)   110   18

SEEDS—see
**NUT BUTTERS/NUTS/SEED
BUTTERS/SEEDS**

† = tobacco company, corporate subsidiary or parent

FROZEN DESSERTS

The products on the following pages can satisfy your craving for ice cream while meeting the AHA criteria for fat, saturated fat and cholesterol. You will find a wide variety of nonfat and low-fat frozen yogurts, frozen dairy desserts, sherbets, sorbets, pops and bars to choose from.

Products listed in this book vary in sodium content. Use the values appearing on the following pages to help plan a daily intake providing no more than 3,000 milligrams of sodium.

You can use the tables below to evaluate products introduced since this book went to press.

AHA Criteria for Frozen Desserts and Cones*

	Tot. Fat (g)	Sat. Fat (g)	Chol. (mg)
Frozen desserts, milk based, such as frozen dairy desserts, frozen yogurt and sherbet	3	2	20
Frozen desserts, not milk based, such as fruit ices, ice pops and sorbets	<0.5	<0.5	<2
Ice cream cones	3	<0.5	<2

* Per serving.

Frozen Desserts Not Recommended for Frequent Consumption

Some types of frozen dessert that are usually too high in fat, saturated fat and/or cholesterol to be recommended for frequent consumption are shown in the table below. Values that exceed AHA criteria are followed by asterisks. The AHA does not have criteria for sodium.

You can use the values in the table to compare these frozen desserts with more-healthful alternatives listed on the following pages.

Frozen Desserts High in Fat, Saturated Fat and/or Cholesterol

	Tot. Fat (g)	Sat. Fat (g)	Chol. (mg)	Sod. (mg)	Cal.
Chocolate ice cream (½ cup)	7.3*	4.5*	22*	50	143
Chocolate soft-serve frozen yogurt (½ cup)	4.3*	2.6*	3	71	115
Vanilla ice cream, rich (½ cup)	12.0*	7.4*	45*	41	178

Adapted from USDA Handbook No. 8 series.

* These values exceed AHA criteria for frozen desserts.

	Tot. Fat (g)	Sat. Fat (g)	Chol. (mg)	Sod. (mg)	Cal.
BARS/POPS					
Blue Bell Pops and Bars					
Big Shot (5 fl oz)	0.0	0.0	0	0	140
Fat Free Fudge Bar (2 fl oz = 1 bar)	0.0	0.0	0	40	50
Gummy Pop (3.75 fl oz)	0.0	0.0	0	0	150
Rainbow Freeze (3.75 fl oz)	0.0	0.0	0	0	90
Sugar Free Bullet Bar (1 bar)	0.0	0.0	0	0	16
Twin Pop (3 fl oz = 1 pop)	0.0	0.0	0	5	70
Crystal Light Bars, all flavors (1 bar)	0.0	0.0	0	10	14
Dole Fruit'N Yogurt Bars					
Mixed Berry (1 bar)	<1.0	(<1.0)	(2)	18	70
Strawberry (1 bar)	<1.0	(<1.0)	(2)	16	70
Strawberry Banana (1 bar)	<1.0	(<1.0)	(2)	15	60
Dole Yogurt Bars, Chocolate (1 bar)	<1.0	(<1.0)	(3)	50	70
Fat Freedom Eskimo Pie Sandwiches					
(1 sandwich)	0.0	0.0	0	150	130
FrozFruit Bars, Chunky Strawberry					
(4 fl oz)	0.0	0.0	0	(10)	70
Fudgsicle Sugar Free Fudge Pops					
(1¾ fl oz = 1 pop)	1.0	(0.6)	(1)	50	35
Jackson's Fudge Jrs. Sugar Free Frozen Dairy Confections					
(1.75 fl oz = 1 pop)	0.0	0.0	(0)	78	32
Jell-O Gelatin Pops Bars, all flavors					
(1 bar)	0.0	0.0	0	25	35
Kemps Frozen Yogurt on a Stick, Raspberry or Strawberry					
(1.75 fl oz)	1.0	(0.6)	3	30	60
Kemps Pops and Bars					
Bomb Pop Jr.'s (2 fl oz)	0.0	0.0	0	6	46
Fudge Bar (2.5 fl oz)	0.0	0.0	0	0	90
Lite Fudge Jr.'s (1.75 fl oz = 1 bar)	0.0	0.0	0	50	55
Lite Pops (1.75 fl oz = 1 pop)	0.0	0.0	0	0	12
Twin Pops, all flavors (2.5 fl oz = 1 bar)	0.0	0.0	0	0	55
Klondike Lite Sandwich (2.8 fl oz = 1 sandwich)	2.0	1.0	5	110	100

	Tot. Fat (g)	Sat. Fat (g)	Chol. (mg)	Sod. (mg)	Cal.
Kool-Aid Kool-Pops, all flavors					
(1.8 fl oz = 1 bar)	0.0	0.0	0	10	40
Lifesavers Flavor Pops (1¾ oz = 1 bar)	0.0	0.0	(0)	5	40
Light N' Lively Nonfat Frozen Dessert Bars					
Chocolate Mousse or Double Chocolate Fudge (1 bar)	0.0	0.0	0	45	50
Orange Vanilla (1 bar)	0.0	0.0	0	15	40
Strawberry (1 bar)	0.0	0.0	0	25	80
Popsicle Ice Pops					
Banana, Lime, Raspberry, Root Beer, Strawberry or Wild Berry (1¾ fl oz = 1 pop)	0.0	0.0	(0)	10	50
Big Stick Orange (3¼ fl oz = 1 pop)	0.0	0.0	(0)	20	80
Sugar Free Ice Pops (1¾ fl oz = 1 pop)	0.0	0.0	(0)	10	18
Sealtest Free Nonfat Frozen Dessert Bars					
Chocolate Fudge Swirl (1 bar)	0.0	0.0	0	30	90
Chocolate with Fudge Swirl or Vanilla with Fudge Swirl (1 bar)	0.0	0.0	0	55	80
Vanilla Fudge Swirl (1 bar)	0.0	0.0	0	30	80
Vanilla Strawberry Swirl (1 bar)	0.0	0.0	0	40	80
Vanilla with Strawberry Swirl (1 bar)	0.0	0.0	0	60	70
Weight Watchers Frozen Novelties					
Chocolate Treat (2.75 fl oz)	1.0	<1.0	10	75	100
Double Fudge Bar (1.75 fl oz = 1 bar)	1.0	(0.5)	5	50	60
Fruit Juice (1 bar)	0.0	0.0	0	10	35
Peanut Butter Fudge (1.75 oz = 1 bar)	<1.0	(0.0)	(1)	120	60
Sugar Free Chocolate Mousse Bar (1.75 fl oz = 1 bar)	<1.0	<1.0	5	30	35
Sugar Free Orange Vanilla Treat Bar (1.75 fl oz = 1 bar)	<1.0	<1.0	5	40	30
Welch's Fruit Juice Bars					
All flavors (1.75 oz = 1 bar)	0.0	0.0	0	0	45
All flavors (3 fl oz = 1 bar)	0.0	0.0	0	0	80
No Sugar Added, all flavors (3 fl oz = 1 bar)	0.0	0.0	0	0	25
Well's Blue Bunny Pops and Bars					
Bomb Pop, Jr. (2 fl oz)	0.0	0.0	0	5	50

	Tot. Fat (g)	Sat. Fat (g)	Chol. (mg)	Sod. (mg)	Cal.
Citrus Snacks (1.75 fl oz)	1.0	1.0	0	5	50
Deluxe Fudge Sticks (1.75 fl oz)	0.0	0.0	0	60	70
Frozen Yogurt and Fruit Snacks (1.75 fl oz)	1.0	<1.0	5	20	50
Fudge Sticks (2½ fl oz)	1.0	1.0	5	90	100
Nonfat Frozen Yogurt and Fruit Snacks (1.75 fl oz)	0.0	0.0	0	25	40
Polar Pops (1.75 fl oz)	0.0	0.0	0	5	40
Rainbow Sticks (1.75 fl oz)	1.0	1.0	0	45	50
Slush Pops (1.75 fl oz)	0.0	0.0	0	10	50
Sugar Free Assorted Pops, Blue Raspberry, Cherry, Orange or Root Beer (1.75 fl oz = 1 bar)	0.0	0.0	0	10	8
Sugar Free Citrus Lites (1.75 fl oz = 1 bar)	0.0	0.0	0	10	16
Sugar Free Deluxe Fudge Lites (1.75 fl oz = 1 bar)	0.0	0.0	0	45	35
Twin Pop Sticks (3 fl oz)	0.0	0.0	0	5	70
Yarnell's Nonfat Bars, Fudge (2½ fl oz = 1 bar)	0.0	0.0	0	105	60

FROZEN DAIRY DESSERTS/ICE MILK

Low-Fat

	Tot. Fat (g)	Sat. Fat (g)	Chol. (mg)	Sod. (mg)	Cal.
Blue Bell Light					
Chocolate Innocence (½ cup)	3.0	2.0	<5	55	110
Cookies 'N Cream (½ cup)	3.0	1.0	10	90	120
Neapolitan (½ cup)	2.0	1.0	10	60	100
Vanilla (½ cup)	2.0	1.0	10	65	100
Vanilla Fudge (½ cup)	2.0	1.3	10	60	110
Borden Ice Milk					
Chocolate (½ cup)	2.0	(1.2)	(9)	80	100
Strawberry or Vanilla Flavored (½ cup)	2.0	(1.2)	(9)	65	90
Breyer's Light Ice Milk					
Strawberry (½ cup)	3.0	2.0	15	50	110
Vanilla Red Raspberry Parfait (½ cup)	3.0	2.0	15	50	130
Carnation Smooth 'N Lite Ice Milk					
Cherry Vanilla (½ cup)	2.0	2.0	10	55	100

FROZEN DESSERTS

	Tot. Fat (g)	Sat. Fat (g)	Chol. (mg)	Sod. (mg)	Cal.
Chocolate (1/2 cup)	2.0	2.0	10	90	90
Dreyer's Low Fat Premium Ice Milk					
Almond Praline (4 fl oz)	2.0	(1.2)	5	80	110
Cookies 'N Cream (4 fl oz)	2.0	(1.2)	5	85	110
Mocha Almond Fudge (4 fl oz)	2.0	(1.2)	5	70	110
Rocky Road (4 fl oz)	2.0	(1.2)	5	60	110
Strawberry (4 fl oz)	2.0	(1.2)	5	55	100
Vanilla (4 fl oz)	2.0	(1.2)	10	60	100
Edy's Low Fat Premium Ice Milk—*see* Dreyer's Low Fat Premium Ice Milk					
Healthy Choice Frozen Dairy Dessert					
Bordeaux Cherry (4 fl oz)	2.0	0.0	5	50	120
Butter Pecan Crunch (4 fl oz)	2.0	<1.0	5	80	140
Chocolate (4 fl oz)	2.0	1.0	5	70	130
Chocolate Chip or Praline & Caramel (4 oz)	2.0	0.0	5	70	130
Coffee Toffee (4 fl oz)	2.0	<1.0	5	80	130
Cookies N' Cream (4 fl oz)	2.0	0.0	5	80	130
Double Fudge Swirl (4 fl oz)	2.0	<1.0	5	70	130
Fudge Brownie (4 fl oz)	2.0	0.0	5	70	140
Mint Chocolate Chip (4 fl oz)	2.0	0.0	5	80	140
Neapolitan or Vanilla (4 fl oz)	2.0	0.0	5	60	120
Old Fashioned Vanilla (4 fl oz)	2.0	1.0	5	60	120
Rocky Road (4 fl oz)	2.0	0.0	5	70	160
Kemps Ice Milk					
Lite Vanilla (4 oz)	2.0	(1.2)	5	60	100
Premium Light, Vanilla (4 oz)	3.0	(1.9)	10	50	100
Land O'Lakes Ice Milk, Vanilla (4 fl oz)	3.0	2.0	10	55	110
Light N' Lively Ice Milk					
Coffee (1/2 cup)	3.0	1.0	10	40	100
Cookies N' Cream (1/2 cup)	3.0	2.0	10	65	110
Vanilla Flavored (1/2 cup)	3.0	2.0	10	40	100
Vanilla Flavored Chocolate-Strawberry (1/2 cup)	3.0	2.0	10	35	100
Vanilla Flavored with Red Raspberry Swirl (1/2 cup)	3.0	1.0	10	35	110
Vanilla Fudge Twirl (1/2 cup)	3.0	2.0	10	45	110
Meadow Gold Frozen Dessert, Vanilla Flavored (4 fl oz)	<1.0	<1.0	0	50	90

	Tot. Fat (g)	Sat. Fat (g)	Chol. (mg)	Sod. (mg)	Cal.
Meadow Gold Light Premium Ice Milk,					
Vanilla (½ cup)	3.0	(1.9)	(9)	55	110
Simple Pleasures Frozen Dairy Dessert					
Chocolate (4 fl oz)	0.9	0.5	5	73	134
Chocolate Chip (4 fl oz)	2.3	0.9	13	54	144
Cookies 'N Cream (4 fl oz)	2.2	0.7	11	85	145
Mint Chocolate Chocolate Chip					
(4 fl oz)	1.6	1.1	4	51	138
Pecan Praline (4 fl oz)	1.5	0.3	4	63	127
Toffee Crunch (4 fl oz)	0.6	0.3	6	105	131
Vanilla (4 fl oz)	0.7	0.2	12	50	116
Ultra Slim-Fast Frozen Delight Lowfat					
Frozen Dessert					
Chocolate (4 fl oz)	<1.0	(<1.0)	0	45	100
Chocolate Fudge (4 fl oz)	<1.0	(<1.0)	0	65	120
Peach (4 fl oz)	<1.0	(<1.0)	0	55	100
Pralines and Caramel (4 fl oz)	<1.0	(<1.0)	0	95	120
Vanilla (4 fl oz)	<1.0	(<1.0)	0	55	90
Vanilla Fudge Cookie (4 oz)	<1.0	(<1.0)	0	90	110
Weight Watchers Premium Ice Milk					
Chocolate (½ cup)	3.0	2.0	10	75	110
Chocolate Swirl (½ cup)	3.0	2.0	5	75	120
Heavenly Hash (4 fl oz)	3.0	1.9	10	90	130
Neapolitan (½ cup)	3.0	1.0	10	75	110
Vanilla (½ cup)	3.0	1.0	10	75	100
Wells' Blue Bunny Hi Lite Ice Milk					
Caramel Pecan (½ cup)	3.0	2.0	10	70	120
Chocolate-Vanilla (½ cup)	3.0	2.0	10	70	110
Strawberry (½ cup)	2.0	2.0	10	65	110
Vanilla (½ cup)	3.0	2.0	10	65	100
Yarnell's Premium Lite					
Old Time Vanilla (4 fl oz)	3.0	(1.9)	14	45	110
Peaches N' Cream or Real Vanilla					
(4 fl oz)	3.0	(1.9)	14	55	110
Strawberries N' Cream (4 fl oz)	3.0	(1.9)	13	55	110
Swiss Milk Chocolate (4 fl oz)	3.0	(1.9)	13	50	110

	Tot. Fat (g)	Sat. Fat (g)	Chol. (mg)	Sod. (mg)	Cal.
Nonfat					
Blue Bell Free					
Chocolate (1/2 cup)	0.0	0.0	0	55	80
Peach (1/2 cup)	0.0	0.0	0	60	80
Strawberry or Vanilla (1/2 cup)	0.0	0.0	0	65	80
Borden Nonfat Frozen Dessert					
Black Cherry or Strawberry (4 fl oz)	<1.0	<1.0	0	40	90
Chocolate (4 fl oz)	<1.0	<1.0	0	50	100
Peach Flavored (4 fl oz)	<1.0	0.0	0	40	90
Vanilla Flavored (4 fl oz)	<1.0	<1.0	0	50	90
Dreyer's Fat Free Cholesterol Free Frozen Dairy Dessert					
Chocolate Fudge or Marble Fudge (4 fl oz)	<1.0	(0.0)	0	80	100
Strawberry (4 fl oz)	<1.0	(0.0)	0	60	90
Vanilla (4 fl oz)	<1.0	(0.0)	0	70	90
Edy's Fat Free Cholesterol Free Frozen Dairy Dessert—*see* Dreyer's Fat Free Cholesterol Free Frozen Dairy Dessert					
Gise Creme Glace					
All flavors except Chocolate (3.5 fl oz)	0.0	0.0	0	0	33
Chocolate (3.5 fl oz)	0.1	(0.0)	(0)	0	34
Gise Creme Glace, Nonfat Frozen Dessert Hardpack, all flavors (3 fl oz)	0.0	0.0	<5	65	80
Kemps Free Nonfat Frozen Dessert, Vanilla (4 oz)	0.0	0.0	0	55	90
Meadow Gold Frozen Dessert					
Black Cherry or Strawberry Flavored (4 fl oz)	<1.0	<1.0	0	40	90
Chocolate (4 fl oz)	<1.0	<1.0	0	50	100
Peach Flavored (4 fl oz)	<1.0	0.0	0	40	90
Vanilla Flavored (4 fl oz)	<1.0	<1.0	0	50	90
Sealtest Free Nonfat Frozen Dessert					
Black Cherry, Peach or Vanilla Flavored (1/2 cup)	0.0	0.0	0	45	100

	Tot. Fat (g)	Sat. Fat (g)	Chol. (mg)	Sod. (mg)	Cal.
Chocolate or Vanilla Fudge Royale (1/2 cup)	0.0	0.0	0	50	100
Strawberry or Vanilla-Chocolate-Strawberry (1/2 cup)	0.0	0.0	0	40	100
Simple Pleasures Frozen Dairy Dessert					
Coffee (4 fl oz)	0.4	0.2	13	69	116
Peach (4 fl oz)	0.4	0.4	5	59	118
Rum Raisin (4 fl oz)	0.5	0.2	13	65	128
Strawberry (4 fl oz)	0.3	0.3	5	57	111
Simple Pleasures Light Frozen Dairy Dessert					
Chocolate (4 fl oz)	0.5	0.3	10	74	74
Chocolate Caramel Sundae (4 fl oz)	0.5	0.2	9	82	86
Vanilla (4 fl oz)	0.4	0.2	9	68	72
Vanilla Fudge Swirl (4 fl oz)	0.2	0.1	10	81	90
Weight Watchers Grand Collection Fat Free					
Chocolate (1/2 cup)	0.0	0.0	5	75	80
Chocolate Swirl (1/2 cup)	0.0	0.0	5	75	90
Neapolitan or Vanilla (1/2 cup)	<1.0	<1.0	5	75	80
Wells' Blue Bunny Nonfat Dairy Dessert					
Burgundy Cherry, Peach or Strawberry (3 fl oz)	0.0	0.0	0	35	70
Chocolate, Neapolitan or Vanilla (3 fl oz)	0.0	0.0	0	45	70
Cookies and Cream (3 fl oz)	0.0	0.0	0	45	80
Wells' Blue Bunny Nonfat Sugar Free Dairy Dessert					
Peach, Raspberry, Strawberry or Vanilla (3 fl oz)	0.0	0.0	0	50	50
Wells' Blue Bunny Nonfat Sugar Free Frozen Dessert, Chocolate (3 fl oz)	0.0	0.0	0	60	50
Yarnell's Guilt Free Frozen Dietary Dairy Dessert					
Banana Nut Crunch, Berry Delicious or Strawberry (4 fl oz)	0.0	0.0	3	60	70
Blueberry Swirl (4 fl oz)	0.0	0.0	3	55	70
Chocolate (4 fl oz)	0.0	0.0	3	60	80
Praline Pecan Crunch (4 fl oz)	0.0	0.0	3	65	70

	Tot. Fat (g)	Sat. Fat (g)	Chol. (mg)	Sod. (mg)	Cal.
Vanilla (4 fl oz)	0.0	0.0	4	60	80
Vanilla Fudge (4 fl oz)	0.0	0.0	3	80	80

FROZEN YOGURT

Low-Fat

	Tot. Fat (g)	Sat. Fat (g)	Chol. (mg)	Sod. (mg)	Cal.
Ben & Jerry's Lowfat Frozen Yogurt					
Banana Strawberry or Raspberry (3 fl oz)	1.0	(0.7)	5	(43)	130
Blueberry Cheesecake (3 fl oz)	1.0	(0.7)	5	(43)	120
Chocolate (3 fl oz)	2.0	(1.3)	6	(43)	130
Blue Bell Light, Pecan Pralines 'N					
Cream (1/2 cup)	3.0	1.0	5	75	120
Blue Bell Lowfat Frozen Yogurt					
Chocolate Cup or Strawberry Cup				55-	
(1 cup = 3 fl oz)	1.0	0.5	5	60	90
Cookies 'N Cream (1/2 cup)	2.0	1.0	5	85	130
Fruit Cocktail (1/2 cup)	2.0	1.0	(5)	75	130
Pecan Pralines 'N Cream (1/2 cup)	2.0	1.0	5	70	130
Strawberry (1/2 cup)	2.0	1.0	9	75	115
Vanilla (1/2 cup)	2.0	1.0	9	90	130
Breyer's Frozen Yogurt					
Peach or Strawberry (1/2 cup)	3.0	2.0	10	55	140
Strawberry Banana (1/2 cup)	3.0	2.0	10	55	130
Carnation Frozen Yogurt, Strawberry					
(4 fl oz)	1.0	(0.6)	<5	80	100
Colombo Shoppe Style Soft Lowfat					
Frozen Yogurt					
Chocolate Cappuccino Twist or					
Vanilla Chocolate Twist (3 fl oz)	1.0	(0.7)	5	45	90
Chocolate Peanut Butter Twist					
(3 fl oz)	3.0	(1.9)	<5	65	110
Old World Chocolate (3 fl oz)	1.0	(0.7)	<5	50	90
Simply Vanilla (3 fl oz)	1.0	(0.7)	5	40	90
Strawberry Cheesecake Twist or					
Vanilla Peach Twist (3 fl oz)	1.0	(0.7)	<5	40	90
Wild Strawberry (3 fl oz)	1.0	(0.7)	<5	35	90
Dannon Lowfat Soft Frozen Yogurt					
Softy Peanut Butter (4 fl oz)	3.0	(2.0)	5	70	130

	Tot. Fat (g)	Sat. Fat (g)	Chol. (mg)	Sod. (mg)	Cal.
Softy Plain (4 fl oz)	1.0	(0.6)	5	60	90
Softy Raspberry (4 fl oz)	2.0	(1.3)	5	65	110
Dreyer's Frozen Yogurt Inspirations					
Almond Praline (4 fl oz)	3.0	(1.9)	10	105	120
Boysenberry-Vanilla Swirl (4 fl oz)	3.0	(1.9)	15	40	100
Chocolate (4 fl oz)	3.0	(1.9)	10	40	100
Chocolate Sundae (4 fl oz)	2.0	(1.3)	10	40	100
Citrus Heights, Peach, Raspberry or Strawberry (4 fl oz)	3.0	(1.9)	10	35	100
Marble Fudge (4 fl oz)	3.0	(1.9)	15	75	120
Orange-Vanilla Swirl (4 fl oz)	2.0	(1.3)	15	65	100
Raspberry-Vanilla Swirl (4 fl oz)	1.0	(0.7)	15	40	100
Vanilla (4 fl oz)	3.0	(1.9)	15	70	110
Edy's Frozen Yogurt Inspirations— *see* Dreyer's Frozen Yogurt Inspirations					
Frusen Gladje Frozen Yogurt, Strawberry (1/2 cup)	3.0	2.0	10	50	120
Kemps Frozen Yogurt, Regular (4 oz)	1.0	(0.7)	7	53	107
Land O'Lakes Frozen Yogurt, Strawberry (4 fl oz)	3.0	2.0	10	60	110
Weight Watchers Sweet Celebrations Desserts, Chocolate Yogurt Shake (7.5 fl oz)	1.0	<1.0	5	140	220
Wells' Blue Bunny Frozen Yogurt					
Burgundy Cherry (1/2 cup)	3.0	2.0	10	50	120
Chocolate (1/2 cup)	3.0	2.0	10	55	115
Peach (1/2 cup)	3.0	2.0	10	60	120
Raspberry (1/2 cup)	3.0	2.0	10	65	110
Strawberry (1/2 cup)	3.0	2.0	10	60	110
Strawberry Banana (1/2 cup)	3.0	2.0	10	50	110
Vanilla (1/2 cup)	3.0	2.0	10	55	100
Wells' Blue Bunny Sugar-Free Lowfat Frozen Yogurt					
Burgundy Cherry, Peach or Strawberry (3 fl oz)	1.0	<1.0	5	40	50
Chocolate (3 fl oz)	1.0	<1.0	5	65	60
Vanilla (3 fl oz)	1.0	<1.0	5	45	60

	Tot. Fat (g)	Sat. Fat (g)	Chol. (mg)	Sod. (mg)	Cal.
Yarnell's Lowfat Frozen Yogurt					
Banana Nut (3 fl oz)	2.0	(1.3)	7	40	80
Chocolate (3 fl oz)	1.0	(0.7)	7	45	90
Peach, Strawberry or Strawberry/					
Banana (3 fl oz)	1.0	(0.7)	7	40	80
Vanilla (3 fl oz)	1.0	(0.7)	7	45	80
Yoplait Soft Frozen Yogurt (3 fl oz)	2.0	(1.3)	5	40	90

Nonfat

	Tot. Fat (g)	Sat. Fat (g)	Chol. (mg)	Sod. (mg)	Cal.
Blue Bell Nonfat Frozen Yogurt					
Banana Split or Fruit Cocktail					
(½ cup)	<0.5	<0.3	0	50	100
Chocolate (½ cup)	<0.5	<0.3	0	55	100
Strawberry (½ cup)	<0.5	<0.3	0	45	100
Vanilla (½ cup)	<0.5	<0.3	0	60	100
Dannon Nonfat Soft Frozen Yogurt					
Softy Chocolate (4 fl oz)	0.0	0.0	0	65	110
Softy Golden Vanilla, Red Raspberry					
or Strawberry (4 fl oz)	0.0	0.0	0	60	100
Softy Rum Raisin (4 fl oz)	0.0	0.0	0	65	100
Dreyer's Nonfat Frozen Yogurt					
Raspberry (4 fl oz)	0.0	0.0	(0)	60	100
Strawberry (4 fl oz)	0.0	0.0	(0)	55	100
Vanilla (4 fl oz)	0.0	0.0	(0)	55	110
Dreyer's Nonfat Frozen Yogurt					
Inspirations					
Banana-Strawberry (4 fl oz)	0.0	0.0	(0)	40	90
Cherry or Mixed Berry (4 fl oz)	0.0	0.0	(0)	55	100
Chocolate (4 fl oz)	0.0	0.0	(0)	55	110
Mixed Berry (4 fl oz)	0.0	0.0	(0)	55	100
Mocha (4 fl oz)	0.0	0.0	(0)	70	110
Edy's Nonfat Frozen Yogurt—see					
Dreyer's Nonfat Frozen Yogurt					
Edy's Nonfat Frozen Yogurt					
Inspirations—see Dreyer's Nonfat					
Frozen Yogurt Inspirations					
Heidi's Light Nonfat Frozen Yogurt,					
Pecan n' Pralines (3 fl oz)	0.0	0.0	(0)	55	65

	Tot. Fat (g)	Sat. Fat (g)	Chol. (mg)	Sod. (mg)	Cal.
I Can't Believe It's Yogurt					
Nonfat (6¾ fl oz = 1 small serving)	0.0	0.0	0	18	135
Sugar Free (6¾ fl oz = 1 small serving)	0.0	0.0	0	18	115
Kemps Frozen Yogurt					
Nonfat (4 oz)	0.0	0.0	0	60	93
Nonfat Soft Serve, Vanilla (1 oz)	0.0	0.0	0	20	25
Sealtest Free Nonfat Frozen Yogurt					
Black Cherry (½ cup)	0.0	0.0	0	50	110
Chocolate (½ cup)	0.0	0.0	0	55	110
Peach or Strawberry (½ cup)	0.0	0.0	0	35	100
Red Raspberry (½ cup)	0.0	0.0	0	40	100
Vanilla (½ cup)	0.0	0.0	0	45	100
TCBY Frozen Yogurt, Non-Fat					
(6 fl oz)	<1.0	0.0	0	68	150
Wells' Blue Bunny Nonfat Frozen Yogurt					
Burgundy Cherry, Neapolitan, Peach, Strawberry or Vanilla (3 fl oz)	0.0	0.0	0	45	60
Chocolate (3 fl oz)	0.0	0.0	0	50	60
Cookies 'N' Cream (3 fl oz)	0.0	0.0	0	55	80
Strawberry Cheesecake (3 fl oz)	0.0	0.0	0	40	80
Yarnell's Nonfat Frozen Yogurt					
Black Cherry or Raspberry (3 fl oz)	0.0	0.0	0	40	80
Lemon (3 fl oz)	0.0	0.0	0	40	70
Pineapple (3 fl oz)	0.0	0.0	0	45	70
ICE CREAM CONES					
Cup-O-Joy Ice Cream Cones, Honey & Bran (1 cone)	0.0	0.0	0	0	20
Delicious Ice Cream Cone					
Cake Cup Cone, Jumbo (.17 oz = 1 cone)	<1.0	(0.0)	0	15	20
Cake Cup Cone, Rainbow (.17 oz = 1 cone)	<1.0	(0.0)	0	15	20
Cake Cup Cone, Vanilla (.17 oz = 1 cone)	<1.0	(0.0)	0	15	20
Sugar Cone (.29 oz = 1 cone)	<1.0	(0.0)	0	5	45

	Tot. Fat (g)	Sat. Fat (g)	Chol. (mg)	Sod. (mg)	Cal.
Sunshine Ice Cream Cones					
Cake Cones (1 cone)	<1.0	(0.0)	0	20	20
Sugar Cones (1 cone)	1.0	(0.3)	0	10	50
ICE MILK—see **FROZEN DAIRY DESSERTS/ICE MILK**					
POPS—see **BARS/POPS**					
SHERBETS/SORBETS					
Blue Bell Sherbet					
Lime, Orange or Rainbow (1/2 cup)	1.0	0.5	5	25	130
Pineapple (1/2 cup)	1.0	0.5	5	25	120
Strawberry (1/2 cup)	1.0	0.5	5	20	120
Borden Sherbet, Orange (1/2 cup)	1.0	(0.6)	(<5)	40	110
Carnation Sherbet					
Lime (1/2 cup)	1.0	<1.0	3	30	105
Orange (1/2 cup)	0.8	<1.0	3	40	110
Raspberry (1/2 cup)	1.0	<1.0	<5	35	110
White Lemon (1/2 cup)	1.0	<1.0	<5	40	110
Dole Fruit Sorbet, Strawberry (4 fl oz)	<1.0	(0.0)	0	10	110
Frusen Gladje Sorbet, Raspberry (1/2 cup)	0.0	0.0	0	10	140
Kemps Sherbet, Orange (4 oz)	1.0	(0.6)	4	25	120
Mama Tish's Gourmet Italian Ices (4 fl oz)	0.0	0.0	0	0	90
Mama Tish's Sorbetto (4 fl oz)	0.0	0.0	0	0	100
Mazzone's Italian Ices					
Cherry (3 1/2 fl oz)	0.0	0.0	0	0	70
Lemon, Lime, Orange, Rainbow or Watermelon (3 1/2 fl oz)	0.0	0.0	0	0	60
Neilson Sherbet					
Lime or Orange (1/2 cup)	1.0	0.6	2	(65)	116
Orange Sherbet Sundae Cup (3 1/3 fl oz = 1 cup)	0.8	0.5	2	(54)	116
Sealtest Sherbet					
Lime or Red Raspberry (1/2 cup)	1.0	0.0	5	30	130
Rainbow (1/2 cup)	1.0	1.0	5	30	130

	Tot. Fat (g)	Sat. Fat (g)	Chol. (mg)	Sod. (mg)	Cal.
Wells' Blue Bunny Ol' Fashion Premium Sherbet, Orange or Raspberry (1/2 cup)	1.0	<1.0	<5	35	120
Wells' Blue Bunny Sherbet Lime, Orange, Rainbow or Raspberry (1/2 cup)	1.0	<1.0	<5	35	120
Pineapple (1/2 cup)	1.0	<1.0	<5	35	140
Strawberry (1/2 cup)	1.0	<1.0	<5	35	125

SORBETS—see **SHERBETS/SORBETS**

FRUITS

Unlike most other sections of this book, the "Fruits" section does *not* list branded products. Because fruits are very low in fat, saturated fat and cholesterol, they all meet the AHA criteria for these food components. Their low sodium content, in addition to their rich nutrient content, is an added advantage.

Avocados and olives, fruits that do contain fat, are listed in the "Fats, Oils, Seeds and Nuts" section, which begins on page 122. Fruit snacks are found in the "Snack Foods" section, starting on page 209.

Products listed in this book vary in sodium content. Use the values appearing on the following pages to help plan a daily intake providing no more than 3,000 milligrams of sodium.

You can use the table on the following page to evaluate products introduced since this book went to press.

AHA Criteria for Fruits*

	Tot. Fat (g)	Sat. Fat (g)	Chol. (mg)
All fruit (except avocados, olives and those listed below)	3	<0.5	<2
Fruit used as ingredients, such as cranberries, lemons and limes	<0.5	<0.5	<2

* Per serving.

	Tot. Fat (g)	Sat. Fat (g)	Chol. (mg)	Sod. (mg)	Cal.
Apples					
Dried (10 rings)	0.2	0.0	0	56	155
Fresh (2¾" diameter)	0.5	0.1	0	1	81
Applesauce					
Canned, with cinnamon or					
sweetened (½ cup)	0.2	0.0	0	4	97
Unsweetened (½ cup)	0.1	0.0	0	2	53
Apricots					
Canned					
in heavy syrup (3 halves)	0.7	0.0	0	3	70
in juice (3 halves)	0.0	0.0	0	3	40
in light syrup (3 halves)	0.0	0.0	0	3	54
in water (3 halves)	0.1	0.0	0	2	22
Dried (10 halves)	0.2	0.0	0	3	83
Fresh (3)	0.4	0.0	0	1	51
Bananas, fresh (8¾" long)	0.6	0.2	0	1	105
Blackberries					
Canned, in heavy syrup (½ cup)	0.1	0.0	0	3	118
Fresh (½ cup)	0.3	0.0	0	0	37
Frozen, unsweetened (½ cup)	0.3	0.0	0	1	49
Blueberries					
Canned, in heavy syrup (½ cup)	0.4	0.0	0	4	112
Fresh (½ cup)	0.6	0.0	0	5	41
Frozen, unsweetened (½ cup)	0.5	0.0	0	1	39
Boysenberries					
Canned, in heavy syrup (½ cup)	0.2	0.0	0	4	113
Frozen, unsweetened (½ cup)	0.2	0.0	0	1	33
Breadfruit, fresh (½ cup)	0.6	0.0	0	2	114
Cantaloupe, fresh (⅓ of a 5"-diameter					
melon)	0.7	0.0	0	23	94
Casabas, fresh, cubed (½ cup)	0.1	0.0	0	10	23
Cherries, sweet					
Canned					
in heavy syrup (½ cup)	0.2	0.0	0	3	107
in juice (½ cup)	0.0	0.0	0	3	68
in light syrup (½ cup)	0.2	0.0	0	3	85
in water (½ cup)	0.2	0.0	0	2	57
Fresh (10)	0.7	0.1	0	0	49
Frozen, sweetened (½ cup)	0.2	0.1	0	3	116
Crabapples, fresh, sliced (½ cup)	0.2	0.1	0	1	42

FRUITS

	Tot. Fat (g)	Sat. Fat (g)	Chol. (mg)	Sod. (mg)	Cal.
Cranberries, fresh, chopped (1/2 cup)	0.1	0.0	0	1	27
Cranberry sauce, canned, sweetened (1/2 cup)	0.2	0.0	0	40	209
Cranberry-orange relish, canned (1/2 cup)	0.1	0.0	0	44	246
Currants					
Dried (1/2 cup)	0.2	0.0	0	6	204
Fresh, red or white (1/2 cup)	0.1	0.0	0	1	31
Dates, dried (10)	0.4	0.0	0	2	228
Figs					
Canned					
in heavy syrup (3)	0.1	0.0	0	1	75
in light syrup (3)	0.1	0.0	0	1	58
in water (3)	0.1	0.0	0	1	42
Dried (2)	0.4	0.1	0	4	95
Fresh (1 medium)	0.2	0.0	0	1	37
Fruit cocktail					
Canned					
in heavy syrup (1/2 cup)	0.1	0.0	0	7	93
in juice (1/2 cup)	0.0	0.0	0	4	56
in light syrup (1/2 cup)	0.1	0.0	0	7	72
in water (1/2 cup)	0.1	0.0	0	5	40
Gooseberries, fresh (1/2 cup)	0.9	0.1	0	1	34
Grapefruit					
Canned					
in juice (1/2 cup)	0.1	0.0	0	9	46
in light syrup (1/2 cup)	0.1	0.0	0	2	76
in water (1/2 cup)	0.1	0.0	0	2	44
Fresh (1/2 of a 3 3/4"-diameter grapefruit)	0.1	0.0	0	0	38
Grapes, fresh (10)	0.1	0.0	0	0	15
Guava, fresh (1)	0.5	0.2	0	2	45
Honeydews, fresh, cubed (1/2 cup)	0.1	0.0	0	9	30
Kiwi fruit, fresh (1 medium)	0.3	0.0	0	4	46
Kumquats, fresh (1)	0.0	0.0	0	1	12
Lemons, fresh (1 medium)	0.2	0.0	0	1	17
Limes, fresh (1)	0.1	0.0	0	1	20
Loganberries, frozen (1/2 cup)	0.2	0.0	0	1	40
Loquats, fresh (1)	0.0	0.0	0	0	5
Lychees, fresh (1)	0.0	0.0	0	0	6

	Tot. Fat (g)	Sat. Fat (g)	Chol. (mg)	Sod. (mg)	Cal.
Mangos, fresh (1)	0.6	0.1	0	4	135
Melon balls, frozen (1/2 cup)	0.2	0.0	0	27	28
Mulberries, fresh (1/2 cup)	0.6	0.0	0	7	31
Nectarines, fresh (21/2" diameter)	0.6	0.0	0	0	67
Oranges, fresh (25/8" diameter)	0.2	0.0	0	0	62
Papayas, fresh, cubes (1/2 cup)	0.1	0.1	0	2	27
Passion fruit, fresh (1)	0.1	0.0	0	5	18
Peaches					
Canned					
in heavy syrup (1/2 cup)	0.1	0.0	0	8	95
in heavy syrup, spiced (1/2 cup)	0.1	0.0	0	5	90
in juice (1/2 cup)	0.0	0.0	0	6	55
in light syrup (1/2 cup)	0.0	0.0	0	7	68
in water (1/2 cup)	0.1	0.0	0	4	29
Dried (10 halves)	1.0	0.1	0	9	311
Cooked without sugar (1/2 cup)	0.3	0.0	0	3	99
Fresh (21/2" diameter)	0.1	0.0	0	0	37
Frozen, sliced, sweetened (1/2 cup)	0.1	0.0	0	8	118
Pears					
Canned					
in heavy syrup (1 half)	0.1	0.0	0	4	58
in juice (1 half)	0.1	0.0	0	3	38
in light syrup (1 half)	0.0	0.0	0	4	45
in water (1 half)	0.0	0.0	0	2	22
Dried					
Cooked without sugar (1/2 cup)	0.4	0.0	0	4	163
Uncooked (5 halves)	0.6	0.0	0	5	230
Fresh (21/2 × 31/2" diameter)	0.7	0.0	0	1	98
Asian (21/4 × 21/2" diameter)	0.3	0.0	0	0	51
Persimmons					
Japanese, fresh (21/2 × 31/2" diameter)	0.3	0.0	0	3	118
Native, fresh (1)	0.1	0.0	0	0	32
Pineapples					
Canned					
Tidbits in heavy syrup (1/2 cup)	0.1	0.0	0	2	100
Tidbits in juice (1/2 cup)	0.1	0.0	0	2	75
Tidbits in light syrup (1/2 cup)	0.1	0.0	0	2	66
Tidbits in water (1/2 cup)	0.1	0.0	0	2	40
Fresh, diced (1/2 cup)	0.3	0.1	0	1	39

FRUITS

	Tot. Fat (g)	Sat. Fat (g)	Chol. (mg)	Sod. (mg)	Cal.
Frozen, chunks, sweetened (1/2 cup)	0.1	0.0	0	2	104
Plantains, fresh, raw (1)	0.7	0.0	0	7	218
Plums					
Canned					
in heavy syrup (3)	0.1	0.0	0	26	119
in juice (3)	0.0	0.0	0	1	55
in light syrup (3)	0.1	0.0	0	26	83
in water (3)	0.0	0.0	0	1	39
Fresh (2 1/8" diameter)	0.4	0.0	0	0	36
Pomegranates, fresh (3 3/8 × 3 3/4"					
diameter)	0.5	0.0	0	5	104
Prickly pears, fresh (1)	0.5	0.0	0	6	42
Prunes					
Canned, in heavy syrup (5)	0.2	0.0	0	2	90
Dried (10)	0.4	0.0	0	3	201
Cooked without sugar (1/2 cup)	0.3	0.0	0	2	113
Pummelo, fresh (5 1/2" diameter)	0.2	0.0	0	7	228
Quince, fresh (1)	0.1	0.0	0	4	53
Raisins (1/4 cup)	0.2	0.1	0	5	127
Raspberries					
Canned, in heavy syrup (1/2 cup)	0.2	0.0	0	4	117
Fresh (1/2 cup)	0.3	0.0	0	0	31
Frozen, sweetened (1/2 cup)	0.2	0.0	0	1	128
Rhubarb					
Fresh, diced (1/2 cup)	0.1	0.0	0	3	13
Frozen, uncooked (1/2 cup)	0.0	0.0	0	1	14
Strawberries					
Canned, in heavy syrup (1/2 cup)	0.3	0.0	0	5	117
Fresh (1/2 cup)	0.3	0.0	0	1	23
Frozen			–		
Sweetened (1/2 cup)	0.0	0.0	0	2	100
Unsweetened (1/2 cup)	0.0	0.0	0	2	26
Tamarinds, fresh (3" long × 1" wide)	0.0	0.0	0	1	5
Tangerines					
Canned					
in juice (1/2 cup)	0.0	0.0	0	7	46
in light syrup (1/2 cup)	0.1	0.0	0	8	76
Fresh (2 3/8 diameter)	0.2	0.0	0	1	37
Watermelons, fresh, diced (1/2 cup)	0.3	0.0	0	2	25

FRUITS

JUICES

Fruit and vegetable juices are a source of vitamins and contain little if any fat, saturated fat and cholesterol.

Keep in mind, however, that some juices are quite high in sodium. Use the values appearing on the following pages to help plan a daily intake providing no more than 3,000 milligrams of sodium.

Most of the foods in this book are brand name products; however, when a brand name is not specified, it means that most brands of that product provide about the same amount of fat, saturated fat and cholesterol and that these amounts do not exceed AHA criteria.

You can use those generic entries and the table below to evaluate products introduced since this book went to press.

AHA Criteria for Juices*

	Tot. Fat (g)	Sat. Fat (g)	Chol. (mg)
All juices	<0.5	<0.5	<2

* Per serving.

	Tot. Fat (g)	Sat. Fat (g)	Chol. (mg)	Sod. (mg)	Cal.
Apple juice (6 fl oz)	<0.2	0.0	0	6	90
Apricot nectar (6 fl oz)	<0.2	0.0	0	6	108
Carrot juice (6 fl oz)	0.3	0.0	0	538	73
Grape juice (6 fl oz)	0.1	0.0	0	6	114
Grapefruit juice					
Sweetened (6 fl oz)	0.2	0.0	0	3	87
Unsweetened (6 fl oz)	0.2	0.0	0	2	72
Lemon juice (2 tbsp)	0.0	0.0	0	3	3
Lime juice (2 tbsp)	0.0	0.0	0	2	3
Orange juice (6 fl oz)	0.2	0.0	0	5	78
Frozen, diluted (6 fl oz)	0.1	0.0	0	2	84
Orange and grapefruit juice (6 fl oz)	0.2	0.0	0	6	78
Papaya nectar (6 fl oz)	0.3	0.0	0	12	108
Passion fruit juice, purple,					
unsweetened (6 fl oz)	0.1	0.0	0	12	96
Peach nectar (6 fl oz)	0.0	0.0	0	12	102
Pear nectar (6 fl oz)	0.0	0.0	0	6	114
Pineapple juice (6 fl oz)	0.1	0.0	0	0	102
Prune juice (6 fl oz)	0.1	0.0	0	6	139
Sauerkraut juice, Bush's Best Kraut					
Juice (1/2 cup)	0.0	0.0	(0)	750	8
Tomato juice (6 fl oz)	0.1	0.0	0	658	3
No salt added (6 fl oz)	0.1	0.0	0	18	32
Tomato juice cocktail, Appletree*					
Tomato Clam Cocktail (6 fl oz)	0.0	0.0	(0)	310	50
Vegetable juice cocktail (6 fl oz)	0.2	0.0	0	664	34

* Appletree products are also marketed under Best Yet, Fine Fare, Food Lion, Hyde Park, Hy-Top, Parade, Piggly-Wiggly, Red & White, Roundy's, Schwegmann, Scot Lad and Tops brand names.

MAIN DISHES AND MEAL-TYPE PRODUCTS

The canned, shelf-stable and frozen main dishes and meal-type products in this section are low in fat, saturated fat and cholesterol as purchased or when prepared according to package directions. The AHA criteria below are given per 100 grams, or about 3½ ounces, of the main dish or meal-type product. The actual amounts of fat, saturated fat and cholesterol in a manufacturer's serving of a food qualifying for this book depend on the total weight of that serving (see the following tables). For example, a meal-type product that weighs 10½ ounces (3 × 3½ oz) can provide a maximum of 9 grams of fat (3 × 3 g), 3 grams of saturated fat (3 × 1 g) and 60 milligrams of cholesterol (3 × 20 mg) and still qualify for inclusion in this book.

Products listed in this book vary in sodium content. Use the values appearing on the following pages to help plan a daily intake providing no more than 3,000 milligrams of sodium.

You can use the tables below to evaluate products introduced since this book went to press.

AHA Criteria for Main Dishes and Meal-Type Products*

	Tot. Fat (g)	Sat. Fat (g)	Chol. (mg)
All main dishes and meal-type products	3 g per 100-g serving** *and* 30% or less of calories from fat	1 g per 100-g serving** *and* less than 10% of calories from fat	20 mg per 100-g serving**

* See also following table.
** 100 g = about 3½ oz.

AHA Criteria for Main Dishes and Meal-Type Products at Various Weights

Weight (oz)	Tot. Fat (g)	Sat. Fat (g)	Chol. (mg)
6	5	2	35
7	6	2	40
8	7	2	45
9	8	3	50
10	9	3	55
11	9	3	60
12	10	3	70
13	11	4	75

Meal-Type Products Not Recommended for Frequent Consumption

Some examples of meal-type products that are usually too high in fat, saturated fat and/or cholesterol to be recommended for frequent consumption are shown in the table below. Values that exceed AHA criteria are followed by asterisks. The AHA does not have criteria for sodium.

You can use the values in the table to compare these meal-type products with more-healthful alternatives listed on the following pages.

Meal-Type Products High In Fat, Saturated Fat and/or Cholesterol

	Tot. Fat (g)	Sat. Fat (g)	Chol. (mg)	Sod. (mg)	Cal.
Beef enchilada dinner (12 ounces)	29.0*	14.6*	81*	2270	750
Beef stroganoff dinner (10 ounces)	14.0*	5.6*	76*	1075	320
Chicken and noodles dinner (12 ounces)	17.6*	6.6*	96*	611	400
Macaroni and cheese dinner (12¾ ounces)	15.8*	7.1*	33	990	382

Adapted from Nutrition Data System, University of Minnesota, Minneapolis.

* These values exceed AHA criteria for meal-type products.

	Tot. Fat (g)	Sat. Fat (g)	Chol. (mg)	Sod. (mg)	Cal.
CANNED AND SHELF-STABLE ENTREES/DINNERS					
Beef—*see also* ***Oriental*** *and* ***Pasta Based***					
Dinty Moore American Classics, Roast Beef & Mashed Potatoes (10 oz)	6.0	(2.3)	45	910	260
Hormel Top-Shelf Entree, Tender Roast Beef (10 oz)	7.0	(2.6)	55	940	250
Chicken—*see also* ***Chili***, ***Oriental*** *and* ***Pasta Based***					
Hormel Top-Shelf Entree					
Chicken Cacciatore (10 oz)	1.0	(0.3)	35	690	200
Glazed Breast of Chicken (10 oz)	2.0	(0.5)	35	780	170
Light 'N Healthy Entrees, Chicken Fiesta with Beans and Rice (7.5 oz)	3.0	<1.0	10	600	170
Lunch Bucket Entrees, Dumplings 'n Chicken (7.5 oz)	2.0	(0.6)	(18)	880	140
Chili					
Hain Spicy Chili with Chicken (7½ oz)	2.0	(0.5)	40	1030	130
Health Valley Foods Vegetarian Chili with Beans, No Salt Added					
Mild (5 oz)	3.0	(0.5)	0	30	160
Spicy (5 oz)	3.0	(0.5)	0	30	160
Health Valley Foods Vegetarian Chili with Lentils, Mild (5 oz)	3.0	(0.5)	0	290	140
No Salt Added (5 oz)	3.0	(0.5)	0	65	140
Nile Spice Meals in a Cup, Chili 'n Beans					
Original (10 fl oz)	1.0	(0.1)	(0)	460	160
Spicy (10 fl oz)	1.0	(0.1)	(0)	460	160

MAIN DISHES AND MEAL-TYPE PRODUCTS

	Tot. Fat (g)	Sat. Fat (g)	Chol. (mg)	Sod. (mg)	Cal.
Oriental					
La Choy Bi-Pack					
Beef Chow Mein (¾ cup)	1.0	0.3	20	840	70
Beef Pepper (¾ cup)	2.0	0.6	17	950	80
Chicken Chow Mein (¾ cup)	3.0	0.8	18	970	80
Chicken Teriyaki (¾ cup)	2.0	0.5	20	850	85
Pork Chow Mein (¾ cup)	4.0	1.3	14	950	80
Shrimp Chow Mein (¾ cup)	1.0	0.2	19	860	70
Sweet and Sour Chicken (¾ cup)	2.0	0.4	13	440	120
La Choy Entree					
Beef Chow Mein (¾ cup)	1.0	0.4	16	890	60
Chicken Chow Mein (¾ cup)	2.0	0.5	16	800	70
Meatless Chow Mein (¾ cup)	<1.0	(0.0)	0	880	25
Sweet and Sour Chicken (¾ cup)	2.0	0.5	19	1420	240
Sweet and Sour Pork (¾ cup)	4.0	1.4	18	1540	250
Pasta Based					
Appletree* Spaghetti with Tomato Sauce and Cheese (7½ oz)	1.0	(0.5)	(2)	760	150
Chef Boyardee					
Beefaroni (7.5 oz)	6.0	(2.0)	(14)	(950)	200
Mini Ravioli (7.5 oz)	4.0	(2.0)	(18)	(955)	190
Sharks (7.5 oz)	1.0	(0.4)	(5)	770	160
Tic Tac Toe (7.5 oz)	1.0	(0.4)	(5)	950	170
Dinty Moore American Classics, Noodles & Chicken (10 oz)	6.0	(2.3)	45	970	240
Franco-American					
CircusO's Pasta in Tomato and Cheese Sauce (7½ oz)	2.0	(0.7)	(5)	860	160
Spaghetti in Tomato Sauce with Cheese (7⅜ oz)	2.0	(0.7)	(5)	840	180
SpaghettiO's in Tomato and Cheese Sauce (7½ oz)	2.0	(0.7)	(5)	880	160

* Appletree products are also marketed under Best Yet, Fine Fare, Food Lion, Hyde Park, Hy-Top, Parade, Piggly-Wiggly, Red & White, Roundy's, Schwegmann, Scot Lad and Tops brand names.

	Tot. Fat (g)	Sat. Fat (g)	Chol. (mg)	Sod. (mg)	Cal.
TeddyO's in Tomato and Cheese Sauce (7½ oz)	2.0	(0.7)	[5]	870	160
WaldO's in Tomato Sauce & Cheese (7.5 oz)	2.0	(1.0)	[2]	860	160
Healthy Choice Shelf Stable Meals or Microwaveable Cups					
Spaghetti Rings (7.5 oz)	0.0	0.0	0	460	140
Spaghetti with Meat Sauce (7.5 oz)	3.0	(0.9)	20	390	150
Hormel Top-Shelf Entree, Spaghettini (10 oz)	6.0	(2.0)	20	980	260
Kraft† Spaghetti Dinner, Mild American (1 cup)	7.0	2.0	0	630	300
Libby's Diner					
Pasta Spirals and Chicken (7.75 oz)	3.0	1.0	15	910	120
Spaghetti & Meatballs in Sauce (7.75 oz)	3.0	1.0	15	870	190
Light 'N Healthy Entrees					
Italian Style Pasta Flavored with Chicken (7.5 oz)	1.0	<1.0	10	630	130
Pasta in Wine Sauce Flavored with Beef (7.5 oz)	3.0	1.0	10	600	130
Pasta 'n Garden Vegetables (7.5 oz)	1.0	<1.0	0	630	150
Lunch Bucket Entrees					
Elbows in Tomato Sauce (7.5 oz)	2.0	(0.3)	[0]	860	190
Lasagna with Meatsauce (7.5 oz)	4.0	(1.4)	[14]	870	220
Spaghetti 'n Meatsauce (7.5 oz)	5.0	(1.7)	[39]	870	240
Nile Spice Meals in a Cup					
Pasta 'n Sauce Mediterranean (10 fl oz)	4.0	(0.5)	[5]	390	210
Pasta 'n Sauce Parmesan (10 fl oz)	4.0	(0.5)	[6]	430	210
Pasta 'n Sauce Primavera (10 fl oz)	3.0	(0.4)	[5]	360	210

Pork—see **Oriental**

Seafood—see also **Oriental**

	Tot. Fat (g)	Sat. Fat (g)	Chol. (mg)	Sod. (mg)	Cal.
Dinty Moore American Classics, Tuna & Noodles (10 oz)	8.0	(1.9)	50	1310	240

	Tot. Fat (g)	Sat. Fat (g)	(mg)	Sod. (mg)	

Turkey

Dinty Moore American Classics, Turkey & Dressing (10 oz)	5.0	(1.5)	40	910	290

FROZEN ENTREES/DINNERS

Beef—see also *Mexican, Oriental* and *Pasta Based*

Armour Classics Lite, Beef Stroganoff (11.25 oz)	6.0	(2.3)	55	510	250
Banquet Healthy Balance					
Homestyle Barbecue (10.5 oz)	5.0	(1.9)	25	680	270
Meat Loaf (11 oz)	7.0	(2.7)	30	800	270
Budget Gourmet Light and Healthy Dinners, Sirloin of Beef in Wine Sauce (11 oz)	8.0	2.0	25	560	280
Healthy Choice Dinners					
Meatloaf (12 oz)	8.0	3.0	40	560	340
Salisbury Steak (11.5 oz)	7.0	3.0	50	550	280
Yankee Pot Roast (11 oz)	4.0	2.0	55	400	260
Healthy Choice Entrees, Mushroom Gravy over Beef Sirloin Tips (9.5 oz)	6.0	2.0	35	580	250
Healthy Choice Homestyle Classics, Salisbury Steak with Mushroom Gravy (11 oz)	6.0	3.0	55	500	280
Kraft† Eating Right Entree, Swedish Meatballs (10 oz)	7.0	2.0	55	470	290
Le Menu New American Cuisine Healthy Frozen Dinners, Old Fashioned Salisbury Steak (10.25 oz)	5.0	2.0	25	480	270
Lean Cuisine Entrees, Beef Pot Roast (9 oz)	7.0	1.0	45	590	220
Ultra Slim-Fast Entrees					
Country Style Vegetables and Beef Tips (12 oz)	5.0	2.0	45	960	230
Mushroom Gravy over Salisbury Steak (10.5 oz)	5.0	(1.7)	35	830	290

	Tot. Fat (g)	Sat. Fat (g)	Chol. (mg)	Sod. (mg)	Cal.
Weight Watchers Stir Fry Single Serve Entrees, Beef Cantonese with Rice (9 oz)	4.0	1.0	15	480	220
Weight Watchers Ultimate 200 Single Serve Entrees					
London Broil (7.5 oz)	3.0	1.0	25	320	110
Veal Patty Parmigiana (8.2 oz)	4.0	1.0	50	550	150

Chicken—see also Mexican, Oriental and Pasta Based

	Tot. Fat (g)	Sat. Fat (g)	Chol. (mg)	Sod. (mg)	Cal.
Armour Classics Lite					
Chicken Ala King (11.25 oz)	7.0	(2.3)	55	630	290
Chicken Burgundy (10 oz)	2.0	(0.6)	45	780	210
Banquet Family Entrees, Chicken and Vegetables Primavera (7 oz)	3.0	(0.8)	(39)	(385)	140
Banquet Healthy Balance, Chicken Parmesan (10.8 oz)	9.0	(2.2)	50	800	300
Budget Gourmet Hearty and Healthy Dinners, Roast Chicken Breast with Herb Gravy (11.2 oz)	9.0	2.0	45	730	290
Budget Gourmet Light and Healthy Dinners					
Chicken Breast Parmigiana (11 oz)	7.0	2.0	40	440	250
Herbed Chicken Breast with Fettucini (11 oz)	6.0	2.0	45	430	240
Mesquite Chicken Breast (11 oz)	5.0	2.0	35	520	280
Budget Gourmet Light Entrees, Orange Glazed Chicken (9 oz)	3.0	1.0	25	800	290
Budget Gourmet Quick Stirs, Chicken Breast and Italian Style Vegetables (11.24 oz)	8.0	2.0	25	780	270
Dining Light Dinners					
Chicken Ala King with Rice (9 oz)	7.0	(1.9)	40	780	240
Chicken with Noodles (9 oz)	7.0	(1.9)	50	570	240
Healthy Choice Dinners					
Chicken Dijon (11 oz)	3.0	1.0	40	470	250
Chicken Parmigiana (11.5 oz)	6.0	3.0	55	340	290
Chicken and Pasta Divan (12.1 oz)	4.0	2.0	50	520	300

	Tot. Fat (g)	Sat. Fat (g)	Chol. (mg)	Sod. (mg)	Cal.
Chicken with Barbecue Sauce (12.75 oz)	6.0	2.0	60	560	390
Herb Roasted Chicken (12.3 oz)	7.0	3.0	50	470	380
Mesquite Chicken (10.5 oz)	3.0	1.0	40	390	300
Southwestern Style Chicken (12.5 oz)	5.0	2.0	60	550	340
Healthy Choice Entrees			—		
Chicken à l'Orange (9 oz)	2.0	<1.0	40	340	260
Chicken and Vegetables (11.5 oz)	3.0	1.0	25	380	280
Chicken Fettucini (8.5 oz)	4.0	2.0	45	370	240
Glazed Chicken (8.5 oz)	3.0	1.0	45	510	220
Honey Mustard Chicken (9.5 oz)	3.0	1.0	40	480	250
Healthy Choice Pasta Classics, Chicken Stir Fry with Pasta (12 oz)	5.0	1.0	30	550	300
Kraft† Eating Right Entree, Glazed Chicken Breast (10 oz)	4.0	1.0	35	560	240
Le Menu New American Cuisine Dinners, Tomato Garden Chicken (10 oz)	6.0	(1.8)	(44)	780	240
Le Menu New American Cuisine Healthy Dinners					
Golden Glazed Chicken (11 oz)	3.0	1.0	30	420	330
Herb Roasted Chicken (10 oz)	4.0	2.0	30	470	300
Mesquite Chicken (10.25 oz)	3.0	1.0	30	290	300
Salsa Chicken (10.75 oz)	4.0	1.0	35	340	300
Lean Cuisine Entrees					
Breast of Chicken Marsala (8 1/8 oz)	4.0	1.0	55	430	180
Breast of Chicken Parmesan (10 7/8 oz)	7.0	2.0	60	580	260
Chicken Cacciatore (10 7/8 oz)	7.0	2.0	45	570	280
Chicken Italiano (9 oz)	6.0	1.0	40	590	270
Chicken à l'Orange (8 oz)	4.0	1.0	55	290	280
Chicken and Vegetables (11 3/4 oz)	5.0	1.0	30	500	240
Chicken in Barbecue Sauce (8 3/4 oz)	4.0	1.0	50	590	250
Chicken in Peanut Sauce (9 oz)	7.0	2.0	45	530	290
Glazed Chicken and Vegetable Rice (8 1/2 oz)	7.0	2.0	50	590	250
Honey Mustard Chicken Breast (7 1/2 oz)	4.0	1.0	40	540	230
Oven Baked Breaded Chicken (8 oz)	5.0	2.0	35	480	200
Tyson Dinner					
Chicken Marsala (9 oz)	3.0	(1.2)	47	600	180

	Tot. Fat (g)	Sat. Fat (g)	Chol. (mg)	Sod. (mg)	Cal.
Chicken Supreme (9 oz)	6.0	(2.3)	51	470	230
Glazed Chicken with Sauce (9.25 oz)	5.0	(1.6)	44	930	250
Ultra Slim-Fast Entrees					
Chicken and Vegetables (12 oz)	3.0	<1.0	30	850	290
Mesquite Chicken (12 oz)	1.0	<1.0	65	300	350
Roasted Chicken in Mushroom Sauce (12 oz)	6.0	2.0	55	830	280
Weight Watchers Frozen Entrees, Homestyle Chicken and Noodles (9 oz)	7.0	2.0	30	450	240
Weight Watchers Smart Ones Single Serve Entrees					
Chicken Francais (8.5 oz)	1.0	<1.0	5	400	150
Chicken Mirabella (9.2 oz)	1.0	<1.0	10	420	160
Lemon Herb Chicken Piccata (7.5 oz)	1.0	<1.0	5	500	160
Weight Watchers Stir Fry Single Serve Entrees, Orange Glazed Chicken with Rice (9 oz)	2.0	<1.0	20	360	200
Weight Watchers Ultimate 200 Single Serve Entrees					
Chicken Kiev (7 oz)	5.0	2.0	15	470	190
Glazed Chicken (7.5 oz)	2.0	1.0	20	520	150
Imperial Chicken (8.5 oz)	3.0	1.0	25	420	200

Mexican

	Tot. Fat (g)	Sat. Fat (g)	Chol. (mg)	Sod. (mg)	Cal.
Banquet Healthy Balance, Chicken Enchilada (11 oz)	4.0	(1.2)	15	630	300
Healthy Choice Dinners					
Beef Enchilada (13.4 oz)	5.0	2.0	30	450	370
Chicken Enchilada (13.4 oz)	6.0	3.0	30	550	320
Salsa Chicken (11.25 oz)	2.0	1.0	50	450	240
Healthy Choice Entrees, Chicken Fajitas (7 oz)	3.0	1.0	35	310	200
Lean Cuisine Entrees, Fiesta Chicken (8 1/2 oz)	5.0	2.0	40	560	240
Lean Cuisine Lunch Express, Mexican Style Rice with Chicken (9 1/8 oz)	5.0	1.0	20	580	270

MAIN DISHES AND MEAL-TYPE PRODUCTS

165

	Tot. Fat (g)	Sat. Fat (g)	Chol. (mg)	Sod. (mg)	Cal.
Weight Watchers Frozen Entrees, Chicken Fajitas (6.75 oz)	5.0	2.0	25	490	210
Weight Watchers Smart Ones Single Serve Entrees, Fiesta Chicken (8 oz)	1.0	<1.0	20	390	210
Weight Watchers Ultimate 200 Single Serve Entrees, Beef Enchiladas Ranchero (9.12 oz)	5.0	2.0	20	500	190

Oriental

	Tot. Fat (g)	Sat. Fat (g)	Chol. (mg)	Sod. (mg)	Cal.
Armour Classics Lite					
Beef Pepper Steak (11.25 oz)	4.0	(1.5)	35	970	220
Chicken Oriental (10 oz)	1.0	(0.3)	35	660	180
Sweet and Sour Chicken (11 oz)	2.0	(0.6)	35	820	240
Banquet Healthy Balance, Sweet & Sour Chicken (10.25 oz)	4.0	(1.2)	35	590	270
Budget Gourmet Entrees, Sweet and Sour Chicken (11 oz)	5.0	(1.5)	30	620	340
Budget Gourmet Hearty and Healthy Dinners, Sweet and Sour Chicken (13 oz)	5.0	1.0	50	800	350
Budget Gourmet Light and Healthy Dinners					
Teriyaki Beef (10.75 oz)	6.0	1.0	35	520	270
Teriyaki Chicken Breast (11 oz)	6.0	1.0	30	480	300
Budget Gourmet Light and Healthy Entrees, Mandarin Chicken (10 oz)	7.0	2.0	40	670	300
Budget Gourmet Quick Stirs					
Oriental Beef with Vegetables (11 oz)	9.0	2.0	25	670	280
Oriental Vegetables and Noodles with Chicken (11 oz)	9.0	2.0	25	760	270
Chun King Entrees					
Beef Pepper Oriental (13 oz)	3.0	(1.2)	40	1300	310
Beef Teriyaki (13 oz)	2.0	(1.2)	(10)	2200	380
Crunchy Walnut Chicken (13 oz)	5.0	(1.4)	45	1700	310
Imperial Chicken (13 oz)	1.0	(0.3)	30	1540	300
Sweet and Sour Pork (13 oz)	5.0	(1.4)	25	1460	400

MAIN DISHES AND MEAL-TYPE PRODUCTS

	Tot. Fat (g)	Sat. Fat (g)	Chol. (mg)	Sod. (mg)	Cal.
Dining Light Dinners, Chicken Chow Mein with Rice (9 oz)	2.0	(0.6)	30	650	180
Healthy Choice Dinners					
Beef Pepper Steak (11 oz)	5.0	2.0	40	500	260
Chicken Oriental (11.25 oz)	1.0	<1.0	35	440	200
Sweet and Sour Chicken (11.5 oz)	2.0	<1.0	35	320	280
Teriyaki Chicken (12.25 oz)	4.0	1.0	55	560	290
Healthy Choice Entrees					
Beef Pepper Steak (9.5 oz)	4.0	2.0	40	560	250
Chicken Chow Mein (8.5 oz)	5.0	2.0	45	530	240
Mandarin Chicken (11 oz)	2.0	<1.0	45	370	240
Oriental Chicken with Spicy Peanut Sauce (9.5 oz)	5.0	1.0	45	400	280
La Choy Entrees, Beef Pepper Oriental (⅓ cup)	1.5	(0.5)	11	160	72
Le Menu New American Cuisine Frozen Dinners, Sweet and Sour Chicken (11.25 oz)	9.0	(2.4)	(43)	720	360
Lean Cuisine Entrees					
Chicken Chow Mein (9 oz)	5.0	1.0	40	500	230
Sweet and Sour Chicken (10⅜ oz)	3.0	1.0	40	370	280
Lean Cuisine Lunch Express					
Mandarin Chicken with Rice and Vegetables (9 oz)	5.0	1.0	35	570	270
Oriental Stir Fry (chicken) (9 oz)	7.0	1.0	25	590	280
Teriyaki Stir Fry (chicken) (9 oz)	5.0	1.0	30	510	260
Ultra Slim-Fast Entrees					
Beef Pepper Steak and Parsleyed Rice (12 oz)	4.0	2.0	45	690	270
Chicken Chow Mein (12 oz)	6.0	(1.7)	60	580	320
Sweet and Sour Chicken (12 oz)	2.0	<1.0	45	340	330
Weight Watchers Smart Ones Single Serve Entrees, Chicken Chow Mein (9 oz)	1.0	<1.0	20	470	170
Weight Watchers Stir Fry Single Serve Entrees					
Chicken Polynesian (9 oz)	1.0	<1.0	20	210	190
Sesame Chicken with Lo Mein Noodles (9 oz)	4.0	2.0	15	420	210

	Tot. Fat (g)	Sat. Fat (g)	Chol. (mg)	Sod. (mg)	Cal.
Vegetable Hunan and Ginger Chicken (9 oz)	2.0	<1.0	15	390	180
Pasta Based					
Banquet Entree Express, Spaghetti with Meat Sauce (8.5 oz)	4.0	(1.2)	(20)	1180	220
Banquet Family Entrees, Mostaccioli and Meat Sauce (7 oz)	3.0	(1.1)	(32)	(695)	170
Banquet Meals					
Italian Style (9 oz)	2.0	(<1.0)	5	790	180
Noodles and Chicken (10 oz)	4.0	(1.5)	40	740	170
Spaghetti and Meat Sauce (8.75 oz)	4.0	(1.2)	10	650	160
Banquet Supreme Entrees, Spaghetti with Meat Sauce (8 oz)	4.0	(1.2)	(30)	1180	220
Budget Gourmet Quick Stirs, Rigatoni with Chicken and Tomato Sauce (11.9 oz)	8.0	2.0	25	540	310
Dining Light Dinners, Lasagna with Meat Sauce (9 oz)	5.0	(2.1)	25	800	240
Healthy Choice Entrees					
Baked Cheese Ravioli (9 oz)	2.0	1.0	20	420	250
Cheese Manicotti (9.25 oz)	3.0	2.0	30	310	220
Lasagna with Meat Sauce (10 oz)	5.0	2.0	20	420	260
Healthy Choice Pasta Classics					
Fettucini with Beef and Broccoli (12 oz)	3.0	1.0	20	520	290
Fettucini with Turkey and Vegetables (12.5 oz)	6.0	3.0	60	480	350
Pasta Italiano (12 oz)	5.0	2.0	30	530	350
Pasta Shells in Tomato Sauce (12 oz)	3.0	2.0	35	470	330
Pasta with Cacciatore Chicken (12.5 oz)	3.0	<1.0	35	430	310
Pasta with Shrimp and Vegetables (12.5 oz)	4.0	2.0	50	490	270
Pasta with Teriyaki Chicken (12.6 oz)	3.0	1.0	45	370	350
Rigatoni with Chicken and Vegetables (12.5 oz)	4.0	2.0	60	430	360
Healthy Choice Quick Meals					
Macaroni and Beef (8.5 oz)	3.0	1.0	15	420	200

	Tot. Fat (g)	Sat. Fat (g)	Chol. (mg)	Sod. (mg)	Cal.
Rigatoni in Meat Sauce (9.5 oz)	6.0	2.0	30	540	260
Spaghetti with Meat Sauce (10 oz)	6.0	2.0	20	480	280
Vegetable Pasta Italiano (10 oz)	1.0	<1.0	0	330	220
Zucchini Lasagna (11.5 oz)	3.0	2.0	15	400	240
Lean Cuisine Entrees					
Angel Hair Pasta (10 oz)	5.0	1.0	10	410	240
Beef Cannelloni (9⅝ oz)	3.0	1.0	25	490	200
Cheddar Bake with Pasta and Vegetables (9 oz)	7.0	2.0	15	540	230
Cheese Lasagna (11½ oz)	6.0	3.0	25	550	280
Fettucini Primavera (10 oz)	7.0	2.0	20	580	260
Linguini with Clam Sauce (9⅝ oz)	8.0	2.0	30	560	280
Macaroni and Beef in Tomato Sauce (10 oz)	6.0	1.0	25	540	250
Marinara Twist (10 oz)	5.0	2.0	10	550	280
Rigatoni Bake (9 oz)	4.0	1.0	25	560	210
Spaghetti with Meat Sauce (11½ oz)	6.0	2.0	20	500	290
Spaghetti with Meatballs (9½ oz)	7.0	2.0	30	550	290
Tuna Lasagna (9¾ oz)	7.0	2.0	20	520	240
Zucchini Lasagna (11 oz)	6.0	2.0	20	520	260
Lean Cuisine Lunch Express					
Cheese Lasagna Casserole (9½ oz)	6.0	2.0	10	560	290
Fettucini with Chicken in Alfredo Sauce (10¼ oz)	6.0	2.0	35	540	240
Pasta with Chicken in Herb Tomato Sauce (9½ oz)	6.0	2.0	35	460	270
Pasta with Turkey in Dijon Sauce (9⅞ oz)	7.0	2.0	35	540	290
Morton Dinners, Spaghetti & Meatsauce (8.5 oz)	2.0	(0.6)	10	930	170
Swanson Frozen Dinners, Pasta with Turkey and Vegetables (11.25 oz)	9.0	(2.7)	35	670	310
Ultra Slim-Fast Entrees					
Cheese Ravioli (12 oz)	3.0	(1.5)	40	770	330
Vegetable Lasagna (12 oz)	4.0	(2.1)	15	730	240
Weight Watchers Frozen Entrees					
Baked Cheese Ravioli (9 oz)	6.0	2.0	15	560	280
Cheese Lasagna (11 oz)	7.0	2.0	20	510	290
Cheese Tortellini (9 oz)	4.0	2.0	25	510	290

	Tot. Fat (g)	Sat. Fat (g)	Chol. (mg)	Sod. (mg)	Cal.
Fettucini Alfredo (8.5 oz)	6.0	2.0	35	590	220
Garden Lasagna (11 oz)	5.0	1.0	15	460	230
Lasagna (10.25 oz)	6.0	2.0	5	510	270
Macaroni and Beef (9.5 oz)	5.0	2.0	15	540	230
Macaroni and Cheese (9 oz)	6.0	2.0	20	550	280
Spaghetti with Meat Sauce (10 oz)	7.0	1.0	5	490	240
Weight Watchers Smart Ones Single Serve Entrees					
Angel Hair Pasta (8.55 oz)	<1.0	<1.0	0	290	120
Lasagna Florentine (10 oz)	1.0	<1.0	10	460	190
Pasta Portofino (9.5 oz)	1.0	<1.0	0	220	160
Weight Watchers Ultimate 200 Single Serve Entrees, Pasta Italiano (8 oz)	4.0	2.0	5	450	190

Pork

Banquet Platters, Ham (8.25 oz)	5.0	(1.5)	35	1050	200
Morton Dinners, Glazed Ham (8 oz)	3.0	(0.9)	35	1120	230
Weight Watchers Ultimate 200 Single Serve Entrees, Ham and Cheese Pocket Sandwich (4 oz)	6.0	2.0	5	490	200

Seafood—see also Pasta Based

Budget Gourmet Hearty and Healthy Dinners, Scallops and Shrimp Marinara (13 oz)	8.0	2.0	65	730	320
Healthy Choice Dinners					
Lemon Pepper Fish (10.7 oz)	5.0	1.0	40	470	300
Shrimp Creole (11.25 oz)	2.0	<1.0	60	430	230
Shrimp Marinara (10.5 oz)	1.0	<1.0	60	320	260
Weight Watchers Smart Ones Single Serve Entrees, Shrimp Marinara with Linguini (8 oz)	1.0	<1.0	60	390	150
Weight Watchers Ultimate 200 Single Serve Entrees, Oven Baked Fish (6.64 oz)	3.0	<1.0	0	370	140

	Tot. Fat (g)	Sat. Fat (g)	Chol. (mg)	Sod. (mg)	Cal.

Turkey—see also Pasta Based

	Tot. Fat (g)	Sat. Fat (g)	Chol. (mg)	Sod. (mg)	Cal.
Banquet Cookin' Bag, Turkey Chili (4 oz)	2.0	(0.6)	15	740	80
Banquet Healthy Balance, Turkey & Gravy with Dressing (11.25 oz)	5.0	(1.5)	35	760	270
Budget Gourmet Light and Healthy Dinners, Stuffed Turkey Breast (11 oz)	6.0	2.0	35	570	250
Budget Gourmet Light and Healthy Entrees, Glazed Turkey (10 oz)	5.0	2.0	35	740	260
Budget Gourmet Quick Stirs, Home Style Turkey Breast with Vegetables (11.25 oz)	8.0	2.0	25	660	290
Healthy Choice Dinners					
Breast of Turkey (10.5 oz)	3.0	1.0	40	560	260
Turkey Tetrazzini (12.6 oz)	6.0	3.0	40	490	340
Healthy Choice Entrees					
Homestyle Turkey with Vegetables (9.5 oz)	3.0	1.0	35	470	230
Roasted Turkey and Mushrooms in Gravy (8.5 oz)	3.0	1.0	40	380	200
Healthy Choice Homestyle Classics, Sliced Turkey with Gravy and Dressing (10 oz)	4.0	2.0	50	530	270
Kraft[†] Eating Right Entree, Sliced Turkey Breast (10 oz)	7.0	2.0	50	560	250
Lean Cuisine Entrees					
Homestyle Turkey (9⅜ oz)	5.0	2.0	50	550	230
Roast Turkey with Dressing (7⅞ oz)	6.0	1.0	30	540	200
Roasted Turkey in Mushroom Sauce (8 oz)	7.0	2.0	35	540	230
Turkey Dijon (9½ oz)	6.0	2.0	45	590	210
Ultra Slim-Fast Entrees					
Glazed Turkey with Dressing (10.5 oz)	5.0	(2.2)	50	570	340
Turkey Medallions in Herb Sauce (12 oz)	6.0	2.0	40	950	280
Weight Watchers Smart Ones Single Serve Entrees, Roast Turkey Medallions (8.5 oz)	1.0	<1.0	25	440	200

MAIN DISHES AND MEAL-TYPE PRODUCTS

	Tot. Fat (g)	Sat. Fat (g)	Chol. (mg)	Sod. (mg)	Cal.

Vegetables—see also Pasta Based

Healthy Choice Entrees, Broccoli & Cheese Sauce with Baked Potato Wedges (9.5 oz)	5.0	2.0	15	510	240
La Choy Vegetables, Chop Suey (1/2 cup)	<1.0	(0.0)	0	320	10
Lean Cuisine Entrees					
Baked Potato with Sour Cream (10 3/8 oz)	6.0	2.0	15	580	220
Stuffed Cabbage and Mashed Potatoes (9 1/2 oz)	6.0	2.0	30	560	210
Weight Watchers Frozen Entrees					
Baked Potato, Chicken Divan (11 oz)	7.0	2.0	30	480	280
Baked Potato, Vegetable Primavera (10 oz)	7.0	3.0	5	460	220

Other Main Dishes and Meal-Type Products

Healthy Choice Breakfast, English Muffin Sandwich (4.25 oz)	3.0	1.0	20	510	200
Healthy Choice Quick Meals French Bread Pizza, Cheese (5.6 oz)	4.0	2.0	15	390	290
Lean Cuisine Entrees, Three Bean Chili with Rice (9 oz)	6.0	1.0	0	490	230

† = tobacco company, corporate subsidiary or parent

MEAT, POULTRY, FISH AND MEAT SUBSTITUTES

Choosing lean cuts of meat and poultry without skin is a good way to help reduce the fat, saturated fat and cholesterol content of your diet. For example, in most supermarkets, the grade of beef lowest in fat is "select." "Choice" grade is higher in fat, and "prime" grade is the highest in fat. Trimming visible fat from meat before cooking is a good way to decrease fat intake. Most fish are naturally low in fat and saturated fat and contain varying amounts of cholesterol.

Products listed in this book vary in sodium content. Use the values appearing on the following pages to help plan a daily intake providing no more than 3,000 milligrams of sodium.

Most of the foods in this book are brand name products; however, when a brand name is not specified, it means that most brands of that product provide about the same amount of fat, saturated fat and cholesterol and that these amounts do not exceed AHA criteria.

You can use those generic entries and the tables below to evaluate products introduced since this book went to press.

AHA Criteria for Meat, Poultry, Fish and Meat Substitutes*

	Tot. Fat (g)	Sat. Fat (g)	Chol. (mg)
Fish and game, cooked (3 ounces)	5	2	95
Fish and poultry, canned (2 ounces)	3	1	20
Luncheon meat, processed, including hot dogs and sausage (2 ounces)	6	2	55
Meat and poultry, cooked (3 ounces)	9	3	80
Meat, canned (2 ounces)	6	2	55
Meat substitutes (2 ounces)	3	1	<2

* Per serving.

Meat, Poultry, Fish and Meat Substitutes Not Recommended for Frequent Consumption

Some types of meat, poultry, fish and meat substitutes that are usually too high in fat, saturated fat and/or cholesterol to be recommended for frequent consumption are shown in the table below. Values that exceed AHA criteria are followed by asterisks. The AHA does not have criteria for sodium.

You can use the values in the table to compare these foods with more-healthful alternatives listed on the following pages.

Meat, Poultry, Fish and Meat Substitutes
High in Fat, Saturated Fat and/or Cholesterol

	Tot. Fat (g)	Sat. Fat (g)	Chol. (mg)	Sod. (mg)	Cal.
Bacon, broiled (1 ounce)	34.9*	4.9*	24	451	162
Beef bologna (1 ounce)	8.1*	3.4*	16	278	88
Beef liver, braised (3 ounces)	4.2	1.6	331*	59	137
Chicken, dark meat with skin, stewed (3 ounces)	12.4*	3.4*	69	59	197
Duck, domesticated, without skin, roasted (3 ounces)	9.5*	3.5*	76	55	171
Ground beef (regular), pan-fried (3 ounces)	19.2*	7.5*	75	71	260
Link pork sausage (2 ounces or about 3½ small links, 2 inches long and ¾ inch in diameter)	18.0*	6.4*	38	851	221
Picnic ham, lean and fat, roasted (3 ounces)	18.2*	6.5*	49	912	238
Prime rib of beef, lean and fat, fat trimmed to ¼ inch (3 ounces)	29.6*	12.3*	72	54	348
Shrimp, boiled, shells removed (3 ounces)	0.9	0.2	166*	190	84

Adapted from USDA Handbook No. 8 series.

* These values exceed AHA criteria for meat, poultry, fish and meat substitutes.

	Tot. Fat (g)	Sat. Fat (g)	Chol. (mg)	Sod. (mg)	Cal.
BEEF, CANNED					
Underwood Light Meat Spreads, Roast Beef (2⅛ oz)	6.0	2.0	30	210	90
BEEF, FRESH AND FROZEN					
Beef bottom round, choice, lean only					
Trimmed of visible fat, roasted (3 oz)	6.6	2.2	66	56	164
Trimmed to ¼" fat, roasted (3 oz)	7.1	2.4	66	56	168
Beef bottom round, select, lean only					
Trimmed of visible fat, roasted (3 oz)	4.6	1.5	66	56	146
Trimmed to ¼" fat, roasted (3 oz)	5.3	1.8	66	56	152
Beef eye of round, choice, lean only					
Trimmed of visible fat, roasted (3 oz)	4.8	1.8	59	53	149
Trimmed to ¼" fat, roasted (3 oz)	4.8	1.8	59	53	149
Beef eye of round, select, lean only					
Trimmed of visible fat, roasted (3 oz)	3.0	1.1	59	53	132
Trimmed to ¼" fat, roasted (3 oz)	3.4	1.2	59	53	136
Beef rib, small end, select, lean only					
Trimmed of visible fat, broiled (3 oz)	7.4	3.0	68	59	168
Trimmed to ¼" fat, broiled (3 oz)	8.2	3.3	68	59	176
Trimmed to ¼" fat, roasted (3 oz)	8.3	3.3	67	61	172
Beef shank, crosscuts, choice, lean only, trimmed to ¼" fat, simmered (3 oz)	5.4	1.9	54	66	171
Beef tenderloin, select, lean only					
Trimmed of visible fat, broiled (3 oz)	7.5	2.8	71	54	170
Trimmed to ¼" fat, broiled (3 oz)	7.4	2.8	71	54	169
Beef tip round, choice, lean only					
Trimmed of visible fat, roasted (3 oz)	5.4	1.9	69	55	153
Trimmed to ¼" fat, roasted (3 oz)	6.2	2.2	69	55	160
Beef tip round, select, lean only					
Trimmed of visible fat, roasted (3 oz)	4.5	1.6	69	55	145
Trimmed to ¼" fat, roasted (3 oz)	5.4	1.9	69	55	153
Beef top loin, choice, lean only, trimmed of visible fat, broiled (3 oz)	8.2	3.1	65	58	177

	Tot. Fat (g)	Sat. Fat (g)	Chol. (mg)	Sod. (mg)	Cal.
Beef top loin, select, lean only					
Trimmed of visible fat, broiled (3 oz)	5.9	2.2	65	58	157
Trimmed to ¼" fat, broiled (3 oz)	6.6	2.5	65	58	164
Beef top round, choice, lean only					
Trimmed of visible fat, braised (3 oz)	4.9	1.7	76	38	176
Trimmed to ¼" fat, broiled (3 oz)	5.0	1.7	71	52	160
Trimmed to ¼" fat, pan-fried (3 oz)	7.3	2.1	82	60	193
Beef top round, select, lean only					
Trimmed of visible fat, braised (3 oz)	3.4	1.2	76	38	162
Trimmed to ¼" fat, braised (3 oz)	3.9	1.3	76	38	166
Trimmed to ¼" fat, broiled (3 oz)	3.1	1.1	71	52	143
Beef top sirloin, choice, lean only					
Trimmed of visible fat, broiled (3 oz)	6.6	2.6	76	56	170
Trimmed to ¼" fat, broiled (3 oz)	6.8	2.7	76	56	172
Beef top sirloin, select, lean only					
Trimmed of visible fat, broiled (3 oz)	4.8	1.9	76	56	153
Trimmed to ¼" fat, broiled (3 oz)	5.3	2.1	76	56	158
Fairbank Farms Tender-Lite Low-Fat Ground Beef, Cooked (4 oz)	8.0	4.0	53	77	160
Ground beef, 7% fat, with carrageenan or oat bran					
No added salt, cooked (3 oz)	7.0	(2.5)	64	(53)	149
Salt added, cooked (3 oz)	7.0	(2.5)	64	(238)	149
Healthy Choice Extra-Lean Ground Beef, Cooked (4 oz)	4.0	1.0	55	240	150

CHICKEN, CANNED

	Tot. Fat (g)	Sat. Fat (g)	Chol. (mg)	Sod. (mg)	Cal.
Underwood Light Meat Spreads, Chunky Chicken (2⅛ oz)	3.0	1.0	30	330	80

CHICKEN, FRESH AND FROZEN

	Tot. Fat (g)	Sat. Fat (g)	Chol. (mg)	Sod. (mg)	Cal.
Chicken breast					
Meat and skin, roasted (3 oz)	6.6	1.9	72	60	167
Without skin, roasted (3 oz)	3.1	0.9	73	63	142
Chicken dark meat, without skin					
Roasted (3 oz)	8.3	2.3	79	79	174
Stewed (3 oz)	7.6	2.1	75	63	163

	Tot. Fat (g)	Sat. Fat (g)	Chol. (mg)	Sod. (mg)	Cal.
Chicken drumstick, without skin, roasted (1.6 oz)	2.5	0.7	41	42	76
Chicken light meat, without skin, roasted (3 oz)	3.8	1.1	72	66	147
Chicken wing, without skin, roasted (3/4 oz)	1.7	0.5	18	19	43
Tyson Frozen Boneless Chicken, Diced Meat (3 oz)	4.0	(1.1)	(65)	43	130
Tyson Fully Cooked Roasted Chicken, Roasted Breast Fillet (1 oz)	2.0	(0.6)	20	160	40
CHICKEN, PRESEASONED					
Banquet Chicken Hot Bites Breast Tenders (2.25 oz)	6.0	(1.2)	(29)	280	150
Southern Fried Breast Tenders (2.25 oz)	7.0	(1.2)	(29)	340	160
Banquet Healthy Balance Baked Boneless Chicken					
Breast Nuggets (2.25 oz)	4.0	(2.0)	30	310	120
Breast Patties (2.25 oz)	4.0	(2.0)	30	310	120
Breast Tenders (2.25 oz)	4.0	2.0	30	310	120
Banquet Snack'n Chicken (3.75 oz)	9.0	(1.5)	(43)	480	140
Chicken By George					
Cajun Style (5 oz)	8.0	(2.3)	80	890	180
Caribbean Grill (5 oz)	6.0	(1.7)	80	610	200
Country Mustard and Dill (5 oz)	7.0	(2.0)	80	640	180
Italian Style Bleu Cheese (5 oz)	8.0	(2.3)	85	890	180
Lemon Herb (5 oz)	6.0	(1.7)	70	870	170
Mesquite Barbecue (5 oz)	6.0	(1.7)	70	790	170
Mexican Style (5 oz)	7.0	(2.0)	80	760	190
Teriyaki (5 oz)	5.0	(1.4)	70	740	180
Tomato Herb with Basil (5 oz)	7.0	(2.0)	80	800	190
Tyson Marinated Chicken Breast Fillets					
Barbecue (3.75 oz)	3.0	(0.8)	(90)	490	120
Italian (3.75 oz)	3.0	(0.8)	(90)	470	120
Lemon Pepper (3.75 oz)	3.0	(0.8)	(90)	260	130
Teriyaki (3.75 oz)	3.0	(0.8)	(90)	360	130

	Tot. Fat (g)	Sat. Fat (g)	Chol. (mg)	Sod. (mg)	Cal.

FISH, CANNED

Appletree*
Chunk Light Tuna in Water (2 oz)	0.0	0.0	(10)	310	60
Solid White Tuna in Water (2 oz)	0.0	0.0	(10)	250	70
Featherweight, Pink Salmon (2 oz)	3.0	(0.8)	20	45	70
Libby's Salmon, Keta (3.7 oz)	6.0	2.0	40	450	130
Romanoff, Lumpfish Caviar (1 tbsp)	1.0	0.0	5	700	16
Salmon, chum, drained solids with bone (3 oz)	4.7	1.3	33	414	120
Tuna, light, in water, drained solids (3 oz)	0.4	0.1	(20)	303	111

FISH, FRESH AND FROZEN

Bass, freshwater, cooked using dry heat (3 oz)	4.0	0.9	74	87	124
Captain Jac					
Choice with Crab Meat (2 oz)	<1.0	0.0	5	530	60
CrabTasties Imitation Crab (2 oz)	<1.0	0.0	5	530	60
Imitation Lobster Chunkstyle (2 oz)	<1.0	0.0	10	240	50
Imitation Shrimp (2 oz)	<1.0	0.0	10	380	60
Clams, cooked, using moist heat (3 oz)	1.8	0.3	57	96	126
Cod					
Atlantic, cooked, using dry heat (3 oz)	0.7	0.1	47	66	89
Pacific, cooked, using dry heat (3 oz)	0.7	0.1	40	77	89
Crab					
Alaska king, cooked, using moist heat (3 oz)	1.3	0.1	45	911	82
Imitation Alaska king, made from surimi (3 oz)	1.1	(0.2)	17	715	87
Flounder, cooked, using dry heat (3 oz)	1.3	0.3	58	89	99

* Appletree products are also marketed under Best Yet, Fine Fare, Food Lion, Hyde Park, Hy-Top, Parade, Piggly-Wiggly, Red & White, Roundy's, Schwegmann, Scot Lad and Tops brand names.

	Tot. Fat (g)	Sat. Fat (g)	Chol. (mg)	Sod. (mg)	Cal.
Grouper, cooked, using dry heat (3 oz)	1.1	0.3	40	45	100
Haddock, cooked, using dry heat (3 oz)	0.8	0.1	63	74	95
Halibut, cooked, using dry heat (3 oz)	2.5	0.4	35	59	119
Healthy Choice Breaded Fish, 2 fillets (3.5 oz)	5.0	<1.0	30	350	160
Lobster, northern, cooked, using moist heat (3 oz)	0.5	0.1	61	323	83
Mrs. Paul's Crunchy Batter Fillets, Haddock (4.5 oz)	5.0	1.0	25	580	190
Mrs. Paul's Healthy Treasures					
Fish Fillets (3 oz)	3.0	1.0	20	210	130
Fish Fillets (4 oz)	3.0	1.0	25	290	170
Fish Sticks (2.25 oz)	3.0	1.0	15	270	110
Ocean perch, cooked, using dry heat (3 oz)	1.8	0.3	46	82	103
Octopus, common, cooked, using moist heat (3 oz)	1.8	0.4	82	(50)	140
Orange roughy, cooked, using dry heat (3 oz)	0.8	0.0	22	69	75
Pike, northern, cooked, using dry heat (3 oz)	0.8	0.1	43	42	96
Pollack, walleye, cooked, using dry heat (3 oz)	1.0	0.2	82	98	96
Redfish—see Ocean perch					
Rockfish, cooked, using dry heat (3 oz)	1.7	0.4	38	65	103
Salmon					
Chinook, smoked (3 oz)	3.7	0.8	20	666	99
Chum, cooked, using dry heat (3 oz)	4.1	0.9	81	54	131
Pink, cooked, using dry heat (3 oz)	3.8	0.6	57	73	127
Scallops, imitation, made from surimi (3 oz)	0.4	0.1	18	676	84
Scrod—see Cod, Atlantic					
Sea bass, cooked, using dry heat (3 oz)	2.2	0.6	45	74	105
Shrimp, imitation, made from surimi (3 oz)	1.3	0.3	31	599	86
Snapper, cooked, using dry heat (3 oz)	1.5	0.3	40	48	109

	Tot. Fat (g)	Sat. Fat (g)	Chol. (mg)	Sod. (mg)	Cal.
Sole—*see* Flounder					
Swordfish, cooked, using dry heat (3 oz)	4.4	1.2	43	98	132
Trout, rainbow, cooked, using dry heat (3 oz)	3.7	0.7	62	29	129
Tuna					
Bluefish, fresh, cooked, using dry heat (3 oz)	5.3	1.4	42	43	157
Yellowfin, fresh, cooked, using dry heat (3 oz)	1.0	0.3	49	40	118
Van de Kamp's Natural Fillets					
Cod (4 oz)	1.0	0.0	25	90	90
Flounder (4 oz)	2.0	0.0	35	100	100
Haddock (4 oz)	1.0	0.0	20	125	90
Ocean Perch (4 oz)	5.0	2.0	40	65	130
Sole (4 oz)	2.0	1.0	35	105	100
Whitefish, smoked (3 oz)	0.8	0.2	28	866	92
Whiting, cooked, using dry heat (3 oz)	1.4	0.3	71	113	98

GAME

	Tot. Fat (g)	Sat. Fat (g)	Chol. (mg)	Sod. (mg)	Cal.
Broken Arrow Ranch Brand Venison					
Chili Grind, Raw (6 oz)	3.1	(1.1)	120	(84)	197
Ground, Raw (6 oz)	3.4	(1.2)	125	(84)	189
Round Steak, Raw (6 oz)	0.9	(0.3)	111	(84)	171
Stew, Raw (6 oz)	3.1	(1.1)	123	(84)	189
Deer, roasted (3 oz)	2.7	1.1	95	46	134
Elk, roasted (3 oz)	1.6	0.6	62	52	124
Goat, roasted (3 oz)	2.6	0.8	64	73	122
Water buffalo, roasted (3 oz)	1.5	0.5	52	48	111

HOT DOGS/SAUSAGE

	Tot. Fat (g)	Sat. Fat (g)	Chol. (mg)	Sod. (mg)	Cal.
Armour 90% Fat Free Hot Dogs, 33% Less Salt (1.6 oz)	5.0	(2.0)	30	410	80
Fairbank Farms Tender-Lite Low Fat Sausage					
Breakfast Sausage (2 oz)	4.0	2.0	33	300	70
Italian Sausage (4 oz)	8.0	4.0	65	830	157

	Tot. Fat (g)	Sat. Fat (g)	Chol. (mg)	Sod. (mg)	Cal.
Healthy Choice Franks					
Beef (1.25 oz = 1 frank)	1.0	<1.0	15	520	60
Bunsize (1 frank)	2.0	1.0	20	570	70
Jumbo (2 oz = 1 frank)	2.0	<1.0	20	570	70
Regular (1.6 oz = 1 frank)	1.0	<1.0	15	460	50
Healthy Choice Lowfat Sausage					
Polska Kielbasa (1 oz)	1.0	<1.0	15	290	35
Smoked (1 oz)	1.0	<1.0	15	290	35
Hormel Light & Lean Dinner Link,					
Smoked (1 oz)	1.0	(0.4)	10	350	30
Hormel Light & Lean 97 Franks					
Beef (1.6 oz = 1 frank)	1.0	(0.4)	15	430	45
Meat (1.6 oz = 1 frank)	1.0	(0.4)	15	390	45
Louis Rich Turkey Sausage					
Breakfast Sausage Link (1 oz)	2.5	0.8	18	234	46
Polska Kielbasa (1 oz)	2.2	0.7	19	250	40
Smoked Sausage (1 oz)	2.3	0.7	18	252	42
Smoked Sausage with Cheese (1 oz)	2.7	0.9	18	270	46
Oscar Mayer Healthy Favorites, Hot					
Dogs (2 oz = 1 link)	1.7	0.6	22	524	55

LAMB

	Tot. Fat (g)	Sat. Fat (g)	Chol. (mg)	Sod. (mg)	Cal.
Lamb, cubed for kabob or stew (leg and shoulder), lean only, broiled (3 oz)	6.2	2.2	77	65	158
Lamb, leg, shank half, lean only, choice, roasted (3 oz)	5.7	2.0	74	56	153
Lamb, loin, lean only, choice					
Broiled (3 oz)	8.3	3.0	80	71	183
Roasted (3 oz)	8.3	3.2	74	56	171
Lamb, loin chops, lean only, broiled (3 oz)	8.3	3.0	80	71	183
Lamb, shoulder, arm, lean only, choice					
Broiled (3 oz)	7.7	2.9	78	70	170
Roasted (3 oz)	7.9	3.1	73	57	163

	Tot. Fat (g)	Sat. Fat (g)	Chol. (mg)	Sod. (mg)	Cal.

LUNCHEON MEAT, PROCESSED

Beef

Carl Buddig

Beef (1 oz)	2.0	1.0	20	430	40
Corned Beef (1 oz)	2.0	1.0	20	380	40
Pastrami (1 oz)	2.0	1.0	20	320	40

Eckrich Lean Slender Sliced, Corned Beef, Chopped, Formed, and

| Smoked (1 oz) | 1.0 | (0.4) | (12) | 290 | 40 |

Healthy Choice

| Beef Bologna (¾ oz = 1 slice) | 1.0 | <1.0 | 10 | 220 | 20 |
| Roast Beef (1 oz = 1 slice) | 1.0 | <1.0 | 15 | 280 | 35 |

Hillshire Farm Deli Select, Oven

| Roasted Cured Beef (1 oz) | 0.5 | (tr) | (15) | 270 | 31 |

Hormel Light & Lean, Roast Beef

| (deli) (1 oz) | 1.0 | <1.0 | 10 | 310 | 30 |

Klement's Deli Lean

Cooked Beef (1 oz)	0.9	(0.5)	20	370	40
Cooked Corned Beef (1 oz)	0.9	(0.4)	20	370	40
Italian Beef (1 oz)	0.9	(0.4)	20	370	40
Jellied Beef (1 oz)	0.6	(0.2)	20	370	29
Pastrami (1 oz)	0.9	(0.4)	20	370	40

Land O' Frost, Beef, Thin Sliced,

| Chopped, Pressed (1 oz) | 2.0 | (0.8) | (12) | (450) | 40 |

Oscar Mayer

| Corned Beef (.6 oz = 1 slice) | 0.3 | 0.2 | 8 | 204 | 17 |
| Pastrami (.6 oz = 1 slice) | 0.3 | 0.2 | 7 | 217 | 16 |

Roast Beef, Thin Sliced (.4 oz =

| 1 slice) | 0.4 | 0.2 | 5 | 55 | 14 |
| Smoked Beef (½ oz = 1 slice) | 0.3 | 0.1 | 7 | 173 | 14 |

Oscar Mayer Deli-Thin Brand, Roast

| Beef (.4 oz = 1 slice) | 0.4 | 0.2 | 6 | 121 | 14 |

Peter Eckrich Deli Lite

Roast Beef, Extra Lean, 97% Fat

| Free (1 oz) | 1.0 | (0.4) | (12) | 370 | 25 |

Roast Beef, Lean, 94% Fat Free

| (1 oz) | 2.0 | (0.8) | (12) | 220 | 40 |

	Tot. Fat (g)	Sat. Fat (g)	Chol. (mg)	Sod. (mg)	Cal.
Weight Watchers, Oven Roasted Cured Beef (1 oz = 1 slice)	<1.0	0.0	15	220	35

Beef and Pork

	Tot. Fat (g)	Sat. Fat (g)	Chol. (mg)	Sod. (mg)	Cal.
Healthy Choice					
Bologna (¾ oz = 1 slice)	1.0	<1.0	10	220	25
Bologna, Thin Sliced (.4 oz = 1 slice)	<1.0	<1.0	5	110	12
Klement's Deli Lean					
Honey Loaf (1 oz)	1.7	(0.5)	17	370	39
Yachtwurst (1 oz)	2.3	(0.7)	17	370	38
Oscar Mayer					
Bar-B-Q Loaf (1 oz = 1 slice)	2.3	1.0	14	333	46
Honey Loaf (1 oz = 1 slice)	0.9	0.4	15	378	33
New England Brand Sausage (.8 oz = 1 slice)	1.3	0.6	13	298	29
Peppered Loaf (1 oz = 1 slice)	1.5	0.8	14	367	39
Weight Watchers, Premium Bologna (1 oz)	3.0	0.0	20	290	45

Chicken

	Tot. Fat (g)	Sat. Fat (g)	Chol. (mg)	Sod. (mg)	Cal.
Butterball Chicken Breast (1 oz)	1.0	(0.3)	(16)	210	30
Butterball Fresh from the Deli, Smoked Chicken Breast (.3 oz = 1 slice)	<1.0	(0.0)	(5)	70	10
Chicken roll, light (3 oz)	6.3	1.7	42	497	135
Eckrich Lite, Smoked Chicken Breast (1 oz = 1 slice)	1.0	(0.4)	(14)	230	30
Healthy Choice Chicken Breast					
Oven Roasted (1 oz = 1 slice)	<1.0	<1.0	15	300	30
Oven Roasted, Thin Sliced (.3 oz = 1 slice)	<1.0	<1.0	5	90	10
Skinless (deli) (1 oz)	<1.0	<1.0	15	240	25
Smoked (1 oz = 1 slice)	<1.0	<1.0	15	240	30
Hillshire Farm Deli Select					
Oven Roasted Chicken Breast (⅓ oz = 1 slice)	<1.0	(tr)	5	100	10
Smoked Chicken Breast (1 oz)	0.2	(tr)	(15)	290	31
Klement's Deli Lean, Chicken Breast (1 oz)	2.3	(0.6)	18	200	42

	Tot. Fat (g)	Sat. Fat (g)	Chol. (mg)	Sod. (mg)	Cal.
Land O' Frost, Chicken Breast (1 oz)	<1.0	(0.0)	(14)	(300)	30
Louis Rich					
Chicken Breast					
Deluxe Oven Roasted (1 oz = 1 slice)	0.8	0.3	14	332	29
Hickory Smoked (1 oz = 1 slice)	0.7	0.3	14	368	29
Oven Roasted, Thin Sliced (.4 oz = 1 slice)	0.3	0.1	5	131	11
White Chicken					
Oven Roasted (1 oz = 1 slice)	1.3	0.5	17	329	34
Oscar Mayer Chicken Breast					
Oven Roasted (1 oz = 1 slice)	0.3	0.1	12	295	25
Smoked (1 oz = 1 slice)	0.2	0.1	11	279	25
Oscar Mayer Deli-Thin Brand, Chicken Breast, Roast (.4 oz = 1 slice)	0.3	0.1	5	152	13
Oscar Mayer Healthy Favorites, Chicken Breast, Oven Roasted (.4 oz = 1 slice)	0.1	tr	5	110	12
Weight Watchers, Roasted & Smoked Chicken Breast (¾ oz = 1 slice)	1.0	0.0	15	230	30
Pork					
Carl Buddig					
Ham (1 oz)	3.0	1.0	20	400	50
Honey Ham (1 oz)	3.0	1.0	20	400	50
Danola Ham, Lower Salt (.8 oz = 1 slice)	<1.0	(0.0)	15	330	25
Eckrich Ham					
Chopped (1 oz = 1 slice)	2.0	(0.6)	(13)	350	35
Cooked (1 oz = 1 slice)	1.0	(0.3)	(13)	380	25
Eckrich Lean 'N Fresh					
Cooked Ham (.3 oz = 1 slice)	<1.0	(0.0)	5	100	10
Smoked Ham (.3 oz = 1 slice)	<1.0	(0.0)	5	100	10
Eckrich Lean Slender Sliced, Smoked Ham, Chopped and Formed (1 oz)	2.0	(0.7)	(13)	400	40
Healthy Choice Ham					
Cooked (1 oz = 1 slice)	1.0	<1.0	10	180	20
Cooked, Baked (1 oz = 1 slice)	1.0	<1.0	10	180	20

MEAT, POULTRY, FISH AND MEAT SUBSTITUTES

185

MEAT, POULTRY, FISH AND MEAT SUBSTITUTES

	Tot. Fat (g)	Sat. Fat (g)	Chol. (mg)	Sod. (mg)	Cal.
Cooked, Thin Sliced (.3 oz = 1 slice)	<1.0	<1.0	5	90	10
Cooked, Virginia Brand (deli) (1 oz)	1.0	<1.0	15	250	30
Honey (1 oz = 1 slice)	1.0	<1.0	10	270	30
Honey, Thin Sliced (.3 oz = 1 slice)	<1.0	<1.0	5	80	10
Smoked (1 oz = 1 slice)	1.0	<1.0	15	270	30
Smoked, Thin Sliced (.3 oz = 1 slice)	<1.0	<1.0	5	90	10
Hillshire Farm Deli Select					
Baked Ham (1/3 oz = 1 slice)	<1.0	(tr)	5	110	10
Cajun Ham (1 oz)	0.9	(tr)	(15)	350	31
Honey Ham (1 oz)	0.9	(tr)	(15)	270	31
Smoked Ham (1 oz)	0.9	(tr)	(15)	300	31
Hormel Light & Lean Ham (.8 oz = 1 slice)	1.0	(0.3)	10	280	25
(Deli) (1 oz)	1.0	(0.3)	15	270	30
Sliced (1 oz)	1.0	(0.3)	15	350	30
Klement's Deli Lean					
Canadian Bacon (1 oz)	0.9	(0.3)	19	370	42
Cooked Ham (1 oz)	1.4	(0.6)	19	370	38
Honey Cured Ham (1 oz)	1.4	(0.5)	19	370	38
New England Ham (1 oz)	2.3	(0.8)	17	370	38
Roast Pork (1 oz)	1.4	(0.5)	19	370	38
Oscar Mayer					
Baked Cooked Ham (3/4 oz = 1 slice)	0.4	0.1	11	237	21
Boiled Ham (3/4 oz = 1 slice)	0.6	0.2	12	279	22
Boiled Ham, Thin Sliced (.4 oz = 1 slice)	0.4	0.1	7	160	13
Cooked Ham, Smoked (3/4 oz = 1 slice)	0.7	0.3	11	268	22
Ham, Lower Salt (3/4 oz = 1 slice)	0.6	0.3	10	173	22
Honey Ham (3/4 oz = 1 slice)	0.6	0.3	11	266	23
Oscar Mayer Deli-Thin Brand					
Cooked Ham, Smoked (.4 oz = 1 slice)	0.4	0.2	7	153	13
Honey Ham (.4 oz = 1 slice)	0.4	0.2	6	152	13
Oscar Mayer Healthy Favorites					
Boiled Ham (.4 oz = 1 slice)	0.3	0.1	7	115	13
Cooked Ham (3/4 oz = 1 slice)	0.6	0.3	10	173	22

	Tot. Fat (g)	Sat. Fat (g)	Chol. (mg)	Sod. (mg)	Cal.
Cooked Ham, Smoked (.4 oz = 1 slice)	0.3	0.2	11	114	13
Honey Ham (.4 oz = 1 slice)	0.4	0.2	6	113	13
Peter Eckrich Deli Lite, Ham					
Extra Lean, 96% Fat Free and 25% Less Sodium (1 oz)	1.0	(0.3)	(13)	240	31
25% Lower Cholesterol and Sodium (1 oz)	1.0	(0.3)	12	240	30
Swift Premium Deli Lite Ham, Extra Lean, 96% Fat Free and 25% Less Sodium (1 oz)	1.0	(0.3)	(13)	240	31
Weight Watchers					
Oven Roasted Ham (⁹⁄₄ oz = 1 slice)	<1.0	(0.0)	5	95	12
Oven Roasted Honey Ham (¹⁄₃ oz = 1 slice)	1.0	0.0	15	290	30
Premium Baked Ham (1 oz)	2.0	0.0	15	220	35
Premium Cooked Ham (1 oz = 1 slice)	1.0	0.0	15	290	30
Wilson Extra Lean Ham (1 oz)	1.0	(0.3)	(13)	(400)	30

Turkey

	Tot. Fat (g)	Sat. Fat (g)	Chol. (mg)	Sod. (mg)	Cal.
Butterball					
Turkey Breast (1 oz)	1.0	(0.3)	(12)	280	30
Honey Roasted (1 oz = 1 slice)	1.0	(0.3)	(12)	230	35
Oven Roasted (1 oz = 1 slice)	1.0	(0.3)	(12)	280	30
Smoked (1 oz = 1 slice)	1.0	(0.3)	(12)	220	30
Turkey Ham (1 oz = 1 slice)	1.0	(0.3)	(12)	390	35
Butterball Fresh from the Deli					
Honey Roasted Turkey Breast (.3 oz = 1 slice)	<1.0	(0.0)	(4)	70	10
Oven Roasted Turkey Breast (.3 oz = 1 slice)	<1.0	(0.0)	(4)	80	10
Smoked Turkey Breast (.3 oz = 1 slice)	<1.0	(0.0)	(4)	70	10
Butterball Lite Deli					
Turkey Breast, Extra Lean, 96% Fat Free and 25% Less Sodium (1 oz)	1.0	(0.3)	(12)	150	30

	Tot. Fat (g)	Sat. Fat (g)	Chol. (mg)	Sod. (mg)	Cal.
Turkey Ham, Extra Lean, 97% Fat Free (1 oz)	1.0	(0.3)	(16)	390	30
Turkey Pastrami, Extra Lean, 97% Fat Free (1 oz)	1.0	(0.3)	(15)	320	35
Carl Buddig					
Turkey (1 oz)	3.0	1.0	15	340	50
Turkey Ham (1 oz)	2.0	1.0	15	430	40
Eckrich Lean 'N Fresh					
Oven Roasted Turkey Breast (.3 oz = 1 slice)	<1.0	(0.0)	(4)	80	10
Smoked Turkey Breast (.3 oz = 1 slice)	<1.0	(0.0)	(4)	70	10
Eckrich Lean Slender Sliced, White Turkey, Smoked (1 oz)	2.0	(0.6)	(12)	300	45
Eckrich Lite					
Oven Roasted Turkey Breast (1 oz = 1 slice)	1.0	(0.3)	(12)	(300)	30
Smoked Turkey Breast (1 oz = 1 slice)	1.0	(0.3)	(12)	(300)	30
Healthy Choice					
Turkey Breast					
Honey Roasted & Smoked (1 oz = 1 slice)	1.0	<1.0	15	230	35
Oven Roasted (1 oz = 1 slice)	1.0	<1.0	10	290	30
Smoked (1 oz = 1 slice)	1.0	<1.0	10	240	30
Turkey Ham (1 oz = 1 slice)	1.0	<1.0	20	300	30
Hillshire Farm Deli Select					
Honey Roasted Turkey Breast (1/3 oz = 1 slice)	<1.0	(tr)	5	100	10
Oven Roasted Turkey Breast (1 oz)	0.2	(tr)	(15)	340	31
Smoked Turkey Breast (1 oz)	0.2	(tr)	(15)	290	31
Turkey Ham (1/3 oz = 1 slice)	<1.0	(tr)	5	100	10
Hormel Light & Lean					
Turkey, Boneless (1 oz)	<1.0	(0.0)	10	270	25
Turkey, Sliced (1 oz)	1.0	(0.3)	10	420	30
Turkey Breast (deli) (1 oz)	<1.0	<1.0	10	140	25
Klement's Deli Lean, Turkey Breast (1 oz)	0.6	(0.2)	22	261	29
Land O' Frost					
Turkey Breast (1 oz)	<1.0	(0.0)	(12)	(400)	30

MEAT, POULTRY, FISH AND MEAT SUBSTITUTES

188

	Tot. Fat (g)	Sat. Fat (g)	Chol. (mg)	Sod. (mg)	Cal.
Turkey Ham, Thin Sliced, Chopped, Pressed (1 oz)	3.0	(1.0)	(16)	(280)	50
Louis Rich					
Turkey					
Smoked (1 oz)	1.0	0.4	11	263	33
Cotto Salami (1 oz)	2.7	0.8	22	289	42
Luncheon Loaf (1 oz = 1 slice)	2.8	0.8	16	271	45
Salami (1 oz)	2.7	0.8	21	285	43
Turkey Breast					
Honey Roasted (1 oz = 1 slice)	0.8	0.3	12	319	32
Oven Roasted (1 oz)	0.7	0.3	11	312	30
Oven Roasted, Thin Sliced (.4 oz = 1 slice)	0.3	0.1	4	123	12
Smoked (¾ oz = 1 slice)	0.3	0.1	9	212	21
Smoked, Thin Sliced (.4 oz = 1 slice)	0.1	tr	5	111	11
Turkey Ham (1 oz)	1.6	0.4	20	317	35
(round) (1 oz = 1 slice)	1.2	0.3	20	303	34
(square) (¾ oz = 1 slice)	0.5	0.2	15	233	22
Chopped (1 oz = 1 slice)	2.3	0.8	22	291	42
Honey Cured (1 oz = 1 slice)	0.6	0.2	15	222	22
Thin Sliced (.4 oz = 1 slice)	0.3	0.1	8	122	11
Turkey Pastrami (1 oz = 1 slice)	1.1	0.3	20	296	32
(square) (.8 oz = 1 slice)	0.8	0.2	15	261	24
Thin Sliced (.4 oz = 1 slice)	0.4	0.2	7	125	11
Louis Rich Deli-Thin Brand					
Hickory Smoked Turkey Breast					
(11 g = 1 slice)	<1.0	(tr)	5	120	10
Oven Roasted Turkey Breast (11 g = 1 slice)	<1.0	(tr)	5	130	12
Smoked Turkey Ham (11 g = 1 slice)	<1.0	(tr)	10	130	12
Mr. Turkey					
Oven Roasted Turkey Breast (1 oz = 1 slice)	1.0	(0.3)	15	280	35
Smoked Turkey (1 oz = 1 slice)	<1.0	(0.0)	15	220	30
Turkey Ham (1 oz = 1 slice)	1.0	(0.3)	20	290	30
Oscar Mayer Turkey Breast					
Oven Roasted (1 oz = 1 slice)	0.4	0.1	8	245	25
Smoked (¾ oz = 1 slice)	0.2	0.1	10	273	19

	Tot. Fat (g)	Sat. Fat (g)	Chol. (mg)	Sod. (mg)	Cal.
Oscar Mayer Deli-Thin Brand					
Turkey Breast, Roast (.4 oz = 1 slice)	0.3	0.1	7	158	12
Turkey Breast, Smoked (.4 oz = 1 slice)	0.1	tr	5	156	11
Oscar Mayer Healthy Favorites Turkey Breast					
Oven Roasted (.4 oz = 1 slice)	0.1	tr	5	101	11
Oven Roasted (1 oz = 1 slice)	0.4	0.1	8	232	25
Smoked (.4 oz = 1 slice)	0.1	tr	5	81	11
Turkey ham, cured, thigh meat (3 oz)	4.3	1.5	(16)	848	110
Turkey pastrami (1 oz)	1.8	0.5	15	297	40
Turkey roll, light and dark meat (3 oz)	5.9	1.7	47	498	126
Weight Watchers					
Oven Roasted Turkey Breast (1 oz)	<1.0	0.0	15	240	30
Smoked Turkey Breast (1 oz)	1.0	0.0	10	260	30

MEAT SUBSTITUTES

	Tot. Fat (g)	Sat. Fat (g)	Chol. (mg)	Sod. (mg)	Cal.
Heartline Lite Meatless Meats					
Beef Fillet, made as directed (1 oz)	0.0	0.0	0	270	44
Canadian Bacon Style, made as directed	0.0	0.0	0	270	44
Chicken Fillet, made as directed (1 oz)	0.0	0.0	0	270	44
Ground Beef, made as directed	0.0	0.0	0	270	44
Pepperoni Style, made as directed	0.0	0.0	0	270	44
La Loma					
Tender Bits (2 oz = 4 pieces)	3.0	(0.5)	0	260	80
Tender Rounds (2.6 oz = 6 pieces)	4.0	(0.6)	0	310	120
Vege-Burger (1/2 cup)	2.0	(0.3)	0	190	110
Worthington					
Bolono (1 1/3 oz = 2 slices)	2.0	(0.5)	0	390	60
Choplets (3 1/4 oz = 2 slices)	2.0	(0.3)	0	440	100
Multigrain Cutlets (3 1/4 oz = 2 slices)	2.0	(0.3)	0	550	90
Vegetable Skallops (3 oz = 1/2 cup)	2.0	(0.3)	0	430	90
No Salt Added (3 oz = 1/2 cup)	1.0	(<1.0)	0	80	80
Vegetable Steaks (3.2 oz = 2 1/2 pieces)	2.0	(0.3)	0	400	110
Vegetarian Burger (4 oz = 1/2 cup)	4.0	1.0	0	780	150

	Tot. Fat (g)	Sat. Fat (g)	Chol. (mg)	Sod. (mg)	Cal.
No Salt Added (4 oz = ½ cup)	4.0	1.0	0	170	150
Vegetarian Cutlets (3¼ oz = 2 slices)	2.0	(0.3)	0	270	100

PORK

	Tot. Fat (g)	Sat. Fat (g)	Chol. (mg)	Sod. (mg)	Cal.
Canadian bacon, grilled (3 oz)	7.2	2.4	49	1316	157
Ham, boneless, extra lean					
Roasted (3 oz)	4.7	1.5	45	1023	123
Roasted, canned (3 oz)	4.1	1.4	25	966	116
Healthy Choice Ham, Honey Cured					
(deli) (1 oz)	1.0	<1.0	15	300	30
Hormel Light & Lean 97 Ham,					
Boneless (1 oz)	1.0	(0.3)	15	320	30
Jones					
Canadian Bacon (½ oz = 1 slice)	1.0	0.3	7	160	30
Family Ham (1 oz = 1 slice)	1.5	0.5	17	330	40
Ham Slices (.8 oz = 1 slice)	1.0	0.2	14	210	30
Oscar Mayer					
Boneless Jubilee Ham (1 oz)	2.4	0.8	15	365	43
Breakfast Ham (1.5 oz = 1 slice)	1.5	0.6	21	536	47
Canadian Style Bacon (.8 oz = 1 slice)	1.0	0.3	11	305	28
Jubilee Ham, Canned (1 oz)	1.0	0.4	14	287	29
Jubilee Ham, Slices (1 oz)	1.0	0.4	14	338	28
Jubilee Ham Steaks (2 oz = 1 slice)	1.8	0.7	30	750	55
Pork, boneless loin chops, lean only, broiled (3 oz)	6.6	2.3	68	55	173
Pork, boneless sirloin chops					
Lean and fat, broiled (3 oz)	7.3	2.5	78	47	177
Lean only, broiled (3 oz)	5.7	1.9	78	48	164
Pork, center loin chops, lean only, broiled (3 oz)	6.9	2.5	70	51	171
Pork, center loin roasts, lean only, roasted (3 oz)	7.7	2.8	67	56	169
Pork, center rib chops, lean only, broiled (3 oz)	8.3	2.9	69	55	186

SAUSAGE—see **HOT DOGS/SAUSAGE**

	Tot. Fat (g)	Sat. Fat (g)	Chol. (mg)	Sod. (mg)	Cal.
TURKEY, CANNED					
Swanson					
Premium Chunk Poultry, White Turkey					
(2.5 oz)	1.0	(0.9)	(56)	260	80
Premium Chunk Turkey (2.5 oz)	3.0	(0.9)	(61)	270	90
Underwood Light Meat Spreads,					
Chunky Turkey (2⅛ oz)	2.0	<1.0	25	330	75
TURKEY, FRESH AND FROZEN					
Healthy Choice Turkey Breast,					
Skinless Honey Roasted &					
Smoked (deli) (1 oz)	<1.0	<1.0	15	220	30
Louis Rich Breast of Turkey					
Barbecued (1 oz)	0.5	0.1	12	336	30
Hickory Smoked (1 oz)	0.3	0.1	13	372	28
Honey Roasted (1 oz)	0.3	0.2	12	340	29
Oven Roasted (1 oz)	0.3	0.1	12	319	26
Louis Rich Hen Turkey Breast with No					
Wing Portion (1 oz)	2.0	0.4	21	19	51
Louis Rich					
Lean Ground Turkey (1 oz)	2.1	0.7	25	32	52
with Natural Flavorings (1 oz)	2.2	0.7	25	33	49
Turkey Breast (1 oz)	1.3	0.6	21	22	45
Roast (1 oz)	0.8	0.3	19	20	42
Slices (1 oz)	0.5	0.1	18	24	39
Smoked (1 oz)	1.0	0.3	15	291	31
Steaks (1 oz)	0.5	0.1	18	24	38
Tenderloins (1 oz)	0.4	0.2	19	23	38
Whole Turkey, Excluding Giblets					
(1 oz)	2.3	0.7	24	24	52
The Turkey Store Turkey Breast					
Ground, raw (3½ oz)	1.0	<1.0	45	65	100
Slices, raw (3½ oz)	1.0	<1.0	45	75	100
Strips, raw (3½ oz)	1.0	<1.0	45	75	100
Tenderloins, raw (3½ oz)	1.0	<1.0	45	75	100
Turkey					
Dark meat, without skin, roasted					
(3 oz)	6.1	2.1	72	67	159

	Tot. Fat (g)	Sat. Fat (g)	Chol. (mg)	Sod. (mg)	Cal.
Light meat, without skin, roasted (3 oz)	2.7	0.9	59	54	133
Turkey, young toms					
Dark meat without skin, roasted (3 oz)	5.9	2.0	75	70	158
Light meat only, roasted (3 oz)	2.5	0.8	59	58	129
Light meat with skin, roasted (3 oz)	6.5	1.8	64	57	163
Meat only, roasted (3 oz)	4.0	1.3	66	63	143
Turkey By George					
Hickory Barbecue (5 oz)	5.0	(1.5)	65	840	190
Italian Style Parmesan (5 oz)	5.0	(1.5)	70	860	170
Lemon Pepper (5 oz)	4.0	(1.2)	50	830	160
Mustard Tarragon (5 oz)	6.0	(1.8)	80	830	180

PASTA, RICE AND OTHER GRAIN PRODUCTS

Pasta, rice and other grain products are naturally very low in fat and saturated fat, and many are low in cholesterol. However, using pastas made with egg yolk or making recipes that include egg yolk increases the cholesterol. Recipes calling for ingredients such as margarine, oil, butter, bacon and cheese can be high in fat and saturated fat. Many packaged mixes are just as good when made with little or none of the margarine or oil called for in the directions.

Products listed in this book vary in sodium content. Use the values appearing on the following pages to help plan a daily intake providing no more than 3,000 milligrams of sodium.

Most of the foods in this book are brand name products; however, when a brand name is not specified, it means that most brands of that product provide about the same amount of fat, saturated fat and cholesterol and that these amounts do not exceed AHA criteria.

You can use those generic entries and the tables below to evaluate products introduced since this book went to press.

AHA Criteria for Pasta, Rice and Other Grain Products*

	Tot. Fat (g)	Sat. Fat (g)	Chol. (mg)
Pasta, rice and other grain products	3	<0.5	<2
Pasta salad	3	1	<2

* Per serving.

Some types of rice and other grain products that are usually too high in fat, saturated fat and/or cholesterol to be recommended for frequent consumption are shown in the table below. Values that exceed AHA criteria are followed by asterisks. The AHA does not have criteria for sodium.

You can use the values in the table to compare these foods with more-healthful alternatives listed on the following pages.

Rice and Other Grain Products
High in Fat, Saturated Fat and/or Cholesterol

	Tot. Fat (g)	Sat. Fat (g)	Chol. (mg)	Sod. (mg)	Cal.
Chinese chow mein noodles (.9 ounce)	7.7*	1.1*	0	110	132
Rice made from commercial seasoned mix with margarine (5 ounces)	6.0*	1.4*	1	833	189

Adapted from USDA Handbook No. 8 series.
* These values exceed AHA criteria for rice and other grain products.

	Tot. Fat (g)	Sat. Fat (g)	Chol. (mg)	Sod. (mg)	Cal.
COUSCOUS—see RICE/OTHER GRAIN PRODUCTS					
KASHI—see RICE/OTHER GRAIN PRODUCTS					

PASTA

Dry Pasta

Macaroni					
Plain, cooked (1 cup)	0.9	0.1	0	1	197
Vegetable, cooked (1 cup)	0.1	0.0	0	9	171
Whole-wheat, cooked (1 cup)	0.8	0.1	0	4	174
Noodles					
Japanese soba, cooked (1 cup)	<1.0	0.0	0	68	113
Japanese somen, cooked (1 cup)	<1.0	0.0	0	284	230
Spaghetti					
Plain, cooked (5 oz = 1 cup)	0.9	0.1	0	1	197
Spinach, cooked (1 cup)	0.9	0.1	0	20	183
Whole-wheat, cooked (1 cup)	0.8	0.1	0	4	174

Frozen/Refrigerated Pasta

Aunt Vi's Pre Boiled Lasagna Sheets, Frozen (1.6 oz)	<1.0	(0.0)	0	10	100

RICE/OTHER GRAIN PRODUCTS

Couscous, cooked (1 cup)	<1.0	0.0	0	9	201
Green Giant Rice Originals, Rice Pilaf (½ cup)	1.0	(<1.0)	2	530	110
Hain 3-Grain Side Dish					
Chicken Meatless Style Side Dish (½ cup)	1.0	(<1.0)	0	390	100
Herb (½ cup)	1.0	(<1.0)	0	470	80
Kashi pilaf					
Breakfast, made with water (2 oz dry = ½ cup cooked)	1.0	(0.1)	0	5	177

	Tot. Fat (g)	Sat. Fat (g)	Chol. (mg)	Sod. (mg)	Cal.
Quicker cooking, made with water (2½ oz dry = ½ cup cooked)	1.0	(0.2)	0	5	177
Regular, made with water (½ cup)	1.0	(0.1)	0	5	177
La Choy Chinese Fried Rice (¾ cup)	1.0	0.1	0	820	190
Lipton Long Grain and Wild Rice, Mushrooms and Herbs (½ cup)	0.0	0.0	0	470	130
Lipton Rice and Sauce Mix, Chicken Flavor (½ cup)	2.0	0.0	(0)	490	130
Mahatma Rice Mix					
Red Beans and Rice, made without butter or margarine (½ cup)	0.0	0.0	0	620	140
Yellow, made without butter or margarine (½ cup)	0.0	0.0	0	480	100
Brown or White, made without butter or margarine (½ cup)	0.0	0.0	0	0	100
Minute Rice					
Boil-in-Bag Rice, made without salt or butter (½ cup)	0.0	0.0	0	0	90
Instant Brown Rice, made without salt or butter (½ cup)	1.0	(0.1)	0	5	120
Original, made without salt or butter (⅔ cup)	0.0	0.0	0	5	120
Old El Paso Spanish Rice (½ cup)	1.0	0.0	0	400	70
Pritikin Brown Rice					
Pilaf, made with water (½ cup)	0.7	0.0	0	40	90
Spanish, made with water (½ cup)	0.7	0.0	0	11	90
Pritikin Dinner Mix					
Cajun, made with water only (1 cup)	1.3	0.1	0	14	170
Mexican, made with water only (1 cup)	1.2	0.1	0	87	170
Oriental, made with water only (1 cup)	1.2	0.0	0	189	170
Rice					
Brown, long-grain, made without salt (1 cup)	2.0	0.0	0	9	216
Carolina, brown or white, made without butter or margarine (½ cup)	0.0	0.0	0	0	100
River, brown, made without butter or margarine (½ cup)	0.0	0.0	0	0	100

PASTA, RICE AND OTHER GRAIN PRODUCTS

197

	Tot. Fat (g)	Sat. Fat (g)	Chol. (mg)	Sod. (mg)	Cal.
White, long-grain, made without salt (1 cup)	1.0	0.0	0	4	264
Wild, made without salt (1 cup)	1.0	0.0	0	6	165
Success Boil-in-the-Bag Rice					
Brown, made without butter or margarine (1/2 cup)	0.0	0.0	0	5	100
White, made without butter or margarine (1/2 cup)	0.0	0.0	0	0	90
Success Rice Mix					
Broccoli and Cheese, made without butter or margarine (1/2 cup)	1.0	0.5	5	310	120
Brown and Wild Rice, made without butter or margarine (1/2 cup)	0.0	0.0	0	500	120
Spanish Rice, made without butter or margarine (1/2 cup)	0.0	0.0	0	450	110
Ultra Slim-Fast Microwaveable Rice Entrees					
Rice and Chicken Sauce (2.3 oz)	1.0	(0.3)	(<1)	1080	240
Rice and Oriental Style Sauce (2.3 oz)	1.0	(0.1)	(0)	900	240

SALAD DRESSINGS AND SANDWICH SPREADS

Some of the salad dressings and sandwich spreads in this section are high in total fat; however, they and the other products on the following pages contain little if any saturated fat and cholesterol as purchased or when prepared according to package directions.

Products listed in this book vary in sodium content. Use the values appearing on the following pages to help plan a daily intake providing no more than 3,000 milligrams of sodium.

You can use the tables below to evaluate products introduced since this book went to press.

AHA Criteria for Salad Dressings and Sandwich Spreads*

	Tot. Fat (g)	Sat. Fat (g)	Chol. (mg)
All salad dressings and sandwich spreads	**	1	<2

* Per serving.

** No criterion; these foods are naturally high in fat but low in saturated fat.

Salad Dressings Not Recommended for Frequent Consumption

Some types of salad dressing that are usually too high in saturated fat and/or cholesterol to be recommended for frequent consumption are shown in the table below. Values that exceed AHA criteria are followed by asterisks. The AHA does not have criteria for sodium.

You can use the values in the table to compare these salad dressings with more-healthful alternatives listed on the following pages.

Salad Dressings High in Saturated Fat and/or Cholesterol

	Tot. Fat (g)	Sat. Fat (g)	Chol. (mg)	Sod. (mg)	Cal.
French dressing (2 tablespoons)	12.8	3.0*	(18)*	427	134
Italian dressing (2 tablespoons)	14.2	2.0*	(0)	232	137
Mayonnaise (1 tablespoon)	11.0	1.6*	8*	78	99

Adapted from USDA Handbook No. 8 series.

* These values exceed AHA criteria for salad dressings.

	Tot. Fat (g)	Sat. Fat (g)	Chol. (mg)	Sod. (mg)	Cal.
BLUE CHEESE SALAD DRESSINGS					
Barondorf Lite Dressing, Bleu Cheese (1 tbsp)	0.0	0.0	(0)	130	7
Healthy Sensations! Salad Dressing, Blue Cheese (1 tbsp)	(<1.0)	(0.0)	0	140	20
Hidden Valley Ranch Low Fat Salad Dressing, Blue Cheese (1 tbsp)	0.0	0.0	0	140	10
Kraft† Free Nonfat Pourable Dressing, Blue Cheese (1 tbsp)	0.0	0.0	0	120	16
Marie's Lite & Luscious Reduced Calorie Dressing, Chunky Blue Cheese (.55 oz = 1 tbsp)	3.0	0.0	0	115	50
CAESAR SALAD DRESSINGS					
Hain No Oil Dry Dressing Mix, Caesar, made as directed (1 tbsp)	<1.0	(0.0)	0	200	6
Weight Watchers Salad Dressing Caesar (1 tbsp)	1.0	0.0	0	200	16
Caesar (¾ oz = 1 single serv)	0.0	0.0	0	270	6
Wish-Bone Salad Dressing, Lite Caesar with Olive Oil (1 tbsp)	3.0	(0.4)	0	170	30
CATALINA SALAD DRESSINGS					
Kraft† Free Nonfat Salad Dressing, Catalina (1 tbsp)	0.0	0.0	0	120	16
Kraft† Reduced Calorie Salad Dressing, Catalina (1 tbsp)	1.0	0.0	0	120	18
CUCUMBER SALAD DRESSINGS					
Henri's Light Salad Dressing, Creamy Cucumber (1 tbsp)	2.0	0.0	0	210	35
Herb Magic Reduced Calorie Dressing, Creamy Cucumber (1 tbsp)	0.0	0.0	0	100	8

SALAD DRESSINGS AND SANDWICH SPREADS

	Tot. Fat (g)	Sat. Fat (g)	Chol. (mg)	Sod. (mg)	Cal.
Weight Watchers Salad Dressing, Creamy Cucumber (1 tbsp)	0.0	0.0	0	85	18

FRENCH SALAD DRESSINGS

	Tot. Fat (g)	Sat. Fat (g)	Chol. (mg)	Sod. (mg)	Cal.
Barondorf Lite Dressing, French Style (1 tbsp)	<1.0	(0.0)	[0]	130	6
Featherweight Salad Dressing, French (1 tbsp)	0.0	0.0	0	15	14
Hain No Oil Dry Dressing Mix, French, made as directed (1 tbsp)	0.0	0.0	0	340	12
Healthy Sensations! Salad Dressing, French (1 tbsp)	(<1.0)	(0.0)	0	120	20
Henri's Choice Fat Free Salad Dressing, French (1 tbsp)	0.0	0.0	0	120	20
Henri's Salad Dressing Light French (1 tbsp)	2.0	0.0	0	135	40
Light Hearty French (1 tbsp)	2.0	0.0	0	105	35
Hidden Valley Ranch Low Fat Salad Dressing, French (1 tbsp)	0.0	0.0	0	115	20
Kraft† Free Nonfat Salad Dressing, French (1 tbsp)	0.0	0.0	0	120	20
Kraft† Reduced Calorie Salad Dressing, French (1 tbsp)	1.0	0.0	0	120	20
Pritikin Salad Dressing, Sweet & Spicy French Style (1 tbsp)	0.1	0.0	0	2	18
Seven Seas Light Reduced Calorie Dressing, French (1 tbsp)	3.0	0.0	0	210	35
Slim-ette Low Calorie Dressing, French Style (1 tbsp)	0.0	0.0	0	130	6
Ultra Slim-Fast Salad Dressings, French (1 tbsp)	<1.0	(0.0)	0	150	20
Western Dressing, Lite French (1 tbsp)	1.0	0.2	0	125	35
Western Fat Free Dressing, French (1 tbsp)	0.0	0.0	0	120	20
Wish-Bone Salad Dressing Lite French Style (1 tbsp)	(<1.0)	(0.0)	0	140	18
Sweet 'n Spicy French Dressing (1 tbsp)	6.0	<1.0	0	160	70

SALAD DRESSINGS AND SANDWICH SPREADS

	Tot. Fat (g)	Sat. Fat (g)	Chol. (mg)	Sod. (mg)	Cal.
HERB SALAD DRESSINGS					
Barondorf Lite Dressing, Dill (1 tbsp)	0.0	0.0	(0)	130	6
Good Seasons Salad Dressing Mix for Fat Free Dressing, Zesty Herb, made with vinegar and water (1 tbsp)	0.0	0.0	0	150	6
Hain No Oil Dry Dressing Mix, Herb, made as directed (1 tbsp)	0.0	0.0	0	140	2
Herb Magic Reduced Calorie Dressing, Herb Basket (1 tbsp)	0.0	0.0	0	170	6
Seven Seas Light Reduced Calorie Dressing, Viva Herbs and Spices! (1 tbsp)	3.0	0.0	0	200	30
ITALIAN SALAD DRESSINGS					
Barondorf Lite Dressing					
Creamy Italian (1 tbsp)	<1.0	(0.0)	0	130	6
Italian (1 tbsp)	<1.0	(0.0)	0	130	4
Bernstein's Light Fantastic Dressing					
Cheese and Garlic Italian (1 tbsp)	5.0	0.0	0	170	50
Italian (1 tbsp)	<1.0	0.0	0	150	18
Good Seasons Lite Salad Dressing Mix					
Cheese Italian, made with vinegar, water and salad oil (1 tbsp)	3.0	(0.4)	0	130	25
Italian, made with vinegar, water and salad oil (1 tbsp)	3.0	(0.4)	0	170	25
Zesty Italian, made with vinegar, water and salad oil (1 tbsp)	3.0	(0.4)	0	130	25
Good Seasons Salad Dressing Mix for Fat Free Dressing					
Creamy Italian, made with skim milk, vinegar and water (1 tbsp)	0.0	0.0	0	140	8
Italian, made with vinegar and water (1 tbsp)	0.0	0.0	0	170	6
Hain Canola Oil Salad Dressing, Italian (1 tbsp)	5.0	(0.3)	0	150	50

	Tot. Fat (g)	Sat. Fat (g)	Chol. (mg)	Sod. (mg)	Cal.
Hain No Oil Dry Dressing Mix, Italian, made as directed (1 tbsp)	0.0	0.0	0	170	2
Healthy Sensations! Salad Dressing, Italian (1 tbsp)	(<1.0)	(0.0)	0	140	6
Henri's Choice Fat Free Salad Dressing, Italian (1 tbsp)	0.0	0.0	0	160	6
Henri's Salad Dressing, Light Creamy Italian (1 tbsp)	2.0	0.0	0	230	30
Herb Magic Reduced Calorie Dressing, Italian (1 tbsp)	0.0	0.0	0	125	4
Hidden Valley Ranch Low Fat Salad Dressing, Italian Parmesan (1 tbsp)	0.0	0.0	0	140	10
Kraft† Free Nonfat Salad Dressing, Italian (1 tbsp)	0.0	0.0	0	210	6
Kraft† Salad Dressing, Oil-Free Italian (1 tbsp)	0.0	0.0	0	220	4
Marie's Lite & Luscious Reduced Calorie Dressing, Creamy Italian Garlic (.55 oz = 1 tbsp)	1.0	0.0	0	120	40
Seven Seas Free Nonfat Dressing, Viva Italian (1 tbsp)	0.0	0.0	0	220	4
Seven Seas Light Reduced Calorie Dressing, Viva Italian (1 tbsp)	3.0	0.0	0	230	30
Slim-ette Low Calorie Dressing Creamy Italian (1 tbsp)	0.0	0.0	(0)	130	6
Italian (1 tbsp)	<1.0	0.0	0	130	6
Ultra Slim-Fast Salad Dressings, Italian (1 tbsp)	<1.0	(0.0)	0	170	6
Walden Farms Reduced Calorie Salad Dressing, Italian (1 tbsp)	0.0	0.0	0	300	9
No Sugar Added (1 tbsp)	0.0	0.0	0	180	6
Sodium Free (1 tbsp)	0.0	0.0	0	5	9
Weight Watchers Salad Dressing Creamy Italian (1 tbsp)	0.0	0.0	0	85	12
Italian Style (1 tbsp)	0.0	0.0	0	200	6
Italian Style (3/4 oz = 1 single serv)	0.0	0.0	0	270	8
Western Dressing, Lite Italian (1 tbsp)	2.0	(0.3)	0	130	30
Wish-Bone Salad Dressing Blended Italian (1 tbsp)	4.0	<1.0	0	210	35
Classic Olive Oil Italian (1 tbsp)	3.0	0.0	0	200	35

	Tot. Fat (g)	Sat. Fat (g)	Chol. (mg)	Sod. (mg)	Cal.
Lite Creamy Italian (1 tbsp)	(<1.0)	(0.0)	0	140	25
Lite Italian (½ oz = 1 tbsp)	0.0	0.0	0	250	6

MAYONNAISE/MAYONNAISE-TYPE DRESSINGS

	Tot. Fat (g)	Sat. Fat (g)	Chol. (mg)	Sod. (mg)	Cal.
Best Foods Cholesterol Free Reduced Calorie Mayonnaise (1 tbsp)	5.0	1.0	0	80	50
Bright Day					
Cholesterol Free Dressing (1 tbsp)	6.0	1.0	0	75	60
Light Cholesterol Free Dressing (1 tbsp)	5.0	1.0	0	140	45
Hain Canola Oil Reduced Calorie Mayonnaise (1 tbsp)	5.0	0.0	0	160	60
Hellmann's Cholesterol Free Reduced Calorie Mayonnaise (1 tbsp)	5.0	1.0	0	80	50
Kraft† Free Nonfat Mayonnaise Dressing (1 tbsp)	0.0	0.0	0	190	12
Kraft† Miracle Whip Free Nonfat Dressing (1 tbsp)	0.0	0.0	0	210	20
Smart Beat					
Light Reduced Calorie Mayonnaise Dressing (1 tbsp)	4.0	<1.0	0	110	40
Nonfat Mayonnaise Dressing (1 tbsp)	0.0	0.0	0	115	12
Weight Watchers, Fat Free Whipped Dressing (1 tbsp)	0.0	0.0	0	115	16

RANCH SALAD DRESSINGS

	Tot. Fat (g)	Sat. Fat (g)	Chol. (mg)	Sod. (mg)	Cal.
Barondorf Lite Dressing, Ranch (1 tbsp)	<1.0	(0.0)	0	130	12
Bernstein's Light Fantastic Dressing, Restaurant Ranch (1 tbsp)	2.0	0.0	0	140	25
Healthy Sensations! Salad Dressing, Ranch (1 tbsp)	(<1.0)	(0.0)	0	140	16
Henri's Choice Fat Free Salad Dressing, Ranch (1 tbsp)	0.0	0.0	0	170	20
Henri's Light Salad Dressing					
Parmesan Ranch (1 tbsp)	2.0	0.0	0	130	35
Ranch (1 tbsp)	2.0	0.0	0	150	40

	Tot. Fat (g)	Sat. Fat (g)	Chol. (mg)	Sod. (mg)	Cal.
Herb Magic Reduced Calorie Dressing, Ranch (1 tbsp)	0.0	0.0	0	110	6
Hidden Valley Ranch Reduced Calorie Salad Dressing, Ranch Italian (1 tbsp)	3.0	(0.5)	0	130	30
Kraft† Free Nonfat Salad Dressing, Ranch (1 tbsp)	0.0	0.0	0	150	16
Seven Seas Free Nonfat Salad Dressing, Ranch (1 tbsp)	0.0	0.0	0	12	16

RUSSIAN SALAD DRESSINGS

	Tot. Fat (g)	Sat. Fat (g)	Chol. (mg)	Sod. (mg)	Cal.
Kraft† Reduced Calorie Salad Dressing, Russian (1 tbsp)	1.0	0.0	0	130	30
Wish-Bone Salad Dressing Lite Russian (1 tbsp)	(0.0)	(0.0)	0	140	20
Russian (½ fl oz = 1 tbsp)	3.0	0.0	0	170	50

THOUSAND ISLAND SALAD DRESSINGS

	Tot. Fat (g)	Sat. Fat (g)	Chol. (mg)	Sod. (mg)	Cal.
Barondorf Lite Dressing, Thousand Island (1 tbsp)	0.0	0.0	(0)	95	9
Hain No Oil Dry Dressing Mix, 1000 Island, made as directed (1 tbsp)	0.0	0.0	<1	150	12
Healthy Sensations! Salad Dressing, Thousand Island (1 tbsp)	(<1.0)	(0.0)	0	135	20
Henri's Choice Fat Free Salad Dressing, Thousand Island (1 tbsp)	0.0	0.0	0	135	20
Herb Magic Reduced Calorie Dressing, Thousand Island (1 tbsp)	0.0	0.0	0	45	8
Hidden Valley Ranch Low Fat Salad Dressing, Thousand Island (1 tbsp)	0.0	0.0	0	140	20
Kraft† Free Nonfat Salad Dressing, Thousand Island (1 tbsp)	0.0	0.0	0	135	20
Ultra Slim-Fast Salad Dressings, Thousand Island (1 tbsp)	<1.0	(0.0)	0	80	18
Wish-Bone Lite Salad Dressing, Thousand Island (1 tbsp)	<1.0	(0.0)	0	140	20

	Tot. Fat (g)	Sat. Fat (g)	Chol. (mg)	Sod. (mg)	Cal.

VINAIGRETTE SALAD DRESSINGS

	Tot. Fat (g)	Sat. Fat (g)	Chol. (mg)	Sod. (mg)	Cal.
Barondorf Lite Dressing, Vinaigrette (1 tbsp)	<1.0	0.0	(0)	130	5
Hain Canola Oil Salad Dressing, Garden Tomato Vinaigrette (1 tbsp)	6.0	(0.3)	0	150	60
Herb Magic Reduced Calorie Dressing, Vinaigrette (1 tbsp)	0.0	0.0	0	170	6
Marie's Zesty Fat Free Vinaigrettes					
Classic Herb (.55 oz)	0.0	0.0	0	130	16
Italian (.55 oz)	0.0	0.0	0	150	16
Red Wine (.55 oz)	0.0	0.0	0	135	20
White Wine (.55 oz)	0.0	0.0	0	135	20
Pritikin Salad Dressing, Herb Vinaigrette (1 tbsp)	0.0	0.0	0	1	8
Seven Seas Free Nonfat Dressing, Red Wine Vinegar (1 tbsp)	0.0	0.0	0	190	6
Wish-Bone Lite Salad Dressing					
Classic Dijon Vinaigrette (1 tbsp)	3.0	0.0	0	200	30
Olive Oil Vinaigrette (1 tbsp)	<1.0	(0.0)	0	130	16
Wish-Bone Salad Dressing, Red Wine Olive Oil Vinaigrette (1 tbsp)	3.0	0.0	0	190	35

OTHER SALAD DRESSINGS

	Tot. Fat (g)	Sat. Fat (g)	Chol. (mg)	Sod. (mg)	Cal.
Bernstein's Light Fantastic Dressing, Creamy Dijon (1 tbsp)	<1.0	0.0	0	130	20
Dorothy Lynch Home Style Dressing					
Reduced Calorie (1 tbsp)	<1.0	(0.0)	0	110	30
Regular (1 tbsp)	3.0	0.5	0	85	55
Good Seasons Salad Dressing Mix for Fat Free Dressing, Honey Mustard, made with vinegar and water (1 tbsp)	0.0	0.0	0	130	10
Hain Canola Oil Salad Dressing, Tangy Citrus (1 tbsp)	5.0	(0.3)	0	75	50
Hain No Oil Dry Dressing Mix, Buttermilk, made as directed (1 tbsp)	<1.0	(0.0)	0	150	11

	Tot. Fat (g)	Sat. Fat (g)	Chol. (mg)	Sod. (mg)	Cal.
Healthy Sensations! Salad Dressing, Honey Dijon (1 tbsp)	(<1.0)	(0.0)	0	130	20
Henri's Salad Dressing, Light Tas-Tee (1 tbsp)	2.0	0.0	0	105	30
Herb Magic Reduced Calorie Dressing, Zesty Tomato (1 tbsp)	0.0	0.0	0	70	14
Marie's Lite & Luscious Reduced Calorie Dressing, Sour Cream & Dill (.55 oz = 1 tbsp)	4.0	0.0	0	120	50
Marie's Salad Dressing, Cole Slaw (1.05 oz)	13.0	(1.9)	(16)	210	140
Weight Watchers Salad Dressing, Creamy Peppercorn (1 tbsp)	0.0	0.0	0	85	10
Western Dressing, Mexican (1 tbsp)	2.0	0.2	0	170	30

SANDWICH SPREADS

	Tot. Fat (g)	Sat. Fat (g)	Chol. (mg)	Sod. (mg)	Cal.
Best Foods Dijonnaise Creamy Mustard Blend (1 tsp)	1.0	(0.1)	0	70	12
Hellmann's Dijonnaise Creamy Mustard Blend (1 tsp)	1.0	(0.1)	0	70	12
La Loma Sandwich Spread (1.7 oz = 3 tbsp)	4.0	(0.6)	0	300	70

† = tobacco company, corporate subsidiary or parent

SNACK FOODS

The snack foods in this section are low in fat, saturated fat and cholesterol as purchased or when made as indicated on the following pages. When preparing dip mixes, use nonfat or low-fat sour cream or yogurt instead of regular sour cream for more-healthful eating.

Products listed in this book vary in sodium content. Use the values appearing on the following pages to help plan a daily intake providing no more than 3,000 milligrams of sodium.

Most of the foods in this book are brand name products; however, when a brand name is not specified, it means that most brands of that product provide about the same amount of fat, saturated fat and cholesterol and that these amounts do not exceed AHA criteria.

You can use those generic entries and the tables below to evaluate products introduced since this book went to press.

AHA Criteria for Snack Foods*

	Tot. Fat (g)	Sat. Fat (g)	Chol. (mg)
All snack foods	3	<0.5	<2

* Per serving.

Snack Foods Not Recommended for Frequent Consumption

Some types of snack food that are usually too high in fat, saturated fat and/or cholesterol to be recommended for frequent consumption are shown in the table below. Values that exceed AHA criteria are followed by asterisks. The AHA does not have criteria for sodium.

You can use the values in the table to compare these snack foods with more-healthful alternatives listed on the following pages.

Snack Foods High in Fat, Saturated Fat and/or Cholesterol

	Tot. Fat (g)	Sat. Fat (g)	Chol. (mg)	Sod. (mg)	Cal.
Barbecue-flavor potato chips (1 ounce)	9.2*	2.3*	0	213	139
Nut and raisin granola bar, soft, uncoated (1 ounce)	5.8*	2.7*	0	72	129
Popcorn, regular microwave (1 ounce or about 2½ cups popped)	8.0*	1.4*	0	251	142
Trail mix with coconut (1 ounce)	8.3*	1.6*	0	65	131

Adapted from USDA Handbook No. 8 series.

* These values exceed AHA criteria for snack foods.

CHIPS

	Tot. Fat (g)	Sat. Fat (g)	Chol. (mg)	Sod. (mg)	Cal.
Barbara's Bakery Basically Baked Chips					
Blue Corn (1 oz = approx. 12 chips)	1.0	(0.2)	0	135	110
Light Salt (1 oz = approx. 12 chips)	1.0	(0.2)	0	135	110
Pesto (1 oz = approx. 12 chips)	1.0	(0.2)	0	100	105
Quinoa (1 oz = approx. 12 chips)	1.0	(0.2)	0	130	100
Unsalted (1 oz = approx. 12 chips)	1.0	(0.2)	0	10	110
Crackle Rice, Cheese & Tomato (1/2 oz)	1.7	0.2	0	92	60
Guiltless Gourmet Baked Tortilla Chips					
White Corn, Salted (1 oz = 22-26 chips)	1.5	0.0	0	180	110
Yellow Corn, Salted (1 oz = 22-26 chips)	1.5	0.0	0	140	110
Yellow Corn, Unsalted (1 oz = 22-26 chips)	1.5	0.0	0	25	110
Happy Heart No Oil Corn Chips, Barbeque, Cheddar Cheese, Nacho Cheese, Original or Sour Cream & Onion (3/8 oz)	<1.0	(0.0)	0	50	40
Heart Lovers No Oil Corn Chips, Barbeque, Cheddar Cheese, Nacho Cheese or Sour Cream & Onion (3/8 oz)	<1.0	(0.0)	0	50	40
Hunger Crunchers					
Apple Cinnamon, Maple Walnut or Natural (1 oz)	3.0	0.0	0	70	100
Chocolate (1 oz)	3.0	0.0	0	80	100
Rice & Bean Tortilla Bites, Jalapeño & Jack (1/2 oz)	0.0	0.2	0	84	60
Smart Temptations Baked Tortilla Chips					
No Salt (1 oz)	1.0	(0.1)	0	0	110
Salted (1 oz)	1.0	(0.1)	0	120	110

	Tot. Fat (g)	Sat. Fat (g)	Chol. (mg)	Sod. (mg)	Cal.
DIPS					
Frito-Lay's Dip					
Jalapeño Bean (1 oz)	1.0	(0.4)	0	180	30
Picante (1 oz)	0.0	0.0	0	160	10
Guiltless Gourmet					
BBQ Black Bean Dip, Mild or Spicy					
(1 oz = 2 tbsp)	0.0	0.0	0	100	15
BBQ Pinto Bean Dip, Mild or Spicy					
(1 oz = 2 tbsp)	0.0	0.0	0	100	20
Black Bean Dip, Mild or Spicy					
(1 oz = 2 tbsp)	0.0	0.0	0	100	15
Cheddar Queso Dip, Mild or Spicy					
(1 oz)	0.0	0.0	0	150	20
Pinto Bean Dip, Mild or Spicy					
(1 oz = 2 tbsp)	0.0	0.0	0	100	20
La Victoria Dip, Chili					
(2 tbsp)	<1.0	(0.0)	0	160	4
Old El Paso Dip					
Chili Bean (2 tbsp)	<1.0	(0.0)	(0)	100	16
Taco (2 tbsp)	<1.0	(0.0)	(0)	74	14
Wise Dip					
Jalapeño Flavored Bean Dip					
(2 tbsp)	0.0	0.0	(0)	100	25
Taco (2 tbsp)	0.0	0.0	(0)	115	12
FRUIT SNACKS					
Barbara's Bakery Real Fruit, all flavors					
(.5 oz)	1.0	(0.1)	(0)	(10)	50
Berry Bears, all varieties					
(1 pouch)	1.0	0.0	0	30	90
Bugs Bunny & Friends or Tazmanian Devil Fruit Snacks					
(1 pouch = .9 oz)	1.0	0.0	0	30	90
Del Monte† Fruit Snacks, Orchard Fruit Mix					
(.9 oz = 1 pouch)	0.0	0.0	(0)	10	70
Fruit By The Foot, all flavors					
(1 roll = .75 oz)	2.0	0.0	0	45	80

SNACK FOODS

	Tot. Fat (g)	Sat. Fat (g)	Chol. (mg)	Sod. (mg)	Cal.
Fruit Corners Fruit Roll-Ups and Peel-Outs, Cherry, Crazy Colors, Grape, Raspberry or Strawberry (1/2-oz roll)	<1.0	(0.0)	0	40	50
Fruit Roll-Ups, Hot Colors (1/2 oz = 1 roll)	<1.0	0.0	0	50	50
Garfield and Friends					
1-2 Punch (1 pouch)	2.0	(0.3)	(0)	65	110
Fruit Party (1/2-oz roll)	<1.0	(0.0)	(0)	40	50
Very Strawberry (1 pouch)	1.0	(0.1)	(0)	65	110
Wild Blue (1/2-oz roll)	<1.0	(0.0)	(0)	20	50
Goelitz Fruit Snacks, Assorted Fruit Nibbles, Fruit Bears, Fruit Circus, Fruit Dinosaurs or Fruit Packets (1.05 oz)	2.0	(0.4)	(0)	10	120
Gushers					
Cherry or Strawberry (1 pouch = .9 oz)	1.0	0.0	0	40	90
Grape (1 pouch = .9 oz)	1.0	0.0	0	40	90
Sour Berry (1 pouch = .9 oz)	1.0	0.0	0	50	90
Mountain House Fruit Crisps					
Mixed Fruit (.55 oz = 1 1/8 cups)	0.0	0.0	0	5	60
Peaches (.55 oz = 1 1/8 cups)	0.0	0.0	0	5	60
Pears (.55 oz = 1 1/8 cups)	0.0	0.0	0	0	60
Strawberries (.55 oz = 1 1/8 cups)	1.0	<1.0	0	0	60
Shark Bites, all varieties (1 pouch)	1.0	(0.0)	(0)	30	90
Soda-Licious, Fruity Mix or Soda Mix (1 pouch = .9 oz)	1.0	0.0	0	20	100
Sunkist Fruit Roll					
Apple or Apricot (3/4 oz = 1 roll)	0.0	0.0	0	15	80
Cherry or Raspberry (3/4 oz = 1 roll)	0.0	0.0	0	20	80
Fruit Punch (3/4 oz = 1 roll)	0.1	0.0	0	10	70
Grape (3/4 oz = 1 roll)	0.0	0.0	0	35	80
Strawberry (3/4 oz = 1 roll)	0.0	0.0	0	10	70
Sunkist Fruit Snacks					
Bunch of Berries, Paaaarrrty Punch, Tiny Toon Adventures or Toony Fruit Assortment (.9 oz)	1.0	(0.1)	(0)	10	100
Hanna Barbera Flintstones, Jetsons or Yogi (1 oz)	(<1.0)	(0.0)	(0)	15	100

	Tot. Fat (g)	Sat. Fat (g)	Chol. (mg)	Sod. (mg)	Cal.
Sunkist Fun Fruit, Galactic Gems, Mario Nintendo, Meteorites, Strawberry Dinosaurs, Wacky Players or Wacky Players Basketball (.9 oz)	1.0	(0.1)	0	10	100
TreeTop Apple Chips					
Cinnamon	0.0	0.0	0	20	55
Crispy (½ oz)	0.0	0.0	0	20	60
Weight Watchers Fruit Snacks					
Apple, Cinnamon or Peach (½ oz = 1 pouch)	<1.0	0.0	(0)	75	50
Apple Chips (¾ oz = 1 pouch)	0.0	0.0	0	110	70
Strawberry (½ oz = 1 pouch)	<1.0	0.0	(0)	140	50

GRANOLA BARS

	Tot. Fat (g)	Sat. Fat (g)	Chol. (mg)	Sod. (mg)	Cal.
Fi-Bar A.M., Apple-Oatmeal Spice (1.5 oz = 1 bar)	3.0	(0.5)	0	25	150
Fi-Bar Original Fruit, Cranberry & Wild Berry, Raspberry or Strawberry (1.2 oz)	2.0	(0.3)	0	15	120
Health Valley Fat-Free Granola Bars, Raspberry (1.5 oz = 1 bar)	<1.0	(0.0)	0	10	140

POPCORN

	Tot. Fat (g)	Sat. Fat (g)	Chol. (mg)	Sod. (mg)	Cal.
Black Jewell Popcorn, hot air popped (½ oz = 1 cup)	0.6	(0.1)	(0)	(<1)	53
Featherweight Microwave Popcorn, Natural Flavor (3 cups popped)	1.0	(0.2)	0	0	80
Health Valley Fat-Free Caramel Corn Puffs					
Apple Cinnamon (1 oz)	<1.0	0.0	0	50	100
Caramel (1 oz)	<1.0	(0.0)	0	45	100
Peanut (1 oz)	<1.0	(0.0)	0	85	100
Healthy Greenfield Foods Air Popped Pop Corn, Caramel (1 oz)	2.0	<1.0	0	100	120

	Tot. Fat (g)	Sat. Fat (g)	Chol. (mg)	Sod. (mg)	Cal.
Jiffy Pop Light Microwave Popcorn, Butter Flavor (3 cups popped)	2.0	(0.3)		70	80
Jolly Time Light Microwave Pop Corn, Butter Flavored (3 cups popped)	2.0	0.5	0	105	60
Jolly Time Pop Corn, White or Yellow, Air Popped (3 cups popped)	<1.0	0.1	0	0	60
Nature's Choice Caramel Corn (1.67 oz)	1.0	(0.3)	(0)	(97)	180
with Peanuts (1.67 oz)	2.0	(0.3)	(0)	(140)	190
Newman's Own Oldstyle Picture Show Microwave Popcorn (3⅓ cups popped)	1.0	(0.0)	0	0	80
Orville Redenbacher's Gourmet Hot Air Popping Corn (3 cups popped)	<1.0	(0.0)	0	0	40
Light Gourmet Microwave Popping Corn					
Butter (3 cups popped)	1.0	0.2	0	70	50
Natural (3 cups popped)	1.0	0.2	0	85	50
Pop*Secret By Request					
Butter Flavor (3 cups popped)	1.0	0.0	0	160	60
Natural Flavor (3 cups popped)	1.0	0.0	0	170	60
Popcorn, made without fat or salt (3½ cups popped)	1.4	0.2	0	1	109
Pops-Rite Light Microwave Popcorn, Butter Flavor or Natural Flavor (3 cups popped)	2.0	0.0	0	70	60
TV Time Merry Poppin "Light" Microwave Popping Corn, Butter Flavor or Natural Flavor (4 cups popped)	3.0	(0.5)	0	225	120
Weight Watchers Popcorn					
Caramel (.9 oz)	1.0	0.0	0	45	100
Microwave (1 oz)	1.0	0.0	(0)	0	90

	Tot. Fat (g)	Sat. Fat (g)	Chol. (mg)	Sod. (mg)	Cal.

PRETZELS

	Tot. Fat (g)	Sat. Fat (g)	Chol. (mg)	Sod. (mg)	Cal.
Andy Capp's Pub Pretzels (1 oz)	1.0	(0.2)	0	500	110
Barbara's Bakery Pretzels					
Bavarian, Honeysweet or 9-Grain (1 oz = 2 pretzels)	<1.0	(0.0)	0	200	110
Bavarian, No Salt Added (1 oz = 2 pretzels)	<1.0	(0.0)	0	10	110
Mini (1 oz = 17 pretzels)	<1.0	(0.0)	0	290	110
Mini, No Salt Added (1 oz = 17 pretzels)	<1.0	(0.0)	0	10	110
Bell Brand Mini-Pretzels (1 oz)	1.0	(0.2)	0	570	110
Delicious Pretzels, Box Dutch, Party, Stick or Twist (1 oz)	1.0	(0.2)	0	500	110
Eagle Brand Pretzels (1 oz)	2.0	(0.4)	0	570	110
Beer (1 oz)	2.0	(0.4)	0	610	110
Keystone Pretzels					
Dutch (1 oz)	1.1	(0.2)	0	538	106
Dutch, No Salt (1 oz)	1.1	(0.2)	0	38	106
Mini (1 oz)	0.9	(0.2)	0	768	102
Mini, No Salt (1 oz)	0.9	(0.2)	0	147	102
Oat Bran (1 oz)	0.8	(0.2)	0	343	104
Oat Bran, No Salt (1 oz)	0.8	(0.2)	0	34	104
Stick (1 oz)	0.5	(0.1)	0	795	105
Superthin (1 oz)	0.3	(0.1)	0	711	98
Thin (1 oz)	0.5	(0.1)	0	918	100
Lance Pretzels (1 oz)	1.0	0.0	0	470	100
Twist (1½ oz = 1 pkg)	1.0	0.0	0	700	150
Mister Salty[1] Pretzels, Fat Free Sticks or Twists (1 oz)	0.0	0.0	0	380	100
Pepperidge Farm Snack Sticks, Pretzel (1.1 oz = 8 crackers)	3.0	0.0	0	430	120
Pretzels (1 oz)	1.4	(0.3)	(0)	504	117
Quinlan Pretzels, Rods (1 oz)	<1.0	0.0	0	480	100
Rold Gold Pretzels					
Bavarian (1 oz = 3 pretzels)	2.0	(0.4)	0	430	120
Pretzel Twist (1 oz = 10 twists)	1.0	(0.2)	0	510	110
Rods (1 oz = 3 rods)	2.0	(0.4)	0	410	110
Sticks (1 oz = 50 sticks)	2.0	(0.4)	0	490	110
Tiny Twists (1 oz = 15 pretzels)	1.0	(0.2)	0	420	110

	Tot. Fat (g)	Sat. Fat (g)	Chol. (mg)	Sod. (mg)	Cal.
Snyder's of Hanover Hard Pretzels, Unsalted (1 oz)	0.0	0.0	0	80	110
Soft pretzel bites (1½ oz = 5 bites)	0.0	0.0	0	95	110
Soft pretzels (2¼ oz)	0.0	0.0	0	140	170
Ultra Slim-Fast Pretzel Twists (1 oz bag)	1.0	(0.2)	0	460	100

SOUPS

The soups in this section are low in fat, saturated fat and cholesterol as purchased or when prepared as indicated on the following pages. If the directions for preparing soup call for the addition of milk, use skim or 1% low-fat milk.

Products listed in this book vary in sodium content. Use the values appearing on the following pages to help plan a daily intake providing no more than 3,000 milligrams of sodium.

You can use the tables below to evaluate products introduced since this book went to press.

	Tot. Fat (g)	Sat. Fat (g)	Chol. (mg)
All soups	3	2	20

* Per serving.

Soups Not Recommended for Frequent Consumption

Some types of soup that are usually too high in fat, saturated fat and/or cholesterol to be recommended for frequent consumption are shown in the table below. Values that exceed AHA criteria are followed by asterisks. The AHA does not have criteria for sodium.

You can use the values in the table to compare these soups with more-healthful alternatives listed on the following pages.

Soups High in Fat, Saturated Fat and/or Cholesterol

	Tot. Fat (g)	Sat. Fat (g)	Chol. (mg)	Sod. (mg)	Cal.
Chicken and dumplings soup, condensed, made with water (1 cup)	5.5*	1.3	34*	861	97
Chunky beef soup, ready-to-serve (1 cup)	5.1*	2.6*	14	867	171
Cream of potato soup, condensed, made with whole milk (1 cup)	6.5*	3.8*	22	1060	148
Oyster stew, condensed, made with whole milk (1 cup)	7.9*	5.1*	32*	1040	134

Adapted from USDA Handbook No. 8 series.

* These values exceed AHA criteria for soups.

	Tot. Fat (g)	Sat. Fat (g)	Chol. (mg)	Sod. (mg)	Cal.

BEAN SOUPS

	Tot. Fat (g)	Sat. Fat (g)	Chol. (mg)	Sod. (mg)	Cal.
Campbell's Home Cookin' Soup					
Bean and Ham (9½ oz)	3.0	(1.2)	(8)	850	180
Bean and Ham (10¾ oz individual size)	3.0	(0.8)	(2)	960	200
Campbell's Soup, Homestyle Bean, made with water (8 fl oz)	1.0	(0.4)	5	700	130
Hambeens 15 Bean Soup					
Cajun, made with seasoning packet (8 oz)	1.0	(0.3)	(0)	280	160
Original, made with seasoning packet (8 oz)	1.0	(0.3)	(0)	165	170
Health Valley Fat-Free Soup, 5 Bean Vegetable (7½ oz)	<1.0	(0.0)	0	290	70
Nile Spice Home Style Soups, Black Bean (10 fl oz)	<1.0	(0.0)	(0)	480	180
Progresso Soup					
Ham & Bean (9½ oz = ½ of a 19-oz can)	2.0	(0.8)	10	950	140
Macaroni and Bean (10.5 oz)	4.0	(1.2)	0	1120	180
Taste Adventure Precooked Soup					
Black Bean, made with water (6 oz)	0.5	(0.1)	0	398	100
Navy Bean, made with water (6 oz)	0.5	(0.1)	0	258	111

BEEF SOUPS

	Tot. Fat (g)	Sat. Fat (g)	Chol. (mg)	Sod. (mg)	Cal.
Campbell's Chunky Soup					
Pepper Steak (9½ oz)	3.0	(1.5)	(10)	930	160
Pepper Steak (10¾ oz individual size)	4.0	(1.5)	(11)	1050	180
Campbell's Cup in a Microwavable Cup, Beef Flavor Noodle, dry (1.35 oz)	2.0	(0.5)	(2)	1330	140
Campbell's Healthy Request Soup, Healthy Vegetable Beef, ready-to-serve (8 oz)	2.0	(0.9)	15	460	120
Campbell's Home Cookin' Soup					
Vegetable Beef (9½ oz)	2.0	(0.9)	(6)	1020	120

	Tot. Fat (g)	Sat. Fat (g)	Chol. (mg)	Sod. (mg)	Cal.
Vegetable Beef (10¾ oz individual size)	3.0	(1.3)	(7)	1160	140
Campbell's Microwave Soup, Vegetable Beef (7¾ oz)	2.0	(0.9)	(5)	930	100
Campbell's Soup					
Beef, made with water (8 fl oz)	2.0	(1.0)	10	830	80
Beef Noodle, made with water (8 fl oz)	2.0	(0.7)	15	840	60
Vegetable Beef, made with water (8 fl oz)	2.0	(0.9)	5	740	70
Healthy Choice Shelf Stable Meals or Microwaveable Cups, Chunky Beef Vegetable Soup (7.5 oz)	1.0	(0.5)	20	490	110
Healthy Choice Soups					
Beef and Potato (7.5 oz)	1.0	<1.0	20	550	110
Chili Beef (7.5 oz)	1.0	<1.0	15	560	150
Hearty Beef (7.5 oz)	1.0	<1.0	20	540	120
Hormel Micro Cup Hearty Soup, Beef Vegetable (7.5 oz)	1.0	(0.4)	5	730	90
Knorr Soupmix, Oxtail Hearty Beef, made with water (8 fl oz)	2.0	(1.0)	(3)	1120	70
Ultra Slim-Fast Instant Soup, Beef Noodle, made with water (6 fl oz)	<1.0	(0.0)	5	700	45

BROTHS/CONSOMMÉS

	Tot. Fat (g)	Sat. Fat (g)	Chol. (mg)	Sod. (mg)	Cal.
Campbell's Consommé, made with water (8 fl oz)	0.0	0.0	5	750	25
Campbell's Healthy Request Soups, Chicken Broth, ready-to-serve (8 oz)	0.0	0.0	0	400	10
Campbell's Low Sodium Soup, Chicken Broth (10½ oz)	1.0	(0.3)	(1)	85	30
Campbell's Soup					
Beef Broth (Bouillon), made with water (8 fl oz)	0.0	0.0	5	820	14
Chicken Broth, made with water (8 fl oz)	2.0	(0.6)	5	710	30
Scotch Broth, made with water (8 oz)	3.0	(1.3)	10	870	80

	Tot. Fat (g)	Sat. Fat (g)	Chol. (mg)	Sod. (mg)	Cal.
College Inn† Broth					
Beef (7 fl oz)	0.0	0.0	0	960	16
Chicken (7 fl oz)	3.0	1.0	5	990	35
Lower Salt (7 fl oz)	2.0	1.0	5	550	20
Featherweight Instant Bouillon					
Beef (1 tsp)	1.0	(0.5)	5	5	12
Chicken (1 tsp)	1.0	(0.2)	5	25	12
Hain Soups					
Vegetable Broth (9½ oz)	0.0	0.0	0	1180	45
Low Sodium (9½ oz)	<1.0	(0.0)	0	85	40
Herb-Ox Instant Broth and Seasoning					
(1 pkt)	<1.0	0.0	(1)	10	11
Knorr Bouillon					
Beef Flavor, made with water					
(8 fl oz)	1.0	(0.5)	(1)	1250	14
Chicken Flavor, made with water					
(8 fl oz)	1.0	(0.2)	(1)	1210	16
Fish Flavor, made with water (8 fl oz)	<1.0	0.0	(1)	1130	10
Vegetarian Vegetable, made with					
water (8 fl oz)	2.0	(0.8)	(4)	990	16
Knorr Granulated Bouillon					
Beef (1 tsp)	<1.0	0.2	2	1010	10
Chicken (1 tsp)	<1.0	0.1	0	1070	10
Lipton Cup-A-Soup, Chicken Flavored					
Broth, made with water (6 fl oz)	<1.0	0.0	0	600	20
Lipton Recipe Soup Mix, Savory Herb					
with Garlic, made with water					
(8 fl oz)	<1.0	(0.0)	0	490	35
Lite-Line Low Sodium Instant Bouillon					
Beef Flavor (1 tsp)	<1.0	(0.0)	(tr)	5	12
Chicken Flavor (1 tsp)	<1.0	(0.0)	(tr)	5	12
Pritikin Broth, Chicken (7.7 oz)	0.3	0.2	1	163	18
Progresso Broth, Chicken (4 oz)	0.0	0.0	<5	360	8
Progresso Seasoned Broth, Beef (4 oz)	<1.0	(0.0)	0	380	10
Swanson Broth					
Beef (7¼ oz)	1.0	(0.5)	(tr)	730	16
Chicken (7¼ oz)	1.0	(0.3)	(1)	900	25
Swanson Natural Goodness Clear					
Broth					
Chicken (7¼ oz)	1.0	(0.3)	(1)	540	20

	Tot. Fat (g)	Sat. Fat (g)	Chol. (mg)	Sod. (mg)	Cal.
Vegetable (7.25 oz)	1.0	(0.2)	(0)	920	20
Weight Watchers Instant Broth Mix					
Beef (1 pkg)	0.0	0.0	(0)	930	8
Chicken (1 pkg)	0.0	0.0	(0)	990	8
Wyler's Instant Bouillon					
Beef Flavor (1 tsp or 1 cube)	<1.0	(0.0)	(tr)	930	6
Chicken Flavor (1 tsp or 1 cube)	<1.0	(0.0)	(tr)	900	8
Onion Flavor (1 tsp)	<1.0	(0.0)	(tr)	670	10
Vegetable Flavor (1 tsp)	<1.0	(0.0)	(tr)	910	6

CHICKEN SOUPS

	Tot. Fat (g)	Sat. Fat (g)	Chol. (mg)	Sod. (mg)	Cal.
Appletree* Chicken Noodle Soup, made with water (8 fl oz)	2.0	(0.5)	(7)	880	60
Campbell's Cup 2 Minute Soup Mix, Chicken Noodle with White Meat, made with water (6 fl oz)	2.0	(0.4)	(2)	890	80
Campbell's Cup in a Microwave Cup, Chicken Flavor Noodle, dry (1.35 oz)	2.0	(0.6)	(1)	1370	140
Campbell's Healthy Request Soup Chicken Noodle, made with water (8 fl oz)	2.0	(0.5)	10	460	60
Chicken with Rice, made with water (8 fl oz)	3.0	(0.7)	10	480	60
Cream of Chicken, made with water (8 oz)	2.0	(0.6)	10	490	70
Hearty Chicken Rice, Ready-to-Serve (8 oz)	3.0	(0.7)	10	480	110
Hearty Chicken Vegetable, Ready-to-Serve (8 oz)	3.0	(0.9)	10	420	120
Campbell's Home Cookin' Soup Chicken Noodle (9½ oz)	3.0	(0.8)	(8)	1010	110
Chicken Noodle (10¾ oz individual size)	4.0	(1.1)	(9)	1150	130

* Appletree products are also marketed under Best Yet, Fine Fare, Food Lion, Hyde Park, Hy-Top, Parade, Piggly-Wiggly, Red & White, Roundy's, Schwegmann, Scot Lad and Tops brand names.

	Tot. Fat (g)	Sat. Fat (g)	Chol. (mg)	Sod. (mg)	Cal.
Chicken Rice, Ready-to-Serve (10¾ oz)	4.0	(1.0)	(9)	1010	160
Chicken Vegetable, Ready-to-Serve (10¾ oz)	4.0	(1.2)	(13)	970	180
Campbell's Microwave Soups, Chicken Noodle (7.75 oz)	3.0	(0.8)	(7)	1090	90
Campbell's Quality Soup and Recipe Mix, Chicken Noodle, made with water (8 fl oz)	2.0	(0.4)	(3)	700	100
Campbell's Soup					
Chicken Alphabet, made with water (8 fl oz)	2.0	(0.5)	10	800	70
Chicken and Stars, made with water (8 fl oz)	2.0	(0.5)	5	830	60
Chicken Gumbo, made with water (8 fl oz)	1.0	(0.3)	5	890	50
Chicken Noodle, made with water (8 fl oz)	2.0	(0.5)	10	870	60
Chicken NoodleO's, made with water (8 oz)	2.0	(0.5)	10	860	70
Chicken Vegetable, made with water (8 fl oz)	2.0	(0.6)	10	820	70
Chicken with Rice, made with water (8 fl oz)	2.0	(0.7)	5	770	60
Curly Noodle with Chicken, made with water (8 fl oz)	2.0	(0.5)	15	800	70
Double Noodle in Chicken Broth, made with water (8 oz)	2.0	(0.5)	(7)	700	90
Homestyle Chicken Noodle, made with water (8 fl oz)	2.0	(0.8)	10	880	60
Souper Stars with Chicken, made with water (8 oz)	2.0	(0.5)	5	850	70
Healthy Choice Soups					
Chicken Pasta (7.5 oz)	2.0	1.0	15	560	100
Chicken with Rice (7.5 oz)	1.0	<1.0	10	510	90
Old Fashioned Chicken Noodle (7.5 oz)	2.0	<1.0	20	540	90
Hormel Micro Cup Hearty Soup					
Chicken Noodle (7.5 oz)	3.0	(0.8)	18	690	110

	Tot. Fat (g)	Sat. Fat (g)	Chol. (mg)	Sod. (mg)	Cal.
Chicken with Rice and Vegetables (7.5 oz)	2.0	(0.5)	5	890	110
Knorr Soupmix, Chick 'N Pasta, made with water (8 fl oz)	2.0	(0.4)	(3)	850	90
Lipton Cup-A-Soup					
Chicken Noodle with Chicken Meat, made with water (6 fl oz)	<1.0	0.0	2	600	50
Chicken Vegetable, made with water (6 fl oz)	<1.0	(0.0)	10	560	60
Chicken'N Rice, made with water (6 fl oz)	<1.0	0.0	5	620	45
Lipton Noodle Soup Mix, Chicken with Diced White Chicken Meat, made with water (8 fl oz)	1.0	0.0	(3)	790	80
Lipton Soup Mix, Chicken Noodle, made with water (8 fl oz)	2.0	(0.5)	(7)	810	80
Lunch Bucket Soups, Chicken Noodle (7.25 oz)	2.0	(0.5)	(7)	810	90
Nile Spice Home Style Soups, Chicken Noodle (10 fl oz)	2.0	(0.5)	(9)	490	120
Pritikin Soup					
Chicken Vegetable (8 oz)	0.9	0.1	4	144	60
Chicken with Ribbon Pasta (8 oz)	1.1	0.2	6	173	80
Progresso Soup					
Chicken Barley (9¼ oz = ½ of an 18½-oz can)	2.0	(0.7)	20	710	100
Escarole in Chicken Broth (9.25 oz)	1.0	(<1.0)	<5	1100	30
Homestyle Chicken (9½ oz = ½ of a 19-oz can)	3.0	(0.9)	20	740	110
Ultra Slim-Fast Instant Soup					
Chicken Leek, made with water (6 fl oz)	<1.0	(0.0)	<2	1070	50
Chicken Noodle, made with water (6 fl oz)	<1.0	(0.0)	5	970	45
Weight Watchers Soup, Chicken Noodle (10.5 oz)	1.0	0.0	0	950	80

	Tot. Fat (g)	Sat. Fat (g)	Chol. (mg)	Sod. (mg)	Cal.

CLAM CHOWDER

	Tot. Fat (g)	Sat. Fat (g)	Chol. (mg)	Sod. (mg)	Cal.
Campbell's Chunky Soup, Manhattan Style Clam Chowder (10¾ oz individual size)	4.0	(0.8)	(3)	1120	160
Campbell's Healthy Request Soups, New England Clam Chowder, Ready-to-Serve (8 oz)	3.0	(0.4)	10	490	100
Campbell's Soup Manhattan Style Clam Chowder, made with water (8 fl oz)	2.0	(0.4)	0	820	70
New England Clam Chowder, made with 2% milk (8 oz)	3.0	(1.1)	10	940	130
New England Clam Chowder, made with water (8 fl oz)	2.0	(0.3)	5	880	80
Progresso Soup, Manhattan Clam Chowder (9.5 oz)	2.0	(0.4)	(2)	1050	120
Snow's Soups, New England Clam Chowder, made with skim milk (8 fl oz)	2.2	(0.5)	(6)	675	108
Weight Watchers Soup, New England Clam Chowder (7.5 oz)	0.0	0.0	5	450	90

CONSOMMÉS—see BROTHS/CONSOMMÉS

LENTIL SOUPS

	Tot. Fat (g)	Sat. Fat (g)	Chol. (mg)	Sod. (mg)	Cal.
Campbell's Home Cookin' Soup, Lentil (10¾ oz individual size)	1.0	(0.4)	(5)	960	160
Hain Savory Soup Mix, Lentil, made with water (¾ cup)	2.0	(0.5)	(0)	810	130
Hain Soups, Vegetarian Lentil (9½ oz)	3.0	(1.4)	5	690	160
No Salt Added (9½ oz)	3.0	(1.4)	5	65	160
Healthy Choice Soups, Lentil (7.5 oz)	1.0	<1.0	0	480	140
Nile Spice Couscous Soups, Lentil Curry (10 fl oz)	<1.0	(0.0)	(0)	590	220
Nile Spice Home Style Soups, Lentil (10 fl oz)	<1.0	(0.0)	(0)	420	190

	Tot. Fat (g)	Sat. Fat (g)	Chol. (mg)	Sod. (mg)	Cal.
Pritikin Soup, Lentil (8.31 oz)	0.8	0.2	0	180	90
Progresso Soup, Lentil (9.25 oz)	4.0	(1.6)	0	1000	140
Taste Adventure Precooked Soup, Curry Lentil, made with water (6 oz)	0.4	(0.1)	0	410	97

MINESTRONE

	Tot. Fat (g)	Sat. Fat (g)	Chol. (mg)	Sod. (mg)	Cal.
Campbell's Healthy Request Soups, Hearty Minestrone, Ready-to-Serve (8 fl oz)	2.0	(0.4)	2	420	90
Campbell's Home Cookin' Soup Minestrone (9½ oz)	3.0	(0.6)	(2)	1080	120
Minestrone (10¾ oz individual size)	3.0	(0.6)	(3)	1220	140
Campbell's Soup, Minestrone, made with water (8 fl oz)	2.0	(0.4)	5	890	80
Hain Savory Soup Mix, Minestrone, made with water (¾ cup)	1.0	(0.2)	(2)	870	110
Hain Soups, Minestrone (9½ oz)	2.0	(0.4)	0	1060	170
Health Valley Fat-Free Soup, Real Italian Minestrone (7½ oz)	<1.0	(0.0)	0	290	70
Healthy Choice Soups, Minestrone (7.5 oz)	1.0	<1.0	0	520	160
Hormel Micro Cup Hearty Soup, Minestrone (7.5 oz)	1.0	(0.2)	5	460	100
Knorr Soupmix, Hearty Minestrone, made with water (10 fl oz)	2.0	(1.0)	(11)	940	130
Nile Spice Couscous Soups, Tomato Minestrone (10 fl oz)	0.0	0.0	(0)	590	200
Pritikin Soup, Minestroni (8.2 oz)	0.9	0.2	0	135	80
Progresso Soup Hearty Minestrone (9.25 oz)	2.0	(1.1)	<5	740	110
Minestrone (10.5 oz)	3.0	(0.6)	0	930	120
Taste Adventure Precooked Soup, Minestrone, made with water (6 oz)	0.5	(0.2)	0	234	93

	Tot. Fat (g)	Sat. Fat (g)	Chol. (mg)	Sod. (mg)	Cal.

MUSHROOM SOUPS

	Tot. Fat (g)	Sat. Fat (g)	Chol. (mg)	Sod. (mg)	Cal.
Campbell's Healthy Request Soups, Cream of Mushroom, made with water (8 oz)	2.0	(0.5)	5	480	60
Campbell's Soup, Golden Mushroom, made with water (8 oz)	3.0	(0.8)	5	850	70
Hain Soups, Mushroom Barley (9½ oz)	2.0	(0.4)	10	600	100
Lipton Recipe and Soup Mix, Beef Flavor Mushroom, made with water (8 fl oz)	0.0	0.0	0	810	35
Weight Watchers Soup, Cream of Mushroom (10.5 oz)	2.0	<1.0	0	1250	90

NOODLE SOUPS

	Tot. Fat (g)	Sat. Fat (g)	Chol. (mg)	Sod. (mg)	Cal.
Campbell's Cup 2 Minute Soup Mix, Noodle with Chicken Broth, made with water (6 fl oz)	2.0	(0.4)	(2)	950	90
Campbell's Cup in a Microwavable Cup, Noodle Soup with Chicken Broth, dry (1.35 oz)	2.0	(0.5)	(1)	1400	140
Campbell's Low Fat Block Ramen Noodle Soup					
Beef Flavor, dry (1.5 oz = ½ pkg)	1.0	(0.2)	(0)	890	160
Chicken Flavor, dry (1.5 oz = ½ pkg)	1.0	(0.2)	(0)	940	160
Oriental Flavor, dry (1.5 oz = ½ pkg)	1.0	(0.2)	(0)	940	150
Pork Flavor, dry (1.5 oz = ½ pkg)	2.0	(0.4)	(0)	450	140
Campbell's Low Fat Ramen Noodle in a Cup					
Beef Flavor with Vegetables, dry (2.2 oz)	2.0	(0.5)	(2)	1600	220
Chicken Flavor with Vegetables, dry (2.2 oz)	2.0	(0.3)	(0)	1500	220
Oriental Flavor with Vegetables, dry (2.2 oz)	2.0	(0.3)	(0)	1400	220
Shrimp Flavor with Vegetables, dry (2.2 oz)	2.0	(0.3)	(0)	1290	230

	Tot. Fat (g)	Sat. Fat (g)	Chol. (mg)	Sod. (mg)	Cal.
Campbell's Quality Soup and Recipe Mix					
Double Noodle, dry (1.8 oz)	2.0	(0.5)	(tr)	770	200
Hearty Noodle, made with water (8 fl oz)	1.0	(0.2)	(3)	840	90
Noodle, made with water (8 fl oz)	2.0	(0.4)	(3)	740	110
Campbell's Ramen Noodle Soup					
Beef Flavor, dry (1.25 oz)	2.0	1.0	2	430	140
Chicken Flavor, dry (1.25 oz)	2.0	1.0	2	420	140
Oriental Flavor, dry (1.25 oz)	2.0	1.0	2	440	140
Pork Flavor, dry (1.25 oz)	2.0	1.0	2	450	140
Campbell's Soup					
Teddy Bear, made with water (8 fl oz)	1.0	(0.4)	5	770	60
Turkey Noodle, made with water (8 oz)	2.0	(0.6)	15	880	70
Knorr Soupmix					
Chicken Flavored Noodle, made with water (8 fl oz)	2.0	(0.4)	(3)	710	100
Tortellini in Brodo, made with water (8 fl oz)	1.0	(0.5)	(3)	820	60
Lipton Cup-A-Soup, Ring Noodle, made with water (6 fl oz)	<1.0	0.0	5	620	60
Lipton Giggle Noodle with Real Chicken Broth, made with water (8 fl oz)	2.0	0.0	(3)	710	70
Lipton Hearty Noodle Soup Mix, Chicken, made with water (8 fl oz)	1.0	0.0	0	790	80
Lipton Hearty Noodle Soup Mix with Vegetables, made with water (8 fl oz)	2.0	0.0	(0)	690	80
Lipton Noodle Soup Mix with Real Chicken Broth, made with water (8 fl oz)	1.0	0.0	0	730	60
Lipton Ring-O-Noodle Soup Mix with Real Chicken Broth, made with water (8 fl oz)	2.0	0.0	(3)	710	70
Progresso Soup, Tortellini (9.5 oz)	3.0	(0.6)	10	840	90

	Tot. Fat (g)	Sat. Fat (g)	Chol. (mg)	Sod. (mg)	Cal.

ONION SOUPS

	Tot. Fat (g)	Sat. Fat (g)	Chol. (mg)	Sod. (mg)	Cal.
Campbell's Quality Soup and Recipe Mix, Onion, made with water (8 fl oz)	1.0	0.0	(0)	650	30
Campbell's Soup, French Onion, made with water (8 fl oz)	2.0	(0.3)	5	890	60
Hain Savory Soup, Dip and Recipe Mix, Onion, made with water (3/4 cup)	2.0	(0.6)	(0)	900	50
No Sodium Added, made with water (3/4 cup)	1.0	(0.3)	(0)	470	50
Knorr Soupmix, French Onion, made with water (8 fl oz)	1.0	(0.2)	(0)	970	50
Lipton Kettle Ready Frozen Soup, French Onion (6 fl oz)	2.0	0.0	0	510	40
Lipton Recipe and Soup Mix Beefy Onion, made with water (8 fl oz)	<1.0	0.0	0	640	30
Onion, made with water (8 fl oz)	0.0	0.0	(0)	630	20
Onion Mushroom, made with water (8 fl oz)	<1.0	0.0	0	740	40
Lipton Soup Mix, Golden Onion with Real Chicken Broth, made with water (8 fl oz)	1.0	0.0	0	730	60
Ultra Slim-Fast Instant Soup, Onion, made with water (6 fl oz)	<1.0	(0.0)	0	930	45

PEA SOUPS

	Tot. Fat (g)	Sat. Fat (g)	Chol. (mg)	Sod. (mg)	Cal.
Campbell's Home Cookin' Soup Split Pea with Ham, ready-to-serve (9.5 oz)	2.0	(0.8)	(9)	1040	190
Split Pea with Ham, ready-to-serve (10.75 oz)	3.0	(1.2)	(10)	1180	220
Campbell's Low Sodium Soup, Split Pea (10 3/4 oz)	4.0	(1.6)	(11)	30	230
Campbell's Soup Green Pea, made with water (8 fl oz)	3.0	(1.4)	5	800	150

	Tot. Fat (g)	Sat. Fat (g)	Chol. (mg)	Sod. (mg)	Cal.
Split Pea with Ham and Bacon, made with water (8 oz)	3.0	(1.2)	5	760	160
Hain Soups, Split Pea (9½ oz)	1.0	(0.5)	0	970	170
No Salt Added (9½ oz)	1.0	(0.5)	0	40	170
Healthy Choice Soups, Split Pea and Ham (7.5 oz)	3.0	1.0	10	460	170
Nile Spice Home Style Soups, Split Pea (10 fl oz)	<1.0	(0.0)	(0)	480	200
Pritikin Soup, Split Pea (8.84 oz)	0.4	0.1	0	160	140
Progresso Soup, Green Split Pea (10.5 oz)	3.0	(1.4)	(0)	920	201
Taste Adventure Precooked Soup, Split Pea, made with water (6 oz)	0.4	(0.1)	0	413	95

TOMATO SOUPS

	Tot. Fat (g)	Sat. Fat (g)	Chol. (mg)	Sod. (mg)	Cal.
Appletree* Tomato Soup, made with water (8 fl oz)	1.0	(0.2)	(0)	620	80
Campbell's Healthy Request Soups, Tomato, made with ½ 2% milk and ½ water (8 oz)	3.0	(0.4)	5	490	140
Campbell's Healthy Request Soups, Tomato, made with water (8 oz)	2.0	(0.4)	0	410	90
Campbell's Home Cookin' Soup Tomato Garden (9½ oz)	3.0	(0.6)	(3)	800	140
Tomato Garden (10¾ oz individual size)	3.0	(0.6)	(4)	910	150
Campbell's Soup Homestyle Cream of Tomato, made with water (8 fl oz)	2.0	(0.0)	5	730	110
Italian Tomato with Basil and Oregano, made with water (8 oz)	0.0	0.0	(0)	740	90
Old Fashioned Tomato Rice, made with water (8 fl oz)	2.0	(0.4)	0	720	110
Tomato, made with water (8 fl oz)	2.0	(0.4)	0	670	90

* Appletree products are also marketed under Best Yet, Fine Fare, Food Lion, Hyde Park, Hy-Top, Parade, Piggly-Wiggly, Red & White, Roundy's, Schwegmann, Scot Lad and Tops brand names.

	Tot. Fat (g)	Sat. Fat (g)	Chol. (mg)	Sod. (mg)	Cal.
Tomato Bisque, made with water (8 fl oz)	3.0	(0.6)	0	820	120
Health Valley Fat-Free Soup, Tomato Vegetable (7½ oz)	<1.0	(0.0)	0	290	40
Healthy Choice Soups, Tomato Garden (7.5 oz)	3.0	1.0	5	510	130
Knorr Soupmix, Tomato Basil, made with water (8 fl oz)	3.0	(1.4)	(1)	940	90
Lipton Cup-A-Soup, Tomato, made with water (6 fl oz)	<1.0	<1.0	0	520	110
Lipton Recipe Soup Mix, Tomato Herb, made with water (8 fl oz)	<1.0	(0.0)	0	570	50
Progresso Soup, Tomato (9.5 oz)	3.0	(0.6)	0	1100	120
Ultra Slim-Fast Instant Soup, Creamy Tomato, made with water (6 fl oz)	<1.0	(0.0)	0	800	60

TURKEY SOUPS

	Tot. Fat (g)	Sat. Fat (g)	Chol. (mg)	Sod. (mg)	Cal.
Campbell's Soup, Turkey Vegetable, made with water (8 fl oz)	2.0	(0.6)	10	770	70
Healthy Choice Soups					
Turkey Vegetable (7.5 oz)	3.0	1.0	15	540	110
Turkey with White and Wild Rice (7.5 oz)	2.0	1.0	15	480	100

VEGETABLE SOUPS

	Tot. Fat (g)	Sat. Fat (g)	Chol. (mg)	Sod. (mg)	Cal.
Appletree* Vegetable Soup with Beef Stock, made with water (8 fl oz)	1.0	(0.2)	(2)	830	80
Campbell's Chunky Soup					
Vegetable (9½ oz)	4.0	(0.6)	(0)	960	150
Vegetable (10¾ oz individual size)	4.0	(0.6)	(0)	1080	160
Campbell's Healthy Request Soups					
Hearty Vegetable, Ready-to-Serve (8 fl oz)	3.0	(0.5)	0	480	90

* Appletree products are also marketed under Best Yet, Fine Fare, Food Lion, Hyde Park, Hy-Top, Parade, Piggly-Wiggly, Red & White, Roundy's, Schwegmann, Scot Lad and Tops brand names.

SOUPS

	Tot. Fat (g)	Sat. Fat (g)	Chol. (mg)	Sod. (mg)	Cal.
Vegetable, made with water (8 fl oz)	2.0	(0.3)	5	500	90
Vegetable Beef, made with water (8 fl oz)	2.0	(0.9)	5	490	70
Campbell's Home Cookin' Soup					
Country Vegetable (9½ oz)	2.0	(0.3)	(0)	760	130
Country Vegetable (10¾ oz individual size)	2.0	(0.3)	(0)	860	150
Campbell's Microwave Soup					
Vegetable (7.75 oz)	2.0	(0.3)	(0)	910	100
Vegetable Beef (7.75 oz)	2.0	(0.9)	(5)	930	100
Campbell's Quality Soup and Recipe Mix, Vegetable, made with water (8 fl oz)	0.0	0.0	(0)	710	40
Campbell's Soup					
Dinousaur Vegetable, made with water (8 oz)	2.0	(0.9)	5	670	100
Golden Corn, made with water (8 oz)	3.0	(1.4)	5	700	110
Hearty Vegetable with Pasta, made with water (8 oz)	0.0	0.0	0	800	70
Homestyle Vegetable, made with water (8 fl oz)	2.0	(0.5)	0	880	60
Old Fashioned Vegetable, made with water (8 fl oz)	2.0	(0.5)	5	850	60
Vegetable, made with water (8 fl oz)	2.0	(0.0)	5	830	90
Vegetarian Vegetable, made with water (8 fl oz)	2.0	(0.3)	0	790	80
Hain Savory Soup Mix					
Vegetable, made with water (¾ cup)	1.0	(0.2)	(0)	730	80
No Sodium Added (¾ cup)	1.0	(0.2)	(0)	330	80
Health Valley Fat-Free Soup					
Country Corn and Vegetable (7½ oz)	<1.0	(0.0)	0	290	60
14 Garden Vegetables (7½ oz)	<1.0	(0.0)	0	290	60
Vegetable Barley (7½ oz)	<1.0	(0.0)	0	290	50
Healthy Choice Soups					
Country Vegetable (7.5 oz)	1.0	<1.0	0	540	120
Garden Vegetable (7.5 oz)	1.0	<1.0	0	560	100
Vegetable Beef (7.5 oz)	1.0	<1.0	15	530	130

	Tot. Fat (g)	Sat. Fat (g)	Chol. (mg)	Sod. (mg)	Cal.
Hormel Micro Cup Hearty Soup, Country Vegetable (7.5 oz)	2.0	(0.5)	2	770	90
Knorr Soupmix					
Asparagus, made with water and milk (8 fl oz)	3.0	(0.9)	(4)	770	80
Cauliflower, made with water and milk (8 fl oz)	3.0	(0.9)	(4)	750	100
Spring Vegetable With Herbs, made with water (8 fl oz)	<1.0	(0.0)	0	640	30
Vegetable, made with water (8 fl oz)	1.0	(0.5)	(tr)	840	35
Lipton Cup-A-Soup					
Country Style Harvest Vegetable, made with water (6 fl oz)	2.0	<1.0	(0)	510	100
Harvest Vegetable, made with water (6 fl oz)	2.0	<1.0	0	510	100
Spring Vegetable, made with water (6 fl oz)	<1.0	0.0	5	520	50
Lipton Recipe and Soup Mix, Vegetable, made with water (8 fl oz)	0.0	0.0	0	680	35
Lipton Soup Mix, Country Vegetable, made with water (8 fl oz)	1.0	0.0	0	790	70
Lunch Bucket Soups, Country Vegetable (7.25 oz)	1.0	(0.2)	(2)	740	70
Nile Spice Couscous Soups, Vegetable Parmesan (10 fl oz)	3.0	(1.1)	(5)	550	200
Nile Spice Home Style Soups, Sweet Corn Chowder (10 fl oz)	3.0	(1.0)	(5)	360	120
Pritikin Soup, Vegetable (8.31 oz)	1.3	0.2	0	161	90
Progresso Soup, Vegetable (10.5 oz)	2.0	(0.4)	<5	1100	90
Snow's Soups, New England Corn Chowder, made with skim milk (7½ oz)	2.2	(0.5)	(8)	645	118
Ultra Slim-Fast Instant Soup					
Creamy Broccoli, made with water (6 fl oz)	<1.0	(0.0)	0	800	75
Hearty Vegetable, made with water (6 fl oz)	<1.0	(0.0)	0	750	50

	Tot. Fat (g)	Sat. Fat (g)	Chol. (mg)	Sod. (mg)	Cal.
Potato Leek, made with water (6 fl oz)	<1.0	(0.0)	0	780	80
Weight Watchers Soup, Vegetable Beef (7.5 oz)	1.0	<1.0	10	450	90

SWEETS, SYRUPS, JAMS AND JELLIES

M ost of the sweets listed on the following pages contain no fat, and none contain saturated fat or cholesterol. Candies that contain chocolate, nuts, peanut butter and/or caramel are not included in this guide because they are high in fat and saturated fat. Be aware, however, that many of the jams, jellies, syrups, toppings and candies in this section are made primarily of sugar.

Products listed in this book vary in sodium content. Use the values appearing on the following pages to help plan a daily intake providing no more than 3,000 milligrams of sodium.

Most of the foods in this book are brand name products; however, when a brand name is not specified, it means that most brands of that product provide about the same amount of fat, saturated fat and cholesterol and that these amounts do not exceed AHA criteria.

You can use those generic entries and the tables below to evaluate products introduced since this book went to press.

AHA Criteria for Sweets, Syrups, Jams and Jellies*

	Tot. Fat (g)	Sat. Fat (g)	Chol. (mg)
All sweets	<0.5	<0.5	<2

* Per serving.

Sweets and Syrups Not Recommended for Frequent Consumption

Some types of sweet and syrup that are usually too high in fat, saturated fat and/or cholesterol to be recommended for frequent consumption are shown in the table below. Values that exceed AHA criteria are followed by asterisks. The AHA does not have criteria for sodium.

You can use the values in the table to compare these sweets and syrups with more-healthful alternatives listed on the following pages.

Sweets and Syrups High in Fat, Saturated Fat and/or Cholesterol

	Tot. Fat (g)	Sat. Fat (g)	Chol. (mg)	Sod. (mg)	Cal.
Chocolate-coated peanuts (1.4 ounces or about 10 pieces)	13.4*	5.8*	4*	16	208
Fondant coated in sweet chocolate (1 patty, about 2½ inches in diameter and ½ inch thick)	3.2*	1.9*	0	9	128
Fudge-type chocolate syrup (2 tablespoons)	5.6*	2.4*	(5)*	54	146

Adapted from USDA Handbook No. 8 series.
* These values exceed AHA criteria for sweets.

CANDY

	Tot. Fat (g)	Sat. Fat (g)	Chol. (mg)	Sod. (mg)	Cal.
Brach's					
Butterscotch Disks (1 oz)	0.0	0.0	(0)	110	110
Cinnamon Disks, Sour Balls or Starlight Mints, Peppermint or Spearmint (1 oz)	0.0	0.0	(0)	15	110
Cinnamon Imperials or Lemon Drops (1 oz)	0.0	0.0	(0)	5	110
Circus Peanuts (1 oz)	0.0	0.0	(0)	10	100
Dessert Mints or Kentucky Mints (1 oz)	0.0	0.0	(0)	0	110
Gummi Bears or Spicettes (1 oz)	0.0	0.0	(0)	15	100
Jelly Beans (1 oz)	0.0	0.0	(0)	5	100
Licorice Twists (1 oz)	0.0	0.0	(0)	50	100
Lolly Drops (1 oz)	0.0	0.0	(0)	35	110
Featherweight Candy					
Berry Patch Blend (1 piece)	0.0	0.0	0	0	12
Butterscotch Candy (1 piece)	0.0	0.0	0	25	25
Cool Blue Mints (1 piece)	0.0	0.0	0	0	25
Orchard Blend or Tropical Blend (1 piece)	0.0	0.0	0	0	12
Peppermint Swirls (1 piece)	0.0	0.0	0	0	20
Strawberry Fruit Drops (1/3 oz)	0.0	0.0	0	15	30
Gumdrops (1 1/2 oz)	0.3	0.0	0	15	147
Hard candy (1 1/2 oz)	0.5	0.0	0	14	164
Heide					
Candy Corn (1 oz)	0.0	0.0	0	40	110
Cinnamon Bears, Fish (assorted), Jujyfruits, Mexican Hats, Sanded Black Bears or Soft Licorice (1 oz)	0.0	0.0	0	0	100
Diamond Licorice Drops (1 oz)	0.0	0.0	0	10	110
Drops, Gourmet Pee Wee Mix, Jersey Cherries or Silly Sours (1 oz)	0.0	0.0	0	0	110
Juicefuls					
Bags (1 piece)	0.0	0.0	0	0	20
Stick Pack (1 piece)	0.0	0.0	0	0	15
Jujubes (1 oz)	0.0	0.0	(0)	10	110

	Tot. Fat (g)	Sat. Fat (g)	Chol. (mg)	Sod. (mg)	Cal.
Kraft†					
Butter Mints (1 piece)	0.0	0.0	0	0	8
Party Mints (1 piece)	0.0	0.0	0	0	8
Lifesavers† Gummisavers (1 piece)	0.0	0.0	0	0	12
Richardson Jellies (1 oz)	0.0	0.0	0	8	108
Richardson Mints					
Anise (1 oz)	0.0	0.0	0	1	109
Butter (1 oz)	0.2	(0.0)	(0)	9	110
Green Jelly (1 oz)	0.0	0.0	0	9	105
Pastel (1 oz)	0.0	0.0	0	1	109
Shari Candies, Assorted Sugar Free					
(1 candy)	0.0	0.0	(0)	0	12
Sunkist Fruit Gems (.37 oz = 1 piece)	0.1	0.0	0	9	35
Velamints					
All flavors except Cocoamint					
(1 piece)	0.0	0.0	0	0	9
Cocoamint (1 piece)	0.0	0.0	0	0	8
Willy Wonka Bottle Caps, Dinasour Eggs, Freckled Eggs, Fruit Runts, Gobstopper, Heart Breakers, Merry Mix, Nerds, Sweet & Sour Hearts, Tangy Bunnys, Tart 'N Tinys or Wacky Wafers (1 oz)	0.0	0.0	0	0	110
Y & S, Twizzlers Strawberry Candy (1.4 oz)	0.5	0.0	0	100	140
HONEY/JAMS/JELLIES/PRESERVES					
Bama Apple Butter (2 tsp)	0.0	0.0	0	5	25
Clement's Apple Butter (2 tsp)	0.0	0.0	0	5	25
Featherweight Low Calorie Fruit Spread					
Apple or Strawberry Jelly or Apricot, Peach, Red Raspberry or Strawberry Preserves (1 tsp)	0.0	0.0	0	0	4
Grape Jelly (1 tsp)	0.0	0.0	0	5	4
Hickory Farms Light Choice Fruit Spread (1 tsp)	0.0	0.0	(0)	0	8
Honey (1 tbsp)	0.0	0.0	0	1	64

	Tot. Fat (g)	Sat. Fat (g)	Chol. (mg)	Sod. (mg)	Cal.
Jams, jellies, marmalades or preserves, all flavors (2 tsp)	0.0	0.0	0	0	35
Kraft† Reduced Calorie Jelly, Grape (1 tsp)	0.0	0.0	0	5	6
Kraft† Reduced Calorie Preserves, Strawberry (1 tsp)	0.0	0.0	0	5	6
Smucker's Apple Butter, Autumn Harvest, Cider, Natural or Simply Fruit (1 tsp)	0.0	0.0	0	0	12
Smucker's Spreads					
Autumn Harvest Pumpkin Butter (1 tsp)	0.0	0.0	0	14	12
Low Sugar (1 tsp)	0.0	0.0	0	<10	8
Orange Marmalade (1 tsp)	0.0	0.0	0	0	18
Peach Butter (1 tsp)	0.0	0.0	0	0	15
Simply Fruit (1 tsp)	0.0	0.0	0	0	16
Slenderella Reduced Calorie (1 tsp)	0.0	0.0	0	0	7
Weight Watchers Fruit Spread, all flavors (1 tsp)	0.0	0.0	0	0	8
Welch's Totally Fruit Spread					
Apricot, Blackberry, Blueberry, Orange Marmalade, Red Raspberry or Strawberry (1 tsp)	0.0	0.0	0	5	14
Grape (2 tsp)	0.0	0.0	0	5	28

JAMS—*see*
HONEY/JAMS/JELLIES/PRESERVES

JELLIES—*see*
HONEY/JAMS/JELLIES/PRESERVES

MARSHMALLOWS

Campfire Marshmallows (2 large or 24 mini)	0.0	0.0	0	10	40
Kraft†					
Funmallows or Regular Marshmallows (1 piece)	0.0	0.0	0	15	30
Funmallows or Regular Miniature Marshmallows (10 pieces)	0.0	0.0	0	5	18

	Tot. Fat (g)	Sat. Fat (g)	Chol. (mg)	Sod. (mg)	Cal.
Jet-Puffed Marshmallows (1 piece)	0.0	0.0	0	5	25
Marshmallows (1½ oz)	0.0	0.0	0	17	135

PRESERVES—*see*
HONEY/JAMS/JELLIES/PRESERVES

SYRUPS

	Tot. Fat (g)	Sat. Fat (g)	Chol. (mg)	Sod. (mg)	Cal.
Aunt Jemima					
Butter Lite Syrup (1 fl oz)	0.0	0.0	0	88	53
Lite Syrup (1 fl oz)	0.1	0.0	0	92	54
Syrup (1 fl oz)	0.0	0.0	0	32	109
Brer Rabbit† Molasses					
Dark (1 fl oz = 2 tbsp)	0.0	0.0	0	20	110
Light (1 fl oz)	0.0	0.0	0	15	110
Brer Rabbit† Syrup, Dark or Light					
(1 fl oz = 2 tbsp)	0.0	0.0	0	0	120
Clement's Syrup					
Reduced Calorie Lite Pancake and					
Waffle (2 tbsp)	0.0	0.0	(0)	65	50
Waffle (2 tbsp)	0.0	0.0	(0)	60	110
Country Kitchen Pancake & Waffle					
Syrup (1 fl oz)	0.0	0.0	0	40	100
Butter Flavored (1 fl oz)	0.0	0.0	0	100	100
Lite Reduced Calorie (1 fl oz)	0.0	0.0	0	85	50
Featherweight Syrup					
Blueberry (1 tbsp)	0.0	0.0	0	35	16
Pancake (1 tbsp)	0.0	0.0	0	30	16
Golden Griddle Syrup (1 tbsp)	0.0	0.0	(0)	15	50
Hershey's Syrup, Chocolate Flavored					
(2 tbsp)	0.0	0.0	0	25	100
Hungry Jack Syrup (2 tbsp)	0.0	0.0	0	25	100
Lite (2 tbsp)	0.0	0.0	0	115	50
Karo Pancake Syrup (1 tbsp)	0.0	0.0	(0)	35	60
Log Cabin Pancake & Waffle Syrup					
(1 fl oz)	0.0	0.0	0	35	100
Lite Reduced Calorie (1 fl oz)	0.0	0.0	0	90	50
Maple syrup (1 tbsp)	0.0	0.0	0	2	50
Molasses					
Blackstrap (1 tbsp)	0.0	0.0	0	39	43

	Tot. Fat (g)	Sat. Fat (g)	Chol. (mg)	Sod. (mg)	Cal.
Light (1 tbsp)	0.0	0.0	0	3	50
Medium (1 tbsp)	0.0	0.0	0	7	46
Nestle Quik Syrup, Strawberry Flavor					
(1.2 oz)	0.0	0.0	0	0	130
Slim-ette Syrup, Maple Flavored					
(1 tbsp)	<1.0	(0.0)	(0)	10	1
Smucker's Syrup					
Chocolate Flavored (2 tbsp)	0.0	0.0	0	35	130
Fruit (2 tbsp)	0.0	0.0	0	<10	100
Weight Watchers Naturally					
Sweetened Syrup (1 tbsp)	0.0	0.0	(0)	40	25

TOPPINGS

	Tot. Fat (g)	Sat. Fat (g)	Chol. (mg)	Sod. (mg)	Cal.
Knorr Sauce, Caramel (1 tbsp)	0.0	0.0	0	5	60
Kraft† Marshmallow Creme (1 oz)	0.0	0.0	0	20	90
Kraft† Topping					
Caramel (1 tbsp)	0.0	0.0	0	45	60
Chocolate (1 tbsp)	0.0	0.0	0	15	50
Pineapple (1 tbsp)	0.0	0.0	0	0	50
Strawberry (1 tbsp)	0.0	0.0	0	5	50
Smucker's Topping					
Light Hot Fudge (2 tbsp)	0.0	0.0	0	35	70
Marshmallow (2 tbsp)	0.0	0.0	0	0	120
Pineapple (2 tbsp)	0.0	0.0	0	0	130
Strawberry (2 tbsp)	0.0	0.0	0	0	120

SWEETS, SYRUPS, JAMS AND JELLIES

† = tobacco company, corporate subsidiary or parent

VEGETABLES

Nature has provided us with a wide array of flavorful, colorful vegetables that contain minimal amounts of fat, no cholesterol, little sodium and few calories. However, beware of adding fat, cholesterol, sodium and/or calories by deep-fat frying or panfrying or by adding ingredients such as butter, bacon, bacon fat, salt pork, cream sauce or cheese to them.

Products listed in this book vary in sodium content. Use the values appearing on the following pages to help plan a daily intake providing no more than 3,000 milligrams of sodium.

Most of the foods in this book are brand name products; however, when a brand name is not specified, it means that most brands of that product provide about the same amount of fat, saturated fat and cholesterol and that these amounts do not exceed AHA criteria.

You can use those generic entries and the tables below to evaluate products introduced since this book went to press.

AHA Criteria for Vegetables*

	Tot. Fat (g)	Sat. Fat (g)	Chol. (mg)
Candied, French fried, hash browned, mashed or stuffed potatoes; potato pancakes; potato skins; potatoes with sauce; or vegetables with sauce	3	1	20
Chili peppers, green onions and garnish, such as parsley and pimiento	<0.5	<0.5	<2
Plain fresh, canned and frozen vegetables (except those listed above)	3	1	<2

* Per serving.

Vegetables Not Recommended for Frequent Consumption

Some types of vegetable that are usually too high in fat, saturated fat and/or cholesterol to be recommended for frequent consumption are shown in the table below. Values that exceed AHA criteria are followed by asterisks. The AHA does not have criteria for sodium.

You can use the values in the table to compare these vegetables with more-healthful alternatives listed on the following pages.

Vegetables High in Fat, Saturated Fat and/or Cholesterol

	Tot. Fat (g)	Sat. Fat (g)	Chol. (mg)	Sod. (mg)	Cal.
Breaded onion rings, frozen, heated in oven (3.9 ounces or about 11 rings)	29.3*	9.4*	0	413	447
French-fried potatoes, frozen, heated in oven (2½ ounces or about 14 strips)	5.3*	0.9	0	21	140
Scalloped potatoes, made from mix with whole milk and butter (about 5 ounces)	6.0*	3.7*	(17)	476	130

Adapted from USDA Handbook No. 8 series.

* These values exceed AHA criteria for vegetables.

	Tot. Fat (g)	Sat. Fat (g)	Chol. (mg)	Sod. (mg)	Cal.
Alfalfa sprouts, raw (1 cup)	0.2	0.0	0	2	10
Artichokes					
Fresh, cooked (1 medium)	0.2	0.0	0	79	53
Frozen (3 oz)	0.4	0.1	0	42	36
Asparagus					
Canned					
No salt added, drained (½ cup)	0.8	0.2	0	(5)	24
Spears, drained (½ cup)	0.8	0.2	0	(425)	24
Fresh					
Cooked (½ cup)	0.3	0.1	0	7	22
Raw (4 spears)	0.1	0.0	0	1	14
Frozen (4 spears)	0.3	0.1	0	2	17
Avocados—see "FATS, OILS, SEEDS AND NUTS," AVOCADOS, page 125					
Bamboo shoots, canned, sliced, drained (½ cup)	1.0	0.1	0	5	13
Bean sprouts, canned					
La Choy Bean Sprouts (1 cup)	0.0	0.0	0	31	11
La Choy Mung Bean Sprouts (⅔ cup)	<1.0	(0.0)	0	20	8
Beans					
Adzuki beans, canned					
Eden Adzuki Beans					
with Kombu (½ cup)	<1.0	(0.0)	0	10	80
with Tamari (½ cup)	<1.0	0.0	0	20	100
Baked beans, canned—see also Vegetarian beans					
Allen Baked Beans (½ cup)	1.0	<1.0	2	410	140
Vegetarian (½ cup)	<1.0	<1.0	2	410	140
Appletree* Baked Beans (½ cup)	1.0	<1.0	(9)	410	140
B & M Brick Oven Baked Beans					
Barbecue (8 oz)	4.0	(1.5)	5	850	280
Honey Baked (8 oz)	2.0	(0.5)	0	940	240
Hot N Spicy (8 oz)	3.0	1.0	3	990	240
Maple (8 oz)	2.0	1.0	<5	890	240
Red Kidney (8 oz)	4.0	(1.0)	5	680	240

* Appletree products are also marketed under Best Yet, Fine Fare, Food Lion, Hyde Park, Hy-Top, Parade, Piggly-Wiggly, Red & White, Roundy's, Schwegmann, Scot Lad and Tops brand names.

VEGETABLES

	Tot. Fat (g)	Sat. Fat (g)	Chol. (mg)	Sod. (mg)	Cal.
Tomato (8 oz)	3.0	1.0	1	1010	230
Vegetarian (8 oz)	2.0	(1.0)	0	750	280
Vegetarian, 50% Less Sodium (8 oz)	2.0	(1.0)	0	370	230
Baked beans with pork and tomato sauce (1/2 cup)	1.3	0.5	9	554	123
Bush's Best Baked Beans (4 oz)	1.0	(0.4)	{0}	550	110
with Onions (4 oz)	1.0	(0.4)	{0}	550	110
Campbell's Beans, Barbecue Baked Beans (4 oz)	2.0	(0.5)	{0}	400	150
Friends Baked Beans, Maple (8 oz)	2.0	1.0	<5	890	240
Green Giant Beans, Baked Style (solids and liquids) (1/2 cup)	2.0	(0.5)	0	670	150
Health Valley Fat-Free Boston Baked Beans with Honey (7.5 oz)	<1.0	(0.0)	0	290	190
Van Camp's Baked Beans (1 cup)	2.0	(0.8)	{0}	1020	260
Deluxe (1 cup)	4.0	(1.5)	{0}	970	320
Black beans, canned					
Eden Black Beans (1/2 cup)	<1.0	(0.0)	0	15	70
Blackeye peas, canned					
Bush's Best Blackeye Peas (4 oz)	0.0	0.0	{0}	350	70
Seasoned with Bacon (4 oz)	0.0	0.0	{0}	420	90
Showboat Blackeye Peas (4 oz)	<1.0	(0.0)	{0}	350	70
Broadbeans, canned (1/2 cup)	0.3	0.0	0	580	91
Butter beans, canned					
Bush's Best Baby Butter Beans (4 oz)	0.0	0.0	{0}	370	70
Large Butter Beans (4 oz)	0.0	0.0	{0}	370	70
Speckled Butter Beans (4 oz)	0.0	0.0	{0}	310	70
Trappey Butterbeans with Sausage (1/2 cup)	2.0	(0.8)	{7}	390	80
Van Camp's Butter Beans (1 cup)	0.5	(0.1)	{0}	710	162
Campbell's Canned Beans					
Barbecue (4 oz)	2.0	(0.5)	{0}	430	130
Home Style (4 oz)	2.0	(0.8)	{8}	430	130
Canellini beans, canned					
Progresso Canellini Beans (1/2 cup)	<1.0	(0.0)	<1	390	80

	Tot. Fat (g)	Sat. Fat (g)	Chol. (mg)	Sod. (mg)	Cal.
Chili beans, canned					
Appletree* Chili Beans (½ cup)	1.0	(0.3)	(0)	470	110
Mexican (½ cup)	1.0	(0.3)	(0)	570	130
Bush's Best Chili Hot Beans (4 oz)	0.0	0.0	(0)	420	70
Campbell's Canned Beans, Hot Chili Beans (4 oz)	2.0	(0.8)	(3)	440	110
Gebhardt Beans, Chili (4 oz)	1.0	0.1	0	580	115
Green Giant Caliente Style Chili Beans (½ cup)	1.0	(0.3)	0	700	100
Van Camp's Chili Beans, Mexican Style (1 cup)	2.4	(0.9)	(0)	730	210
Cowpeas, cooked (½ cup)	0.7	0.2	0	4	89
Cream peas, canned					
East Texas Fair Peas, Cream Peas (½ cup)	<1.0	(0.0)	(0)	400	90
Fava beans, canned					
Progresso Fava Beans (½ cup)	<1.0	(0.0)	<1	420	90
Field peas, canned					
Bush's Best Field Peas with Snaps (4 oz)	1.0	0.2	(0)	550	80
Garbanzo beans, canned (½ cup)	1.4	0.1	0	359	143
Bush's Best Garbanzo Beans (4 oz)	0.0	0.0	(0)	350	80
Eden Garbanzo Beans with Kombu (½ cup)	1.0	(0.1)	0	10	90
with Tamari (½ cup)	2.0	(0.2)	0	15	110
Green Giant Garbanzo Beans (½ cup)	2.0	0.0	0	320	90
50% Less Salt (½ cup)	2.0	0.0	0	160	90
Great northern beans—see Northern Beans					
Green or snap beans					
Canned (½ cup)	0.1	0.0	0	170	13
Appletree* Green Beans and New Potatoes (3.2 oz)	0.0	0.0	(0)	5	40
Bush's Best Cut Green & Shelly Beans (4 oz)	0.0	0.0	(0)	290	35

* Appletree products are also marketed under Best Yet, Fine Fare, Food Lion, Hyde Park, Hy-Top, Parade, Piggly-Wiggly, Red & White, Roundy's, Schwegmann, Scot Lad and Tops brand names.

VEGETABLES

	Tot. Fat (g)	Sat. Fat (g)	Chol. (mg)	Sod. (mg)	Cal.
No salt added, drained (1/2 cup)	0.1	0.0	0	1	13
Fresh, cooked (1/2 cup)	0.2	0.0	0	2	22
Frozen (1/2 cup)	0.1	0.0	0	9	18
Birds Eye Combination Vegetables, French Green Beans with Toasted Almonds (3 oz)	2.0	(0.4)	0	340	50
Green Giant Cut Green Beans in Butter Sauce (1/2 cup)	1.0	<1.0	5	230	30
Green Giant One-Serve Green Beans in Butter Sauce (5.5 oz)	2.0	1.0	5	370	60
Kidney beans					
Canned, all types (1/2 cup)	0.4	0.1	0	445	104
Eden Kidney Beans (1/2 cup)	<1.0	(0.0)	0	20	60
Trappey Red Kidney Beans with Chili Gravy (1/2 cup)	1.0	(0.1)	(0)	430	100
Van Camp's New Orleans Style Red Kidney Beans (1 cup)	0.6	(0.1)	(0)	940	178
Cooked, boiled (1/2 cup)	0.4	0.1	0	2	112
Lentils, cooked, boiled (1/2 cup)	0.4	0.1	0	2	115
Lima beans					
Canned, undrained (1/2 cup)	0.4	0.1	0	309	93
No salt added (1/2 cup)	0.4	0.1	0	5	93
Frozen					
Baby (1/2 cup)	0.3	0.1	0	26	94
Cooked (1/2 cup)	0.3	0.1	0	26	94
Green Giant Lima Beans in Butter Sauce (1/2 cup)	3.0	1.0	5	390	100
Mexe-Beans					
Old El Paso Mexe-Beans (1/2 cup)	1.0	0.0	0	627	163
Mixed beans, canned					
Bush's Best Mixed Beans (4 oz)	0.0	0.0	(0)	410	70
Hambeens 15 Bean Soup, Original, made with seasoning pkt (8 oz)	1.0	(0.3)	(0)	280	170
Cajun, made with seasoning pkt (8 oz)	1.0	(0.3)	(0)	280	180
Navy beans					
Canned					
Bush's Best Navy Beans (4 oz)	0.0	0.0	(0)	370	60
Eden Navy Beans (1/2 cup)	<1.0	(0.0)	0	15	70
Cooked, boiled (1/2 cup)	0.5	0.1	0	1	129

	Tot. Fat (g)	Sat. Fat (g)	Chol. (mg)	Sod. (mg)	Cal.
Northern beans, canned					
Bush's Best Great Northern Beans (4 oz)	0.0	0.0	(0)	380	70
Eden Great Northern Beans (½ cup)	<1.0	0.0	0	15	110
Pinto beans					
Canned (½ cup)	0.4	0.1	0	499	93
Appletree* Pinto Beans, Jalapeño with Bacon (½ cup)	1.0	(0.4)	(9)	480	90
Bush's Best Pinto Beans Seasoned with Pork (4 oz)	0.0	0.0	(0)	470	70
Eden Pinto Beans with Kombu (½ cup)	<1.0	(0.0)	0	15	70
Eden Pinto Beans with Tamari (½ cup)	<1.0	(0.0)	0	20	110
Gebhardt Beans, Pinto (4 oz)	<1.0	(0.0)	0	600	100
Cooked, boiled (½ cup)	0.4	0.1	0	1	117
Pork and beans, canned					
Appletree* Pork and Beans in Tomato Sauce (½ cup)	1.0	(0.4)	(9)	590	140
Bush's Deluxe Pork & Beans (4 oz)	1.0	(0.4)	(9)	350	110
Showboat Pork & Beans (4 oz)	<1.0	(0.0)	(9)	470	80
Campbell's Beans, Pork & Beans in Tomato Sauce (4 oz)	2.0	(0.8)	0	370	120
Trappey Pork & Beans with Jalapeños (½ cup)	1.0	(0.3)	(0)	430	110
Van Camp's Pork and Beans (1 cup)	1.9	1.0	0	1000	216
Wagon Master Extra Fancy Beans Pork & Beans (½ cup)	1.0	(0.4)	(9)	540	130
Red beans, canned					
Bush's Best Red Beans (4 oz)	0.0	0.0	(0)	350	70
Van Camp's Red Beans (1 cup)	0.6	(0.1)	(0)	928	194
Refried beans, canned					
Gebhardt Refried Beans (4 oz)	2.0	0.8	2	490	100
Jalapeño (4 oz)	2.0	0.7	2	270	115
Little Pancho Refried Beans and Green Chili (½ cup)	0.0	0.0	(0)	330	80

* Appletree products are also marketed under Best Yet, Fine Fare, Food Lion, Hyde Park, Hy-Top, Parade, Piggly-Wiggly, Red & White, Roundy's, Schwegmann, Scot Lad and Tops brand names.

VEGETABLES

	Tot. Fat (g)	Sat. Fat (g)	Chol. (mg)	Sod. (mg)	Cal.
Old El Paso Refried Beans (1/2 cup)	<1.0	0.0	1	200	55
Spicy (1/4 cup)	1.0	0.0	1	280	35
Vegetarian (1/4 cup)	1.0	<1.0	0	730	70
with Green Chilies (1/4 cup)	<1.0	(0.0)	(1)	252	49
with Jalapeños (1/4 cup)	1.0	0.0	1	265	31
Rosarita Refried Beans (4 oz)	2.0	0.8	2	470	120
Spicy (4 oz)	2.0	0.8	2	460	130
Vegetarian (4 oz)	2.0	0.5	0	470	100
with Bacon (4 oz)	2.0	0.9	14	560	110
with Green Chilies (4 oz)	2.0	0.7	2	430	120
with Nacho Cheese (4 oz)	2.0	0.9	2	490	140
with Onions (4 oz)	2.0	0.8	2	500	130
Roman beans, canned					
Progresso Roman Beans (1/2 cup)	<1.0	(0.0)	<1	420	110
Snap beans—*see* Green or snap beans					
Three bean salad, canned					
Green Giant Three Bean Salad (1/2 cup)	<1.0	0.0	0	470	70
Vegetarian beans, canned—*see also* Baked beans					
Bush's Deluxe Vegetarian Beans (4 oz)	0.0	0.0	(0)	350	110
Campbell's Canned Beans, Vegetarian Beans in Tomato Sauce (8 oz)	1.0	(0.1)	(0)	400	110
Van Camp's Vegetarian Style Beans (1 cup)	0.6	(0.1)	(0)	950	206
White beans, cooked (1/2 cup)	0.4	0.1	0	7	153
Beets					
Canned, slices, drained (1/2 cup)	0.1	0.0	0	(324)	27
Harvard, undrained (1/2 cup)	0.1	0.0	0	199	89
No salt added, drained (1/2 cup)	0.1	0.0	0	(57)	27
Pickled, slices, undrained (1/2 cup)	0.1	0.0	0	301	75
Fresh, sliced, cooked (1/2 cup)	0.0	0.0	0	42	26
Blackeye peas—*see* Beans, Blackeye peas					
Broccoli					
Fresh					
Chopped, cooked (1/2 cup)	0.1	0.0	0	22	25

VEGETABLES

251

	Tot. Fat (g)	Sat. Fat (g)	Chol. (mg)	Sod. (mg)	Cal.
Chopped, raw (1/2 cup)	0.2	0.0	0	12	12
Spears, boiled (1 spear)	0.5	0.1	0	19	53
Frozen					
Chopped, cooked (1/2 cup)	0.2	0.0	0	8	23
Green Giant					
Broccoli Spears in Butter Sauce (1/2 cup)	2.0	<1.0	5	350	40
Broccoli Spears in Cheese Flavored Sauce (1/2 cup)	2.0	<1.0	2	530	60
One-Serve Broccoli Cuts in Butter Sauce (4 1/2 oz)	2.0	<1.0	5	420	45
One-Serve Broccoli Cuts in Cheese Flavored Sauce (5 oz)	3.0	<1.0	5	660	70
Brussels sprouts					
Fresh, cooked (1/2 cup)	0.4	0.1	0	17	30
Frozen, cooked (1/2 cup)	0.3	0.1	0	18	33
Green Giant Baby Brussels Sprouts in Butter Sauce (1/2 cup)	1.0	<1.0	5	280	40
Cabbage					
Fresh					
Chinese, shredded, cooked (1/2 cup)	0.1	0.0	0	29	10
Chinese, shredded, raw (1/2 cup)	0.1	0.0	0	23	5
Green, shredded, cooked (1/2 cup)	0.2	0.0	0	14	16
Green, shredded, raw (1/2 cup)	0.1	0.0	0	6	8
Red, shredded, cooked (1/2 cup)	0.2	0.0	0	6	16
Red, shredded, raw (1/2 cup)	0.1	0.0	0	4	10
Carrots					
Canned, slices (1/2 cup)	0.1	0.0	0	176	17
No salt added (1/2 cup)	0.1	0.0	0	31	17
Fresh					
Baby, raw, 2 3/4" long (1 medium)	0.1	0.0	0	3	4
Raw (7 1/2" × 1" diam)	0.1	0.0	0	25	31
Sliced, cooked (1/2 cup)	0.1	0.0	0	52	35
Frozen, sliced (1/2 cup)	0.1	0.0	0	43	26
Cauliflower					
Fresh					
Cooked, 1" pieces (1/2 cup)	0.1	0.0	0	4	15
Raw, 1" pieces (1/2 cup)	0.2	0.0	0	16	17

VEGETABLES

	Tot. Fat (g)	Sat. Fat (g)	Chol. (mg)	Sod. (mg)	Cal.
Frozen					
Green Giant Cauliflower					
in Cheese Flavored Sauce (¹/₂ cup)	2.0	<1.0	2	500	60
in Cheese Flavored Sauce (5.5 oz)	2.0	<1.0	5	640	80
Celery					
Fresh					
Diced, cooked (¹/₂ cup)	0.8	0.0	0	48	11
Raw (1 stalk = 7¹/₂″ × 1″)	0.1	0.0	0	35	6
Chayote					
Fresh					
Cooked, 1″ pieces (¹/₂ cup)	0.4	0.0	0	1	19
Raw, 1″ pieces (¹/₂ cup)	0.2	0.0	0	3	16
Cilantro, fresh (coriander leaf) (¹/₄ cup)	0.1	(0.0)	0	1	1
Corn					
Canned					
Cream style (¹/₂ cup)	0.5	0.1	0	365	93
No salt added (¹/₂ cup)	1.0	0.1	0	4	93
Whole kernel, drained (¹/₂ cup)	0.8	0.1	0	(286)	66
No salt added, drained (¹/₂ cup)	0.8	0.1	0	(3)	66
Fresh, sweet, cooked (¹/₂ cup)	1.1	0.2	0	14	89
Frozen (¹/₂ cup)	0.1	0.0	0	4	67
Green Giant					
Cream Style Corn (¹/₂ cup)	1.0	0.0	0	370	110
Niblets Corn in Butter Sauce (¹/₂ cup)	2.0	1.0	5	310	100
One-Serve Niblets Corn in Butter Sauce (4.5 oz)	2.0	<1.0	5	350	120
Shoepeg White Corn in Butter Sauce (¹/₂ cup)	2.0	<1.0	5	280	100
Cowpeas—*see* Beans, Cowpeas					
Cream peas—*see* Beans, Cream peas					
Cucumbers, fresh, raw (¹/₂ cup)	0.1	0.0	0	1	7
Eggplant, fresh, cubes, cooked (¹/₂ cup)	0.1	0.0	0	2	13
Endive, fresh, chopped, raw (¹/₂ cup)	0.1	0.0	0	6	4
Field peas—*see* Beans, Field peas					
Garlic, fresh, raw (1 clove)	0.0	0.0	0	1	4
Greens					
Beet, fresh, pieces, cooked (¹/₂ cup)	0.1	0.0	0	173	20

	Tot. Fat (g)	Sat. Fat (g)	Chol. (mg)	Sod. (mg)	Cal.
Collard, canned					
Bush's Best Collard Greens, Chopped (4 oz)	0.0	0.0	(0)	320	30
Dandelion, fresh, chopped, cooked (1/2 cup)	0.3	0.0	0	23	17
Kale					
Canned					
Bush's Best Kale Greens, Chopped (4 oz)	0.0	0.0	(0)	230	25
Fresh, chopped, cooked (1/2 cup)	0.3	0.0	0	15	21
Mixed, canned					
Bush's Best Mixed Greens (Turnip and Mustard) (4 oz)	0.0	0.0	(0)	300	20
Mustard					
Canned					
Bush's Best Mustard Greens, Chopped (4 oz)	0.0	0.0	(0)	220	20
Fresh, chopped, cooked (1/2 cup)	0.2	0.0	0	11	11
Frozen (1/2 cup)	0.2	0.0	0	19	14
Turnip					
Canned, undrained (1/2 cup)	0.4	0.1	0	325	17
Bush's Best Turnip Greens with Diced Turnips (4 oz)	0.0	0.0	(0)	370	25
Fresh, chopped, cooked (1/2 cup)	0.2	0.0	0	21	15
Frozen (1/2 cup)	0.4	0.1	0	12	24
Hominy, canned					
Bush's Best Golden Hominy (4 oz)	0.0	0.0	(0)	390	45
Bush's Best White Hominy (4 oz)	0.0	0.0	(0)	450	45
Jicama (yam bean), fresh, slices, raw (1 cup)	0.1	(0.0)	0	5	46
Kale—see Greens, Kale					
Kohlrabi, fresh, slices, cooked (1/2 cup)	0.1	0.0	0	17	24
Leeks					
Fresh, chopped, cooked (1/4 cup)	0.1	0.0	0	3	8
Raw (1/4 cup)	0.1	0.0	0	5	16
Lentils—see Beans, Lentils					
Lettuce, fresh, iceberg (1/4 head)	0.3	0.0	0	12	18
Mixed vegetables					
Canned, drained (1/2 cup)	0.4	0.0	0	122	39

	Tot. Fat (g)	Sat. Fat (g)	Chol. (mg)	Sod. (mg)	Cal.
La Choy					
Fancy Mixed Chinese Vegetables					
(½ cup)	<1.0	(0.0)	0	30	12
Vegetables (½ cup)	<1.0	(0.0)	0	320	10
Frozen (½ cup)	0.1	0.0	0	32	54
Appletree* Mixed Vegetables					
California Mix (3.2 oz)	0.0	0.0	(0)	25	25
Country Style Blend (3.2 oz)	0.0	0.0	(0)	24	50
Italian Style (3.2 oz)	0.0	0.0	(0)	30	40
Oriental Mix (3.2 oz)	0.0	0.0	(0)	20	20
Rancho Fiesta (3.2 oz)	0.0	0.0	(0)	110	70
Vegetable Gumbo Mix (3.2 oz)	(0.0)	(0.0)	(0)	20	90
Appletree* Stew Vegetables					
(3.2 oz)	0.0	0.0	(0)	30	50
Birds Eye Custom Cuisine					
Chow Mein Vegetables in Oriental					
Sauce (4.6 oz)	2.0	(0.5)	0	570	80
Vegetables with Creamy Mushroom					
Sauce for Beef (4.6 oz)	2.0	(0.7)	5	450	60
Vegetables with Dijon Mustard					
Sauce for Chicken or Fish (4.6 oz)	3.0	(0.3)	5	310	70
Vegetables with Savory Tomato					
Basil Sauce for Chicken (4.6 oz)	3.0	(0.5)	0	360	110
Vegetables with Wild Rice in					
White Wine Sauce for Chicken					
(4.6 oz)	0.0	0.0	0	510	100
Birds Eye Farm Fresh Mixtures					
Broccoli, Baby Carrots and Water					
Chestnuts (4 oz)	0.0	0.0	0	35	45
Broccoli, Cauliflower and Red					
Peppers (4 oz)	0.0	0.0	0	25	30
Broccoli, Corn and Red Peppers					
(4 oz)	1.0	0.0	0	15	60
Broccoli, Green Beans, Pearl					
Onions and Red Peppers (4 oz)	0.0	0.0	0	15	35

* Appletree products are also marketed under Best Yet, Fine Fare, Food Lion, Hyde Park, Hy-Top, Parade, Piggly-Wiggly, Red & White, Roundy's, Schwegmann, Scot Lad and Tops brand names.

VEGETABLES

255

	Tot. Fat (g)	Sat. Fat (g)	Chol. (mg)	Sod. (mg)	Cal.
Broccoli, Red Peppers, Bamboo Shoots and Straw Mushrooms (4 oz)	0.0	0.0	0	20	30
Brussels Sprouts, Cauliflower and Carrots (4 oz)	0.0	0.0	0	30	40
Cauliflower, Baby Whole Carrots and Snow Pea Pods (4 oz)	0.0	0.0	0	35	40
Cauliflower, Zucchini, Carrots and Red Peppers (4 oz)	0.0	0.0	0	25	30
Sugar Snap Peas, Baby Carrots and Water Chestnuts (3.2 oz)	0.0	0.0	0	20	50
Zucchini, Carrots, Pearl Onions and Mushrooms (4 oz)	0.0	0.0	0	15	30
Birds Eye Stir-Fry Vegetables					
Chinese Style (3.3 oz)	0.0	0.0	0	540	35
Japanese Style (3.3 oz)	0.0	0.0	0	510	30
Green Giant American Mixtures					
California (1/2 cup)	0.0	0.0	0	40	25
Heartland (1/2 cup)	0.0	0.0	0	35	25
Manhattan Style (1/2 cup)	0.0	0.0	0	15	25
New England (1/2 cup)	1.0	(0.0)	0	75	70
San Francisco (1/2 cup)	0.0	0.0	0	35	25
Santa Fe (1/2 cup)	1.0	(0.0)	0	0	70
Seattle (1/2 cup)	0.0	0.0	0	35	25
Western Style (1/2 cup)	2.0	0.0	0	25	60
Green Giant Broccoli, Cauliflower and Carrots					
in Butter Sauce (1/2 cup)	1.0	<1.0	5	240	30
in Cheese Flavored Sauce (1/2 cup)	2.0	<1.0	2	490	60
Green Giant Garden Medley (1/2 cup)	0.0	0.0	0	350	35
Green Giant Mixed Vegetables in Butter Sauce (1/2 cup)	2.0	<1.0	5	300	60
Green Giant One-Serve					
Broccoli, Cauliflower and Carrots in Cheese Sauce (5 oz)	2.0	<1.0	5	650	80
Broccoli, Carrots and Rotini in Cheese Sauce (5.5 oz)	2.0	<1.0	5	440	100

	Tot. Fat (g)	Sat. Fat (g)	Chol. (mg)	Sod. (mg)	Cal.
Green Giant Pantry Express					
Corn, Green Beans, Carrots, Pasta in Tomato Sauce (solids and liquids) (1/2 cup)	2.0	0.0	0	330	80
Green Beans, Potatoes and Mushrooms in a Lightly Seasoned Sauce (1/2 cup)	3.0	<1.0	0	440	60
Mixed Vegetables (Green Beans, Potatoes, Carrots, Corn) (1/2 cup)	<1.0	0.0	0	300	35
Green Giant Valley Combinations					
Broccoli Cauliflower Medley (1/2 cup)	2.0	0.0	0	340	60
Broccoli Fanfare (1/2 cup)	2.0	0.0	0	340	80
Le Sueur Style (1/2 cup)	2.0	0.0	0	400	70
La Choy, Stir Fry Vegetables 'N Sauce					
Mandarin (4 oz)	1.0	(<1.0)	0	903	161
Spicy Szechuan (4 oz)	1.0	(<1.0)	0	723	191
Sweet & Sour (4 oz)	1.0	(<1.0)	0	743	171
Teriyaki (4 oz)	1.0	(<1.0)	0	953	120
Tropical Fruit & Vegetable Medley (5/8 cup)	0.2	(0.0)	0	10	30
Vegetable Chow Mein (1/3 cup)	1.6	(0.4)	0	256	45
Vegetables, Oriental Stir-Fry (3/4 cup)	0.2	(0.0)	0	20	35
Ore-Ida Stew Vegetables (3 oz)	<1.0	0.0	0	35	50
PictSweet Vegetables					
California (3.2 oz)	0.0	0.0	0	25	25
Del Sol (3.2 oz)	0.0	0.0	0	35	30
Grande (3.2 oz)	0.0	0.0	0	15	45
Italian (3.2 oz)	0.0	0.0	0	10	20
Japanese (3.2 oz)	0.0	0.0	0	10	25
Milano (3.2 oz)	0.0	0.0	0	40	40
New England (3.2 oz)	0.0	0.0	0	25	40
Oriental (3.2 oz)	0.0	0.0	0	10	25
Parisian (3.2 oz)	0.0	0.0	0	20	30
Romano (3.2 oz)	0.0	0.0	0	50	50
Swiss (3.2 oz)	0.0	0.0	0	20	25

VEGETABLES

	Tot. Fat (g)	Sat. Fat (g)	Chol. (mg)	Sod. (mg)	Cal.
Vegetables for Stir-Fry, made without fat (3.5 oz)	0.0	0.0	0	30	35
Western (3.2 oz)	0.0	0.0	0	5	50
Mushrooms					
Canned, pieces, drained (½ cup)	0.6	0.0	0	(330)	19
Fresh (1)	0.1	0.0	0	1	5
Pieces, cooked (½ cup)	0.4	0.1	0	2	21
Pieces, raw (½ cup)	0.2	0.0	0	1	9
Okra					
Canned					
Trappey Mixed Vegetables					
Creole Okra Gumbo (½ cup)	<1.0	(0.0)	(0)	420	25
Okra, Tomatoes & Corn (½ cup)	<1.0	(0.0)	(0)	440	25
Fresh, slices, cooked (½ cup)	0.1	0.0	0	4	25
Frozen (½ cup)	0.3	0.1	0	3	34
Onions					
Fresh					
Chopped, cooked (½ cup)	0.2	0.0	0	8	29
Raw (½ cup)	0.2	0.0	0	2	27
Frozen					
Appletree* Onions, Diced (1 oz)	0.0	0.0	(0)	0	6
Parsnips, fresh, slices, cooked (½ cup)	0.2	0.0	0	8	63
Pea pods, frozen					
Chun King Chinese Pea Pods (1.5 oz)	0.0	0.0	(0)	<10	20
Peas and carrots					
Canned, undrained (½ cup)	0.4	0.1	0	332	48
No salt added, undrained (½ cup)	0.4	0.1	0	5	48
Frozen (½ cup)	0.3	0.1	0	55	38
Peas and onions					
Canned, undrained (½ cup)	0.2	0.0	0	265	30
Frozen (½ cup)	0.2	0.0	0	(78)	40
Peas, green					
Canned (½ cup)	0.3	0.1	0	186	59
No salt added, drained (½ cup)	0.3	0.1	0	2	59
Fresh, cooked (½ cup)	0.2	0.0	0	2	67
Frozen (½ cup)	0.2	0.0	0	70	63

* Appletree products are also marketed under Best Yet, Fine Fare, Food Lion, Hyde Park, Hy-Top, Parade, Piggly-Wiggly, Red & White, Roundy's, Schwegmann, Scot Lad and Tops brand names.

VEGETABLES

	Tot. Fat (g)	Sat. Fat (g)	Chol. (mg)	Sod. (mg)	Cal.
Green Giant					
Le Sueur Baby Early Peas in Butter Sauce (½ cup)	2.0	<1.0	5	440	80
One-Serve Le Sueur Baby Early Peas in Butter Sauce (4.5 oz)	2.0	<1.0	5	400	90
Sweet Peas in Butter Sauce (½ cup)	2.0	<1.0	5	410	80
Le Sueur Early Peas in Butter Sauce (½ cup)	2.0	<1.0	5	400	80
Peppers, hot					
Canned, hot chili, no salt added, undrained (1 pepper)	0.1	0.0	0	(470)	18
Progresso Roasted Peppers (½ cup)	<1.0	<1.0	0	2	20
Fresh, raw (1)	0.1	0.0	0	3	18
Peppers, sweet					
Canned, green, halves (½ cup)	0.2	0.0	0	958	13
Fresh					
Green or red, chopped, raw (½ cup)	0.2	0.0	0	2	12
Red, cooked (1 oz)	0.0	0.0	0	1	5
Yellow, raw, 5″ long × 3″ diam (1 large)	0.4	(0.0)	0	3	50
Potato					
Canned, whole, drained (½ cup)	0.2	0.0	0	(452)	54
Fresh					
Baked with skin (1)	0.2	0.1	0	16	220
Boiled (½ cup)	0.1	0.0	0	3	68
Frozen					
Ore-Ida Country Style Dinner Fries, Baked (3 oz)	3.0	<1.0	0	15	110
Ore-Ida Hash Browns Cheddar, Baked (3 oz)	2.0	1.0	5	420	80
Potatoes O'Brien, Baked (3 oz)	<1.0	0.0	0	15	50
Shredded Hash Browns, Baked (3 oz)	<1.0	0.0	0	25	70
Southern Style, Baked (3 oz)	<1.0	0.0	0	25	70
Ore-Ida Home Style Potato Wedges, Baked (3 oz)	3.0	<1.0	0	25	110
Ore-Ida Lites Crinkle Cuts, Baked (3 oz)	2.0	<1.0	0	35	80

VEGETABLES

259

	Tot. Fat (g)	Sat. Fat (g)	Chol. (mg)	Sod. (mg)	Cal.
Instant					
Arrowhead Mills Potato Flakes (2 oz = 1 cup)	0.0	0.0	0	42	140
Idahoan Complete Mashed Potatoes, made with water (1/2 cup)	1.0	(0.3)	(0)	175	80
Pumpkin					
Canned (1/2 cup)	0.3	0.0	0	6	41
Fresh, cooked, mashed (1/2 cup)	0.9	0.1	0	2	24
Radicchio, fresh, raw, shredded (1/2 cup)	0.1	0.0	0	4	5
Radishes, fresh, raw, 1" diameter (10)	0.2	0.0	0	11	7
Rutabagas, fresh, cubed, cooked (1/2 cup)	0.2	0.0	0	15	29
Sauerkraut, canned, undrained (1/2 cup)	0.2	0.0	0	780	22
Bush's Best Bavarian Kraut (4 oz)	0.0	0.0	(0)	400	60
Vlasic Old Fashioned Sauerkraut (1 oz)	0.0	0.0	(0)	280	4
Shallots, fresh, chopped, raw (1 tbsp)	0.0	0.0	0	1	7
Snow peas					
Fresh					
Cooked (1/2 cup)	0.2	0.0	0	3	34
Raw (1/2 cup)	0.1	0.0	0	3	30
Frozen (1/2 cup)	0.3	0.1	0	4	42
La Choy Snow Pea Pods (7/8 cup)	0.2	(0.0)	0	4	42
Spinach					
Canned, drained (1/2 cup)	0.5	0.1	0	(269)	25
No salt added, drained (1/2 cup)	0.5	0.1	0	29	25
Fresh					
Chopped, cooked (1/2 cup)	0.2	0.0	0	63	21
Raw (1/2 cup)	0.1	0.0	0	22	6
Frozen (1/2 cup)	0.2	0.0	0	82	27
Green Giant					
Creamed Spinach (1/2 cup)	3.0	1.0	2	480	70
Cut Leaf Spinach in Butter Sauce (1/2 cup)	2.0	<1.0	5	380	40
Squash					
Summer, fresh, all varieties, slices					
Cooked (1/2 cup)	0.3	0.1	0	1	18
Raw (1/2 cup)	0.1	0.0	0	1	13

	Tot. Fat (g)	Sat. Fat (g)	Chol. (mg)	Sod. (mg)	Cal.
Winter, fresh, all varieties, cubed, cooked (1/2 cup)	0.6	<1.0	0	1	39
Zucchini					
Canned, Italian-style, undrained (1/2 cup)	0.1	0.0	0	427	33
Progresso Italian Style Zucchini (1/2 cup)	2.0	<1.0	<1	540	50
Fresh, sliced, boiled (1/2 cup)	0.1	0.0	0	2	14
Succotash					
Canned					
With corn (1/2 cup)	0.6	0.1	0	283	81
With cream-style corn (1/2 cup)	0.7	0.1	0	325	102
Frozen, cooked (1/2 cup)	0.8	0.1	0	16	111
Sweet potatoes—*see also* Yams					
Canned, in syrup, drained (1/2 cup)	0.3	0.1	0	38	106
Mashed (1/2 cup)	0.3	0.1	0	96	129
Fresh, mashed, cooked (1/2 cup)	0.1	0.0	0	10	103
Frozen, cubed (1/2 cup)	0.1	0.0	0	7	88
Mrs. Paul's					
Candied Sweet Potatoes (4 oz)	1.0	(0.4)	(0)	140	190
Candied Sweets 'N Apples (4 oz)	0.0	0.0	(0)	55	160
Taro, slices					
Fresh, cooked (1/2 cup)	0.1	0.0	0	10	94
Raw (1/2 cup)	0.1	0.0	0	6	56
Tomatillos					
Canned					
La Victoria					
Tomatillo, Crushed (4 tbsp)	<1.0	0.0	0	80	8
Tomatillo Entero, drained (2 tbsp)	<1.0	(0.0)	0	95	4
Fresh, raw (1 med = 1 5/8" diameter)	0.4	(0.0)	0	0	11
Tomato paste, canned (1/2 cup)	1.2	0.2	0	1035	110
Contadina Italian Paste (1/4 cup)	1.0	(0.1)	(0)	520	65
No salt added (1/2 cup)	1.2	0.2	0	86	110
Tomato puree, canned (1/2 cup)	0.1	0.0	0	499	51
No salt added (1/2 cup)	0.1	0.0	0	25	51
Tomatoes					
Canned					
Contadina					
Italian Style (Pear) Tomatoes (1/2 cup)	<1.0	(0.0)	(0)	220	25

	Tot. Fat (g)	Sat. Fat (g)	Chol. (mg)	Sod. (mg)	Cal.
Italian Style Stewed Tomatoes (½ cup)	<1.0	(0.0)	(0)	250	35
Mexican Style Stewed Tomatoes (½ cup)	0.3	0.1	0	230	35
Pasta Ready Tomatoes (½ cup)	2.0	0.3	0	560	50
Recipe Ready (½ cup)	0.2	0.1	0	570	25
Eden Organic Crushed Tomatoes, No Salt Added (4 oz)	0.0	0.0	0	0	35
Old El Paso					
Tomatoes and Green Chilies (¼ cup)	<1.0	(0.0)	0	480	14
Tomatoes and Jalapeños (¼ cup)	<1.0	0.0	0	150	11
Red, stewed (½ cup)	0.2	0.0	0	325	34
Whole (½ cup)	0.3	0.0	0	195	24
With green chilies (½ cup)	0.0	0.0	0	481	18
Fresh					
Cooked (½ cup)	0.3	0.0	0	13	30
Green, raw (1 tomato = 2⅗″ diameter)	0.3	0.0	0	16	30
Red, raw (1 tomato = 2⅗″ diameter)	0.3	0.0	0	10	24
Sun-dried (1 tbsp)	0.1	0.0	0	71	9
Whole, no salt added (½ cup)	0.3	0.0	0	16	24
Turnips, fresh, cubed, cooked (½ cup)	0.1	0.0	0	39	14
Water chestnuts					
Canned, sliced, undrained (½ cup)	0.0	0.0	0	6	35
Fresh, raw (½ cup)	0.1	0.0	0	9	66
Yams—see also Sweet Potatoes					
Canned					
Trappey Yams, Orange-Pineapple (½ cup)	<1.0	(0.0)	(0)	60	180
Fresh, cubed, cooked (½ cup)	0.1	0.0	0	6	79

OTHER SOURCES FOR FOOD DATA

USDA Handbook No. 8 Series

Series No.	Food Group Issued	Year
8–1	Dairy and Egg Products	1976
8–2	Spices and Herbs	1977
8–4	Fats and Oils	1979
8–5	Poultry Products	1979
8–6	Soups, Sauces and Gravies	1980
8–7	Sausages and Luncheon Meats	1980
8–8	Breakfast Cereals	1982
8–9	Fruits and Fruit Juices	1982
8–10	Pork Products	1992
8–11	Vegetables and Vegetable Products	1984
8–12	Nut and Seed Products	1984
8–13	Beef Products	1990
8–14	Beverages	1986
8–15	Finfish and Shellfish Products	1987
8–16	Legumes and Legume Products	1986
8–17	Lamb, Veal and Game Products	1989
8–18	Baked Products	1992
8–19	Snacks and Sweets	1991
8–20	Cereal, Grains and Pasta	1989
8–21	Fast Foods	1988

USDA Handbook No. 456, 1975.

USDA Provisional Table on the Fatty Acids and Cholesterol Content of Selected Foods, 1984.

The Living Heart Brand Name Shopper's Guide—Revised and Updated.

ALSO FROM THE

American Heart Association

Fighting Heart Disease and Stroke

American Heart Association
Cookbook, 5th Edition:
New and Revised

American Heart Association
Low-Fat, Low-Cholesterol Cookbook

American Heart Association
Low-Salt Cookbook

American Heart Association
Kids' Cookbook

American Heart Association
Family Guide to Stroke

Available in bookstores everywhere
or call
1-800-733-3000
to order direct